Launching the Imagination

A Guide to Three-Dimensional Design

Launching
the Imagination

A Guide to Three-Dimensional Design

second edition

Mary Stewart

Boston   Burr Ridge, IL   Dubuque, IA   Madison, WI   New York   San Francisco   St. Louis
Bangkok   Bogotá   Caracas   Kuala Lumpur   Lisbon   London   Madrid   Mexico City
Milan   Montreal   New Delhi   Santiago   Seoul   Singapore   Sydney   Taipei   Toronto

Higher Education

LAUNCHING THE IMAGINATION: A GUIDE TO THREE-DIMENSIONAL DESIGN
Published by McGraw-Hill, a business unit of The McGraw-Hill Companies, Inc., 1221 Avenue of the Americas, New York, NY, 10020.

This book is printed on acid-free paper.

1 2 3 4 5 6 7 8 9 0 DOW/DOW 0 9 8 7 6 5

ISBN   0-07-287063-X

Editor in Chief: *Emily Barrosse*
Publisher: *Lyn Uhl*
Sponsoring Editor: *Joe Hanson*
Developmental Editor: *Cynthia Ward*
Editorial Assistant: *Elizabeth Sigal*
Executive Marketing Manager: *Suzanna Ellison*
Managing Editor: *Jean Dal Porto*
Project Manager: *Catherine R. Iammartino*
Art Director: *Jeanne Schreiber*
Senior Designer and Interior Designer: *Kim Menning*
Cover Designer: *Bill Stanton*
Senior Photo Research Coordinator: *Alexandra Ambrose*
Photo Research: *Photo Search, Inc., New York*
Art Editor: *Emma C. Ghiselli*
Cover Credits:
[1] Tanija & Graham Carr, *Untitled*, 2001. Courtesy of the artists. Photo: Victor France.
[2] © Lee Snider/CORBIS.
[3] Ted Gall, *Plaza Facets*, 2001. Courtesy of the artist.
[4] Adele Linarducci, *Slingshot Wheelchair*, 1989. © Adele Linarducci, 1989. Photo: Robert Stave, 1989.
[5] Museo Arqueologico del Banco Central, Quito, Ecuador. © 2005 Dirk Bakker.
Lead Media Producer: *Shannon Gattens*
Media Project Manager: *Michele Borrelli*
Production Supervisor: *Janean A. Utley*
CD-ROM Development and Design: *Creative Myndz*
Composition: *10.5/14 Palatino by Prographics*
Printing: *70# Sterling Ultra Web Dull, R.R. Donnelley and Sons, Inc./Willard, OH*

Credits: The credits section for this book begins on page 305 and is considered an extension of the copyright page.

Library of Congress Cataloging-in-Publication Data
Stewart, Mary, 1952-
    Launching the imagination. A comprehensive guide to three-dimensional design / Mary Stewart.
    p. cm.
    Also issued as pt. 2-3 of Launching the imagination : a comprehensive guide to basic design.
    Includes bibliographical references and index.
    ISBN 0-07-287063-X (softcover : alk. paper)
    1. Design. I. Title.
NK1510.S743 2006
730'.1'8--dc22
                                                                                2005041660

The Internet addresses listed in the text were accurate at the time of publication. The inclusion of a website does not indicate an endorsement by the authors of McGraw-Hill, and McGraw-Hill does not guarantee the accuracy of the information presented at these sites.

Launching the Imagination:
A Guide to Three-Dimensional Design
is dedicated to my inventive and hardworking graduate
teaching assistants at Northern Illinois University.

dedication

In the beginning of my teaching career, I had the good fortune to audit the courses of two master teachers of design, William Itter and David Hornung. Itter's fundamentals course, derived from Joseph Albers' approach, featured assignments that were methodical, systematic, and highly analytical. Hornung's course, which focused on conceptual and visual patterns, was exuberant, synthetic, and often irreverent. Despite significant differences in their assignments, both teachers brilliantly presented substantial design information.

Based on these experiences and my own teaching, I concluded that a comprehensive approach to design requires experimentation as well as analysis, and that rambunctiousness is the natural partner to rigor. Thus, when McGraw-Hill invited me to write a design textbook, I was determined to present substantial information in the liveliest possible way.

An Approach for 21st Century Students

Launching the Imagination treats design as both a verb and a noun—as a problem-solving process as well as a well-crafted product. It challenges students to use design to explore their own ideas while encouraging them to look closely and learn from the work of other artists. My aim was to write a book that would help students create designs that are both conceptually inventive and visually compelling. I hope that students will be inspired to see the foundations course as a launching pad for their future work, for their entry into the community of artists.

Thorough coverage of 3D design. This book covers all of the topics common to three-dimensional design courses, recognizing that artists and designers benefit from a strong shared vocabulary. This second edition has benefitted from the feedback of many foundations teachers, whose suggestions are reflected in the expanded and refined discussions of elements, principles, materials, and concepts. (For instructors who would like a book that includes 2D and time design as well, a comprehensive edition is available.)

Unique coverage of creativity and concept development. Because foundations courses are as much about process as product, *Launching the Imagination* covers such topics as generating and developing ideas, managing time, and making the most of critiques. This material, found in Part Two, can be assigned any time in the course. Some instructors find it valuable to discuss the material during class time, while others prefer it as supplemental reading.

Hundreds of full-color images. An art textbook is only as good as the images it offers—and I've sought images that are diverse and compelling. The stylistic range represents both time-honored masterworks and works by contemporary artists. There are examples from many different cultures, representing a wide range of media. A Maori meeting house is included in a discussion on cultural meaning, a kinetic Japanese tower is presented in a discussion of time, and contemporary and historic masks have been analyzed throughout. Many forms of visual culture are represented, from product design, furniture, and jewelry to sculpture, architecture, installations, and earthworks.

Conversations with practicing artists. Guest speakers have enhanced my own courses, and I tried to recreate that experience in book form through the "Profiles" at the end of each chapter. In these interviews, students learn about working processes and career choices from a remarkable group of masters. The "Profiles" help students see connections between basic design and professional practice. An interview with sculptor Todd Slaughter has been added to the second edition of this book.

New to the Second Edition

Working with invaluable feedback from adopters of the first edition, I have expanded, reorganized, refined, and updated the presentation—all with an eye to creating

preface

a better learning experience. The following summarizes the key changes in this edition:

- **Expanded and improved coverage of 3D design.** Part Three has been expanded to four chapters, making for a more coherent and manageable presentation of 3D elements, principles, materials, and concepts. Because an understanding of the practical and expressive qualities of materials is essential to work in 3D, I have created a separate chapter (10) on construction methods and materials. Throughout, illustrations have been added and concepts have been explained in greater detail.

- **New coverage of visual communication.** The unit on Concepts and Critical Thinking (Part Two) has been strengthened by the addition of a new Chapter 7, entitled "Constructing Meaning." This new chapter provides a lively and concise introduction to the theory and practice of visual communication. In it, students will explore the role of audience in communication and consider the importance of intent, context, visual drama, and metaphor.

- **Better placement of "Key Questions."** To help students immediately see the relevance of a topic to their own studio work, the "Key Questions" now appear at the end of sections within the chapter rather than at the end of the chapter.

- **New media resource guides.** This book is supported by a website and CD-ROMs that adds another dimension to the learning environment. A page at the end of Parts Two and Three shows you what types of media resources are available. These guides also include lists of studio projects that are available in the extensive Instructor's Manual.

Multimedia Resources for Students and Instructors

Please contact your local McGraw-Hill representative for details on the following supplements, including policies, prices, and availability, as some restrictions may apply. If you are not sure who your representative is, you can find him or her by using the rep locator at www.mhhe.com.

For Students:

- **The Core Concepts CD-ROM** is made up of five components to offer students essential study material in conjunction with this text. *Elements and principles of art* are illustrated with interactive exercises and animations. *Art techniques* are demonstrated and explained with brief video segments. *Chapter Resources* include study guides and quizzes. *Internet Resources* provides a guide to using the Internet for research. *Study Skills Primer* provides students with essential advice on how to be successful when studying during college.

- **The Online Learning Center,** located at **www.mhhe.com/launching2,** offers resources for each chapter of the text, including chapter objectives, discussion questions, online testing, and links to websites for additional research of the topics covered. In addition, the site hosts links to promote getting involved in art and in conducting research on the Web.

For Instructors:

- **The Instructor's Manual** includes more than 50 studio assignments, with examples, in a consistent format that makes them easy for instructors to use as is or adapt to their own purposes. For new foundations teachers, the IM offers suggestions for constructing a syllabus. The Instructor's Manual is available on the instructor's section of the Online Learning Center, located at **www.mhhe.com/launching2,** and on the **Instructor's Resource CD-ROM.** Adopters may obtain a password and/or CD-ROM from their local McGraw-Hill representative.

Acknowledgments

Writing this book has been an enormous undertaking and I've received a lot of help from my colleagues. At Northern Illinois University, I am especially indebted to Dr. Harold Kafer, who has been encouraging and supportive throughout this process, to Professor Leif Allmendinger, who reviewed Chapter Seven and suggested improvements, and to Foundations Program secretary Florence Butler, whose reserves of energy and wit seem bottomless.

I would like to thank the following artists and designers who contributed so generously to the Profiles, which accompany each chapter:

Nancy Callahan, Professor of Art, *The State University of New York at Oneonta*

Bob Dacey, Associate Professor of Art, *Syracuse University*

Diane Gallo, Independent Writer

Heidi Lasher-Oakes, Independent Sculptor

David MacDonald, Professor of Art, *Syracuse University*

Rodger Mack, Professor of Art, *Syracuse University*

Rick Paul, Professor of Art, *Purdue University*

Todd Slaughter, Professor of Art, *The Ohio State University*

I am also grateful for the advice of the following reviewers, who responded so thoughtfully to the project in various stages of development. Their opinions, suggestions, criticisms, and encouragement helped shape *Launching*:

For the Second Edition:

Kathleen A. Arkles, *College for Creative Studies*

Donald Barrie, *Seattle Central Community College*

Julie Baugnet, *St. Cloud State University*

Donna Bechis, *Fitchburg State College*

Nancy Blum-Cumming, *University of Wisconsin-Stout*

Debra K.D. Bonello, *Lansing Community College*

Jeff Boshart, *Eastern Illinois University*

Jacquelin Boulanger, *New College of Florida*

Stephanie Bowman, *Pittsburg State University*

Peter Brown, *Ringling School of Art*

John Carlander, *Westmont College*

Steven Cost, *Amarillo College*

Michael Croft, *University of Arizona*

Cat Crotchett, *Western Michigan University*

Claire Darley, *Art Academy of Cincinnati*

Anita M. DeAngelis, *East Tennessee State University*

Beverly Dennis, *Jowes County Junior College*

Tracy Doreen Dietzel, *Edgewood College*

Tim Doud, *American University*

James Elniski, *School of The Art Institute of Chicago*

John Ford, *Labette Community College*

Corky Gross, *Cazenovia College*

Arlene Grossman, *Art Institute of Boston at Lesley University*

Danielle Harmon, *West Texas A & M University*

Christopher Hocking, *University of Georgia*

Carol Hodson, *Webster University*

Sara M. Hong, *University of Arizona*

Lorie Jesperson, *Lake Michigan College*

Cheryl Ann Kittredge, *University of Maine, Presque Isle*

Michelle LaPerriere, *Maryland Institute College of Art*

In Shik Lee, *Tompkins Cortland Community College*

Richard F. Martin, *New York Institute of Technology*

Christine McCullough, *Youngstown State University*

Julie McWilliams, *Sussex County College*

Nancy Morrow, *Kansas State University*

Byron Myrich, *Jones Junior College*

Kelly Nelson, *Longwood University*

Lara Nguyen, *California State University, Long Beach*

Grace O'Brien, *Purdue University*

Mark O'Grady, *Pratt Institute*

William Potter, *Herron School of Art-IUPUI*

Patsy C. Rainey, *University of Mississippi*

Cherri Rittenhouse, *Rock Valley College*

Gil Rocha, *Richland Community College*

William B. Rowe, *Ohio Northern University*

Kim Schrag, *Tompkins Cortland Community College*

Jean Sharer, *Front Range Community College*

Gail Simpson, *University of Wisconsin-Madison*

Todd Slaughter, *Ohio State University*

Robert Smart, *Lawrence University*

Karen Spears, *Eastern Kentucky University*

Mindy Spritz, *The Art Institute of Atlanta*

Teresa Stoll, *Lake City Community College*

Katherine Strause, *University of Arkansas at Little Rock*

Rob Tarbell, *Limestone College*

William Travis, *Rowan University*

Gerson M. Rapaport, *New York Institute of Technology*

Linda Vanderkolk, *Purdue University*

Carolynne Whitefeather, *Utica College*

Reid Wood, *Lorain County Community College*

Marilyn H. Wounded Head, *Mesa State College*

Alice Zinnes, New York City College of Technology, *City University of New York*

For the First Edition:

Scott Betz, *Winston-Salem State University*

Jeff Boshart, *Eastern Illinois University*

Peter Brown, *Ringling School of Art and Design*

Brian Cantley, *California State University, Fullerton*

Laurie Beth Clark, *University of Wisconsin, Madison*

Michael Croft, *The University of Arizona*

John Fillwalk, *Ball State University*

David Fobes, *San Diego State University*

Albert Grivetti, *Clarke College*

Ken Horii, *Rhode Island School of Design*

Imi Hwangbo, *University of Louisville*

Michelle Illuminato, *Bowling Green State University*

Ann Baddeley Keister, *Grand Valley State University*

Margaret Keller, *St. Louis Community College*

Dan Lowery, *Southwestern Illinois College*

Karen Mahaffy, *University of Texas at San Antonio*

Richard Moses, *University of Illinois*

Gary Nemcosky, *Appalachian State University*

Helen Maria Nugent, *Art Institute of Chicago*

Rick Paul, *Purdue University*

Ron Saito, *California State University, Northridge*

Karen Schory, *Johnson County Community College*

Susan Slavick, *Carnegie Mellon University*

Paul Wittenbraker, *Grand Valley State University*

William Zack, *Ball State University*

Finally, the McGraw-Hill team has been knowledgeable, supportive, and enthusiastic. Senior Editor Joe Hanson contributed a great deal to the book design, continually expanded the use of new technologies, and enthusiastically promoted the book at every opportunity. Developmental Editor Cynthia Ward encouraged me to pursue a wide range of revisions, and the book is greatly improved as a result. Editorial assistants Torii Yamada and Elizabeth Sigal have been prompt and helpful throughout the process. Designer Kim Menning and layout genius Glenda King greatly increased the visual impact of the book. As head of the photo research team, Alexandra Ambrose was prompt, inventive, and helpful. Project Manager Cathy Iammartino and Executive Marketing Manager Suzanna Ellison were highly accessible, enthusiastic, and consistently supportive. Bonnie Mitchell and her CreativeMyndz team have been resilient, dedicated, and endlessly inventive in their approach to the CD-ROM.

Mary Stewart

part two

Concepts and Critical Thinking

part three

Three-Dimensional Design

Concepts and Critical Thinking

part two

Three-Dimensional Design

part three

Launching the Imagination

A Guide to Three-Dimensional Design

A Guide to *Core Concepts in Art* CD-ROM, Version 3.0

 ## GETTING STARTED

System Requirements

In order to run this CD-ROM properly, please make sure that your computer meets the minimum system requirements:

WINDOWS

- Intel Pentium II 200
- 128 MB RAM (64 MB available RAM)
- Windows 95/98, 2000, XP, or NT 4.0+
- 4x (or better) CD-ROM drive
- SVGA or higher monitor with 800x600 resolution running 16-bit color

MACINTOSH OSX

- G3 running 10.1 or better
- 128 MG of available RAM
- Color monitor with 800x600 resolution running 16-bit color

MACINTOSH CLASSIC

- Power Macintosh 180 (G3 recommended)
- 128 MG of available RAM
- System 8.6 or later
- 4x (or better) CD-ROM drive
- Color monitor with 800x600 resolution running 16-bit color
- Sound capability

QuickTime Requirements

QuickTime is required to run the program. You can click the InstallQuicktime.html file on this CD-ROM, which will bring you directly to the Apple QuickTime website, where you can download the program. The website is www.apple.com/quicktime/download

Starting the CD-ROM

Follow these steps to install the CD-ROM and begin working with the program:

WINDOWS

1. Insert the CD into the CD-ROM drive.
2. Double click on My Computer on your desktop.
3. Double click on the CD-ROM drive, most commonly called the D:/drive.
4. Double click on the Start_HerePC.exe file from the CD-ROM.

MACINTOSH

1. Insert the CD into the CD-ROM drive.
2. Double click on the "Launching the Imagination" CD-ROM.
3. Double click on the Start_Here (OSX) or Start_Here (Classic) file from the CD-ROM. Use Start_Here (OSX) for Macintosh 0SX 10.1 or higher, and Start_Here (Classic) for System 9.2 or lower.

If you need help installing this program, please call 1-800-331-5094 between 9am and 5pm EST.

CD-ROM CONTENTS

The five icons on the main menu correspond to the five components of the *Core Concepts in Art* CD-ROM.

Main menu of *Core Concepts in Art*

 ## Elements and Principles of Art

Explore the elements of 2D, 3D, and time design through interactive exercises and animated demonstrations. Experiment with the principles of unity and variety, pattern and rhythm, balance, scale and proportion, emphasis and focal point, and illusion of space.

 ## Art Techniques

Observe techniques for painting, sculpture, printmaking, glass, jewelry, photography, and new media in a series of video demonstrations.

 ## Chapter Resources

Review the content of each chapter in *Launching the Imagination*, Second Edition, in this section of the CD-ROM.

 More extensive chapter review materials are also available at the McGraw-Hill **Online Learning Center** (www.mhhe.com/launching2), which can be launched from the Internet Resources section.

1

Internet Resources

This section is helpful if you are new to using the Internet for research. It offers basic "how-to's" on using the Web, along with an introduction to computer terminology and netiquette.

Study Skills Primer

Applicable to all your courses, this primer offers tips on study and organizational skills. It also includes advice on documenting sources.

You can also access the McGraw-Hill **Online Learning Center** through a link in this section.

EXPLORING ELEMENTS, PRINCIPLES, AND TECHNIQUES

The following screen shots are examples of the types of demonstrations and interactive exercises found in the CD-ROM. For a guide to correlating the CD-ROM with this text, see the "Multimedia Resources" pages at the end of every part.

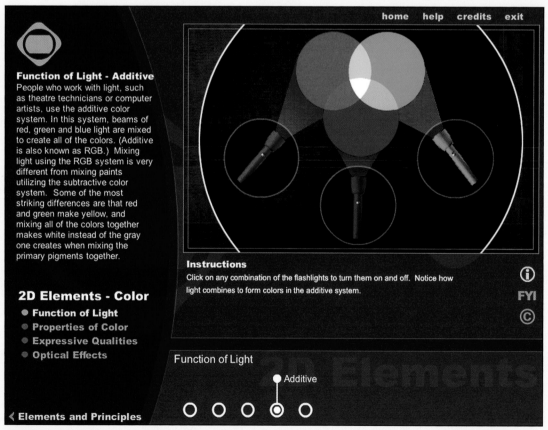

An interactive activity that allows you to experiment with additive color, found in "Elements and Principles of Art"

An interactive activity that allows you to experiment with positive and negative space, found in "Elements and Principles of Art"

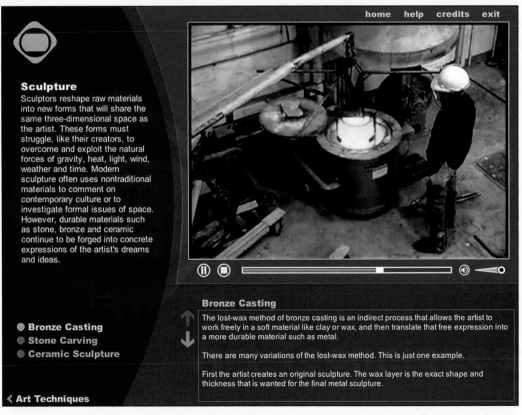

A video demonstration of the lost-wax method of bronze casting, found in "Techniques"

An interactive activity that allows you to experiment with positive and negative space, found in "Elements and Principles of Art"

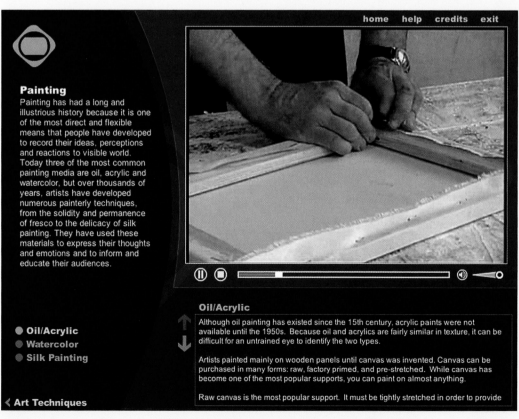

A video demonstration of painting with oils and acrylics, found in "Techniques"

Author Mary Stewart with *Labyrinth* book.

Learning to Breathe #4, **1999.** Photocopy transfer and colored pencil. 82″ × 42″.

Author **Mary Stewart** is currently the Foundations Program Coordinator for the School of Art at Northern Illinois University. Strongly committed to first-year students, Stewart has taught Two-Dimensional Design, Three-Dimensional Design, and Drawing for over twenty-five years. She also serves as a Regional Coordinator for Foundations in Art: Theory and Education, a professional organization devoted to excellence in college-level teaching.

As an artist, Stewart uses the dialogs of Plato as a beginning point for visual narratives using drawing, visual books, and computer graphics. *Labyrinth,* shown in the top photo, is composed of eleven etchings based on cave paintings, fragments of early writing, and Greek sculpture. When collapsed, the book presents a cohesive composition; when opened, the images become fragmented, creating a sense of mystery. The second photograph represents *Learning Series,* a twelve-part installation. The size and shape of each drawing suggest a doorway, while photocopies of train stations, water, gates, and architectural ruins suggest the universal nature of memory described by Plato. Stewart is now developing a series of computer animation projects exploring interpretations of reality.

about the author

i.1 Bill Viola, *Slowly Turning Narrative*, 1992. Bill Viola's *Slowly Turning Narrative* consists of a large, rotating screen onto which moving images are projected. One side of the screen is a mirror, which reflects distorted images back into the room.

Beginner's Mind, Open Mind

You are ready to embark on a marvelous journey. New technologies and exhibition venues offer dazzling new ways to produce, perform, and publicize visual ideas. Contemporary sculpture has expanded to include performance art and installations (i.1), and metalsmiths now use everything from plastics to precious metals to create inventive small-scale sculptures (i.2). Graphic designers develop many forms of visual communication, from shopping bags and exhibitions (i.3) to Websites, logos, and brochures. Film and video, the most popular forms of public storytelling worldwide, are becoming increasingly integrated with the Internet, which promises to extend visual communication even further (i.4). And, as a result of the extensive experimentation with expression and abstraction in the twentieth century,

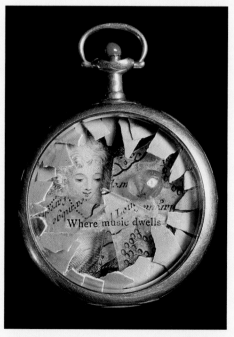

i.2 Keith E. LoBue, *Where the Music Dwells*, 1993. A broken pocket watch can become an evocative artwork when images and words are added.

i.3 Bill Cannan & Co., NASA's Participating Exhibit at the 1989 Paris Air Show. To suggest the mystery of space travel and highlight individual displays, this NASA exhibition used dramatic pools of light within a mysterious dark setting.

i.4 Hans-Jürgen Syberberg, *Parsifal,* 1982. Syberberg combined live actors with oversized projections of dreamlike landscapes in his filmic interpretation of Richard Wagner's opera.

i.5 Christian Marclay, *Amplification,* **1995.** The photographic images in this installation shift, fuse, and divide, depending on the position of the viewer.

the traditional arts of painting, printmaking, and photography (i.5) now offer expanded opportunities for introspective thinking and the development of a personal vision. The opportunities for exploration are endless. It is a great time to be studying art and design!

A journey of a thousand miles begins with one step. As a beginner, your first steps are especially important. Free of the preconceptions or habitual patterns that often paralyze more advanced students, beginners enter the learning experience with an open mind and an intense desire to learn. With no reputation to defend, they can more easily make the mistakes that are so essential to learning. Having taught students at all levels (from freshmen to graduate students and beyond), I have found that beginners of any age are the most courageous students by far. The open, unencumbered "beginner's mind" is wonderfully receptive and resilient. As a result, remarkable changes occur during the first year of study.

Defining Design

The ideas and implications of basic design are extensive and complex. The compositions created by fine artists and the designs used in the applied arts are all derived from the same raw material. As a verb, *design* can be defined four ways:

- To plan, delineate, or define, as in designing a building
- To create a deliberate sequence of images or events, as in developing a film storyboard (i.6)

i.6 Harold Michelson, Storyboard for Alfred Hitchcock's *The Birds.* Storyboards are used to plan the sequence of events and compose the specific shots in a film. Alfred Hitchcock, who began his career as an artist, preplanned his films with exacting care.

- To create a functional object, as in product design (i.7)
- To organize disparate parts into a coherent whole, as in composing a brochure

As a noun, *design* may be defined as

- A plan or pattern, such as the layout for a garden (i.8)
- An arrangement of lines, shapes, colors, and textures into an artistic whole, as in the composition of a painting or sculpture (i.9)

i.7 Designworks/USA, Home Pro Garden Tool Line. These five gardening tools are all based on the same basic combination of handle, blades, and simple pivot. Variations in proportion determine their use.

30J

3A

3E 40L

24H

i.8 Garden Design. An extensive layout is generally used for planning a garden. Matching the plants to the soil conditions, setting, climate, and overall intent saves money and improves results. In this case, the design is not an artwork in itself but, rather, a plan of action.

i.9 Claude Monet, *Waterlily Pond (Le Bassin des Nymphéas)*, 1904. Impressionist Claude Monet moved to the village of Giverny in 1883 and built an extensive water garden. The waterlilies he grew there inspired his last major series of paintings. Monet combined lines, shapes, textures, and colors to create a compelling illusion of a shimmering space.

Design is deliberate. Rather than hope for the best and accept the result, artists and designers explore a wide range of solutions to every problem, then choose the most promising option for further development. Even when chance is used to generate ideas, choices are often made before the results are shown. Design creates a bridge between artistic intention and compositional conclusion. As painter Joseph Albers noted, "To design is to plan and to organize, to order, to relate and to control."

i.10 Sam Francis, *Flash Point*, 1975. Surrounded by explosive energy, the white square in the center of this painting provides a unifying focal point.

Two-dimensional compositions are constructed from lines, shapes, textures, values, and colors that have been arranged to create a unified whole (i.10). Lines, planes, volumes, masses, and space are the basic components of a three-dimensional composition (i.11). Time design, including video, photography, performance, kinetic sculpture, and the book arts (i.12), is based on the juxtaposition of images and events. A great idea never saved a bad painting. Art and design are visual forms of communication: without careful composition, a great idea may be lost.

i.11 Alice Aycock, *Tree of Life Fantasy: Synopsis of the Book of Questions Concerning the World Order and/or the Order of Worlds,*
1990–92. Inspired by the double-helix structure of DNA and by medieval illustrations representing the entrance to paradise as a spinning hole in the sky, Aycock has combined a linear structure with a series of circular planes and a lot of open space. The resulting sculpture is as open and playful as a roller coaster.

i.12 Paul Jenkins and Jae Lee, from _Inhumans:_ "First Contact," March 1999. Comic books, like films, rely on the development of characters, the use of "camera" angles, and the organization of multiple images.

Developing a wide range of solutions to every problem is the quickest way to master composition. Small, quick studies are often used to explore the possibilities. By translating a mental image into a rough sketch, you can immediately see whether the idea has potential. Furthermore, the best way to have a good idea is to have a lot of ideas (i.13). If you explore only one idea, you are far less likely to produce an inventive image. By selecting the best rough composition from 20 sketches, you will have a good beginning point for your final design.

In the pages that follow, the basic elements, principles, and implications of design are explored in depth. Over 600 images supply visual examples from many cultures and in all areas of art and design. Fourteen interviews with living artists provide insight into the creative process.

Reading this book, however, is just the first step. True understanding comes through your own efforts, combined with the direction your teachers can provide. Remember that basic drawing and design courses provide the foundation on which all subsequent courses are built. You are only a beginner once in your entire life: this is not a rehearsal. By using your time well, you really _can_ get the rocket off the launching pad.

i.13 Mary Stewart, *Formal Relationships* (Exercise), 2001. The relationships among the parts and the whole determine the visual quality of a design. To explore a wide range of relationships, artists and designers often complete many small studies before developing more elaborate work.

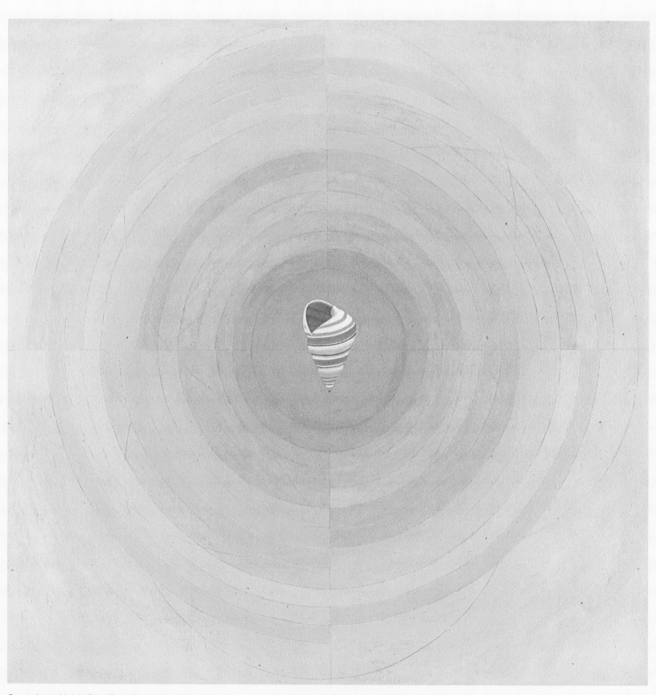

Georgiana Nehl, *Sun/Star* **(Detail), 1996.** Oil paint on gessoed wood, 25¾ in. w. × 13¼ in. h. × 1 in. d. (65 × 34 × 3 cm).

Concepts and Critical Thinking

In *A Kick in the Seat of the Pants,* Roger Von Oech identifies four distinct roles in the creative process.

First, the *explorer* learns as much as possible about the problem. Research is crucial. Ignorance of a topic may result in a superficial solution, while finalizing the first solution envisioned often results in a cliché.

Second, the *artist* experiments with a wide variety of solutions, using all sorts of combinations, proportions, and materials. By creating 10 answers to each question, the artist can select the best solution rather than accepting the only solution.

Third, the *judge* assesses the work in progress and determines what revisions are required. Innovative ideas are never fully developed when first presented; most need extensive revision and expansion. Rather than discard an underdeveloped idea, the judge identifies its potential and determines ways to increase its strength.

Finally, the *warrior* implements the idea. When the project is large and complex, implementation can be a challenge. When obstacles appear, the warrior assesses the situation, determines the best course of action, and then completes the project.

We will explore each of these roles in the next four chapters. Strategies for cultivating creativity and improving time management are discussed in Chapter Four. Chapter Five deals with concept development and visual problem solving. Chapter Six is devoted to critical thinking and provides specific ways to improve any design. In Chapter Seven, we expand our discussion of visual communication and consider ways to make more meaningful designs.

Part Two

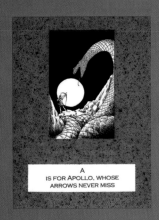

A
IS FOR APOLLO, WHOSE
ARROWS NEVER MISS

U
IS FOR URANIA THE MUSE OF
CELESTIAL FORCES IS SHE

Cultivating Creativity

"The heart of all new ideas lies in the borrowing, adding, combining or modifying of old ones. Do it by accident and people call you lucky. Do it by design and they'll call you creative."

Michael LeBoeuf, in *Imagineering*

DESIGN AND CREATIVITY

Design and creativity are natural partners. The quality of a design is determined by the integration of its parts into a cohesive whole. The design will work when the parts fit together well. Many compositional possibilities are invented and discarded during the design process. Likewise, creative thinking requires extensive exploration and experimentation. Old ideas are recombined to create new structures. These new structures suggest new questions, which then suggest new answers. By looking at familiar elements in a new way and by combining ideas that have traditionally been separate, we can cultivate a cycle of creativity.

Once viewed as peripheral, creativity and innovation have become highly valued in the current business climate. In the Information Age, intellectual property can be the most important asset in a business. Innovation in art and design, always highly valued in Western culture, has accelerated. New technologies have expanded the range of approaches available, and new ideas drawn from literature, science, philosophy, and history inspire contemporary artists and designers. The sky is the limit. An effective artist or designer cannot simply follow instructions. Cultivating creative thinking is as fundamental as mastering any technical skill.

SEVEN CHARACTERISTICS OF CREATIVE THINKING

Creativity is inherently unpredictable. Through creative thinking, old habits are broken and familiar patterns of thought are transformed. Anything can happen. Predicting the future based on past experience becomes inadequate when a creative breakthrough occurs. Like a shimmering drop of mercury, creativity eludes capture.

We can actively encourage creative thinking, however. Rather than waiting for inspiration, we can set up the conditions favorable to creativity. Based on observation and on interviews, various researchers have noted the following characteristics in many creative people.

Receptivity

Creative people are open to new ideas and welcome new experiences. Never complacent, they question the status quo and embrace alternative solutions to existing problems. Listening more and talking less is helpful. As journalist Larry King says, "I never learn anything new when I'm the one talking!"

Curiosity

A good designer brings an insatiable curiosity to each project. Researching unfamiliar topics and analyzing unusual systems is a source of delight rather than a cause for concern. Like a child, the designer is eager to learn new things and explore new places. "How does it work?" and "How can it work better?" are frequently asked questions.

Wide Range of Interests

With a broad knowledge base, a creative person can make a wider range of connections. Consider the number of words you can create from the letters in the word *image:*

age, game, gem, am, aim, a, I, me

Try the same game with the word imagination:

gin, nation, gnat, ton, tan, not, man, again, gain, oat, got, tag, am, aim, ant, no, on, tin, gamin, inn, ingot, main, a, I

With more components, the number of combinations increases. Likewise, an artist who has a background in literature, geology, archery, music, and history can make more connections than a single-minded specialist.

Attentiveness

Realizing that every experience is potentially valuable, creative people pay attention to seemingly minor details. Scientists often develop major theories by observing small events, which they then organize into complex patterns. Artists can often see past superficial visual chaos to discern an underlying order. Playwrights develop dramatic works by looking past the surface of human behavior to explore the substance of the human condition. By looking carefully, creative people see possibilities that others miss.

Connection Seeking

Seeing the similarity among seemingly disparate parts has often sparked a creative breakthrough. For example, Egyptian hieroglyphs became readable when a young French scholar realized that they carried the same message as an adjacent Greek inscription on a slab of stone. By comparing the two and cracking the code, Jean-François Champollion opened the door for all subsequent students of ancient Egyptian culture.

Conviction

Creative people value existing knowledge. Since new ideas are often derived from old ideas, it is foolish to ignore or dismiss the past. However, creative people also love change. Never satisfied with routine answers to familiar questions, they constantly consider new possibilities and often challenge the authorities. Convinced of the value of their ideas, they tenaciously pursue an independent path.

Complexity

In lecture classes, we must accurately take notes, memorize facts, and collect and analyze data. We are encouraged to think rationally, write clearly, and present our ideas in a linear progression. In studio classes, exploration, experimentation, and intuition are encouraged, especially during brainstorming sessions. Synthesis, emotion, visualization, spatial perception, and nonlinear thinking are highly valued.

To be fully effective, a creative person needs to combine the rational with the intuitive. While intuition may be used to generate a new idea, logic and analysis are often needed for its realization. As a result, the actions of creative people are often complex or even contradictory. As noted by psychologist Mihaly Csikszentmihalyi,[1] creative people often combine

- Physical energy with a respect for rest. They work long hours with great concentration, then rest and relax, fully recharging their batteries. They view balance between work and play as essential.

- Savvy with innocence. They use common sense as well as intellect in completing their work yet remain open to experience. Creative people tend to view the world and themselves with a sense of wonder, rather than cling to preconceptions or stereotypes.

- Responsibility with playfulness. When the situation requires serious attention, creative people are remarkably diligent and determined. They realize that there is no substitute for hard work and drive themselves relentlessly when nearing completion of a major project. On the other hand, when the situation permits, a playful, devil-may-care attitude may prevail, providing a release from the previous period of work.

- Risk-taking with safe-keeping. Creativity expert George Prince has noted two behavioral extremes in people.[2] Safe-keepers look before they leap, avoid surprises, punish mistakes, follow the rules, and watch the clock. A safe-keeper is most comfortable when there is only one right answer to memorize or one solution to produce. Risk-takers are just the opposite. They break the rules, leap before they look, like surprises, are impetuous, and may lose track of time. A risk-taker enjoys inventing multiple answers to every question.

    An imbalance in either direction inhibits creativity. The safe-keeper lives in fear, while the extreme risk-taker lives brilliantly — but dangerously. Creative thinking requires a mix of risk-taking and safe-keeping. When brainstorming new ideas, open-ended exploration is used: anything is possible. But, when implementing new ideas, deadlines, budgets, and feasibility become major concerns. The risk-taker gets the job started; the safe-keeper gets the job done.

- Extroversion with introversion. When starting a new project, creative people are often talkative and gregarious, eager to share insights and explore ideas. When a clear sense of direction develops, however, they often withdraw, seeking solitude and quiet work time. This capacity for solitude is crucial. Several studies have shown that talented teenagers who cannot stand solitude rarely develop their creative skills.

- Passion with objectivity. Mature artists tend to plunge into new projects, convinced of the significance of the work and confident of their skills. Any attempt to distract or dissuade them at this point is futile. However, when the model or rough study is done, many will pause to assess their progress. This period of analysis and judgment may occur in a group setting or may be done by the artist alone. In either case, the emotional attachment required while creating is now replaced by a dispassionate objectivity. Work that does not pass this review is redone or discarded, regardless of the hours spent in its development. In major projects, this alternating process of creation and analysis may be repeated many times.

- Disregard for time with attention to deadlines. Time often dissolves when studio work begins. An artist or a designer can become engrossed in a project: when the work is going well, 6 hours can feel like 20 minutes. On the other hand, an acute attention to deadlines is necessary when preparing an exhibition or working for a client.

- Modesty with pride. As they mature, creative people often become increasingly aware of the contributions to their success made by teachers, family, and colleagues. Rather than brag about past accomplishments, they tend to focus on current projects. On the other hand, as creative people become aware of their significance within a field, they gain a powerful sense of purpose. Distractions are deleted from the schedule, and increasingly ambitious goals are set. When the balance is right, all these complex characteristics fuel even greater achievement.

GOAL SETTING

As humans, our behavior is strongly goal-directed. Every action occurs for a reason. When we focus our attention on a specific task, we can accomplish just about anything. Goals help us channel our energy and manage our time. When we reach our goals,

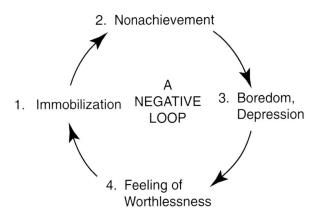

4.1 Michael LeBoeuf, *Imagineering*, 1980

our self-esteem increases, which then helps us overcome obstacles. And, with each goal met, our knowledge increases. Michael LeBoeuf has diagrammed this effect clearly (4.1).

A Goal-Setting Strategy

Self-knowledge is essential. To be effective, goals must be authentic. No matter how hard we try, we can never really fulfill our potential when pursuing goals set by others. Identifying our true interests, strengths, and objectives can be liberating. The following exercise can help clarify personal interests.

1. Get a package of small Post-it notes. Working spontaneously, write one of your characteristics on each note, such as "I am creative," "I love music," "I write well." Identify as many attributes as possible.

2. When you finish, lay out the notes on a table and look at them for a while. Consider the type of person they describe. What are this person's strengths? What additional interests might this person need to develop?

3. On a fresh stack of notes, write a new set of responses, this time dealing with the question "Why not?" as an expansion of these interests. Why not travel to Tibet? Why not learn Spanish? Why not master canoeing? Add these to the grid.

4. Then, leave the room. Go for a walk, have dinner, or head to class. Let your subconscious mind play with the possibilities suggested by your notes.

5. Next, organize the notes into four general categories: intellectual goals, personal-relationship goals, spiritual or emotional goals, physical fitness goals. If you are an extreme safe-keeper, add a category called "Adventure." If you are an extreme risk-taker, add a category called "Organization." Since a mix of activities helps feed the psyche, working with each of these categories is important. Even though spiritual, emotional, or social development is fluid and continuous, recognition of these categories can contribute to effective time management.

6. Prioritize the notes within each category. On the top note, write "This is first because _____." One the second, write "This is second because _____." Continue until you complete the grid. Discard notes that you now realize are unnecessary.

7. Choose one goal from each of the four categories. It is tempting to choose the top goal in each case, but this is unrealistic. Even the most experienced businessperson can rarely manage more than three major goals at a time. Choose one primary goal and three secondary goals.

8. Now, specify your goals. "I want to become a better artist" is too vague. Consider specific actions you can take to improve your artwork. "I need to improve my drawing" is more specific. "I want to learn anatomy" is better still. To learn anatomy, you can take a class, study an anatomy book, or draw from a skeleton. These are tangible actions: you now know what to do.

9. Determine how to achieve your goals and develop a rough timetable, listing weekly goals,

semester goals, and one-year goals. It is not necessary to list career goals just yet. Most of us explore many ideas during our first year of college, and formalizing career goals prematurely is counterproductive. After you are clearly committed to a major field of study, you can add a page of long-term goals, projecting your priorities for the next three to five years.

10. At least once a month, review your chart and add or delete information as necessary. If you realize that you are overextended this term, shift one of your minor goals to next semester or delete it altogether. This system is intended to provide you with a target, not to create a straitjacket. Make adjustments as necessary, so that your primary goals are met.

11. If you achieve all your goals, congratulate yourself — then set more ambitious goals next term. If you achieve half of your goals, congratulate yourself — then prioritize more carefully next term. You may have taken on too many tasks and thus dissipated your energy. Because there is always a gap between intention and outcome, a 70 to 80 percent completion rate is fine.

Characteristics of Good Goals

Challenging but Attainable

Too modest a goal will provide no sense of accomplishment. Too ambitious a goal will reduce, rather than increase, motivation. No one wants to fight a losing battle! Knowing your strengths and weaknesses will help you set realistic goals.

Compatible

Training for the Boston Marathon while simultaneously trying to gain 20 pounds is unwise, since you will burn off every calorie you consume. Trying to save a thousand dollars while touring Europe is unrealistic, since travel always costs more than you expect. On the other hand, by taking a dance class or joining a hiking club, you may be able to combine a fitness goal with a social goal.

Self-Directed

Avoid goals that are primarily dependent on someone else's actions or opinions. "I want to earn an *A*

in drawing" is a common example. Since the grade is determined by a teacher, your control in this area is limited. Instead, focus on improving your drawing as much as possible. This will increase your receptivity to learning and will focus your attention on actions you can control. When you do your best work, good grades generally follow.

Clearly Defined

We all have "too much to do." No matter how carefully we organize our time, there are only 24 hours in a day. Identifying daily and weekly priorities can help focus attention, increase productivity, and reduce stress.

1. Identify your target. It may be a specific action (such as doing your laundry) or a broader intention (such as improving your knowledge of anatomy). Specificity is important. It is nearly impossible to hit a target you cannot see.

2. Focus. Reduce distractions as much as possible. If visiting friends have taken over your living space, plan another time for socializing; then chase them out. If you need music to improve your concentration, put on an appropriate CD. If you can't seem to focus due to an assortment of worries, try writing them down; then refocus on the task at hand. Getting worries off your mind often helps.

3. Then, hit your target with the necessary force and energy.

Temporary

Set clear target dates, get the job done, and move on to the next project. Each completed task increases your self-confidence and adds momentum. Unfinished work, on the other hand, can drain energy and decrease momentum. If you are overloaded, delete secondary goals, so that you can complete primary goals.

TIME MANAGEMENT

Time management can help you achieve your goals. Working smarter is usually more effective than simply working harder. In a world bursting with opportunity, using your work time well can increase the time available for travel, volunteer work, or socializing. The following time-management strategies have been used by many artists and designers.

Set the Stage

Choosing when and where to work can significantly increase your output. If you are a lark, bursting with energy and enthusiasm in the morning, tackle major projects before noon. If you are an owl, equipped with night vision and able to hunt after dark, work on major projects after dinner. If you are distracted by clutter, clean your desk before beginning your workday, and tidy up your desk before you leave. These seemingly minor actions can substantially increase your productivity.

Prioritize

Use your goal list to help determine your priorities. Note which tasks are most *urgent* and which tasks are most *important*. Timing can be crucial. When you pay your phone bill on time, you easily complete an urgent but unimportant task. When your phone bill is overdue and the service is cut off, this unimportant task becomes a major headache. Dispense with urgent tasks quickly. Distribute important tasks over several weeks if necessary.

See the Big Picture

Use monthly calendar pages to record your major projects and obligations. A calendar that is organized by months can help you see which weeks will be packed with deadlines and which weeks will be relatively quiet. To avoid all-nighters, distribute large, important tasks over several weeks. To avoid missing a pivotal lecture or critique, schedule out-of-town trips during "slow" weeks.

Work Sequentially

Many activities are best done in a specific sequence. If you are writing a 20-page paper, it is best to start with research, make an outline, complete a rough draft, make corrections, then write the final draft. If you are designing a poster, it is best to start with research, make thumbnail sketches, assess the results, make a full-size rough layout, consult the client, and

then complete the poster. It is tempting to try to cut out the intermediate steps and move directly to the final draft, but this is rarely effective. With most large projects, you learn more, save time, and do better work by following the right sequence of events.

Use Parts to Create the Whole

Seen as a whole, a major project can become overwhelming. In an extreme case, creative paralysis sets in, resulting in a condition similar to writer's block. Breaking down big jobs into smaller parts helps enormously. In *Bird by Bird*, Anne Lamott gives a wonderful description of this process:

> Thirty years ago my other brother, who was ten years old at the time, was trying to get a report on birds written that he'd had three months to write. [It] was due the next day. . . . He was at the kitchen table close to tears, surrounded by binder paper and pencils and unopened books on birds, immobilized by the hugeness of the task ahead. Then my father sat down beside him, put his arm around my brother's shoulder, and said, "Bird by bird, buddy. Just take it bird by bird.[3]

By doing the job incrementally, you are likely to learn more and procrastinate less.

Make the Most of Class Time

Psychologists tell us that beginnings and endings of events are especially memorable. An experienced teacher knows that the first 10 minutes of class sets the tone for the rest of the session and that a summary at the end can help students remember the lesson. A choreographer knows that the first 10 minutes of a performance can set the stage for the next 2 hours and that the end of a dance determines the overall impact. Similarly, the wise student arrives 5 minutes early for class and maintains attention to the end of class.

Be an active learner. You can use that 5 minutes before class to review your notes from the previous session and organize your supplies. This helps create a bridge between what you know and the new information to be presented. Try to end the class on a high note, either by completing a project or by clearly determining the strengths and weaknesses of the work in progress. By analyzing your progress, you can organize your thinking and provide a solid beginning point for the next work session.

Start Early

Momentum is extremely powerful. It is much easier to climb a hill when you are already moving forward, rather than reclining. When you receive a long-term assignment, such as a 20-page paper, start it right away. Even one hour of research will help focus your attention on the problem and get you going. A slow start is better than no start!

When in Doubt, Crank It Out

Fear is one of the greatest obstacles to creative thinking. When we are afraid, we tend to avoid action and consequently miss opportunities. It is difficult to act decisively or pursue the unknown potential of a new idea. Both habit and perfectionism feed fear. If you consistently repeat the same activities and limit yourself to the most familiar friendships, you will become more and more fearful of new experiences. If you insist on doing each job perfectly, you can waste time on minor defects and avoid exploring new ideas. Perfectionism is especially destructive during brainstorming, which requires a loose, open approach.

Creativity takes courage. As IBM founder Thomas Watson noted, "If you are not satisfied with your rate of success, try failing more." Baseball player Reggie Jackson is renowned for his 563 home runs—but he also struck out 2,597 times. Thomas Edison's research team tried over 6,000 materials before finding the carbon-fiber filament used in lightbulbs.

"When in doubt, don't!" is the safe-keeper's motto. "When in doubt, do!" is the risk-taker's motto. Creativity requires risk-taking. By starting each project with a sense of adventure, you increase your level of both learning and creativity.

Work Together

Many areas of art and design, including filmmaking, industrial design, and advertising design, are often done collaboratively. Working together, artists and designers can complete projects that are too complex or time-consuming to be done alone. Collaborative thinking helps us break familiar patterns and teaches us to listen to alternative or opposing ideas.

Here is one example. Gather 20 people. Start with a copied fragment from an existing image, such as *Metamophosis II*, an 8 × 160 in. banner by M. C. Escher (4.2). In this case, students in a design class were provided with a 1-inch strip of the banner to create a beginning point and another 1-inch strip of the banner to create the ending point (4.3A). Each person invented an 8½ × 11 in. connection between the two strips. Buildings, plants, abstract shapes, chess pieces, and other images were used to bridge the gap between the strips at the beginning and the end. The images were then connected end to end, like cars in a train. When combined, they created a collaborative banner, 20 feet long (4.3B). Students had to negotiate with the person ahead of them in the line and with the person behind them,

4.2 M. C. Escher, Part of *Metamorphosis II*, 1939–40. Woodcut in black, green, and brown, printed from 20 blocks on three combined sheets, 7½ × 153⅜ in. (19 × 390 cm). © 2002 Cordon Art B. V. Baarn, Holland. All rights reserved.

4.3 A Examples of Escher Starter Images

4.3 B Mary Stewart and Jesse Wummer, **Expanded Escher Collaboration.** Student work.

in order to make a continuous image with graceful transitions. In effect, all 20 participants become members of a creative team. Finally, each 8½ × 11 in. section was photocopied and traded, providing each person with the completed artwork. In a collaboration of this kind, everyone gains, both in the learning process and in the sharing of the product.

Reduce Stress

Finally, good time management can help you avoid excessive stress. When you are pushing beyond familiar limits, some stress is inevitable. Excessive stress, however, leads to illness, anger, insomnia, mental paralysis, exhaustion, and depression. Here are some strategies that can help.

No Blame

No matter what happens, blaming yourself or others is never useful. Work on the solution rather than remaining stuck in the problem.

Keep Your Balance

A mix of emotional, spiritual, physical, and intellectual activities will help feed all areas of your psyche. No matter how significant a particular assignment may appear to be, remember that it is only one aspect of your life. Taking a break can often give you the fresh perspective you need to solve a difficult problem. Value rest. When the balance is right, your time off can actually increase your productivity.

Remember That Positives Attract

A creative person seeks change. Any change tends to present a combination of obstacles and opportunities. Focusing on the opportunities rather than on the obstacles increases confidence. Furthermore, an upbeat, positive attitude attracts other creative thinkers, while a negative, excessively critical attitude drives creative thinkers away. By assuming that you *can* do the job well, you start the spiral of accomplishment needed to fully realize your creative potential. Accentuate the positive!

SUMMARY

- Creativity and design both require new combinations of old ideas.

- Creative people are receptive to new ideas, are curious, have a wide range of interests, are attentive, seek connections, and work with great conviction.

- Creative people combine rational and intuitive thinking. While intuition may be used to generate a new idea, logic and analysis are often needed for its completion. As a result, the actions of creative people are often complex or even contradictory.

- Goals you set are goals you get. Establishing priorities and setting appropriate goals will help you achieve your potential. Good goals are challenging but attainable, compatible, self-directed, clearly defined, and temporary. Deadlines encourage completion of complex projects.

- Creating a good work area, completing tasks in an appropriate sequence, making the most of each work period, maintaining momentum, and reducing stress are major aspects of time management.

- Collaborative work can help us expand our ideas, explore new fields, and pursue projects that are too complex or time-consuming to do alone.

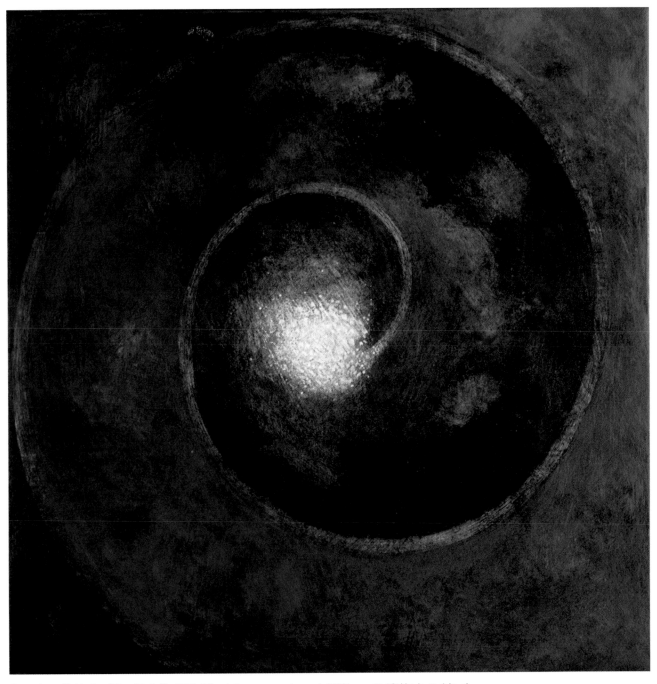

Georgiana Nehl, *Sun/Star* **(Detail), 1996.** Oil paint on gessoed wood, 25¾ in. w. × 13¼ in. h. × 1 in. d. (65 × 34 × 3 cm).

Profile:
Nancy Callahan, Artist, and Diane Gallo, Writer

Storefront Stories: Creating a Collaborative Community

Nancy Callahan (left in photo) is a leader in the field of artists' books and is known for her creative work in screen printing. She has exhibited her work widely, and, in 1994, she was one of four artists chosen to represent the United States at the International Book and Paper Exhibition in Belgium. In 1999, she participated in the International Artists' Book Workshop and Symposium in Mor, Hungary. In addition to her full-time teaching at the State University of New York at Oneonta, Callahan has taught workshops at major book centers around the country, including the Center for Book Arts in New York City and The Women's Studio Workshop.

Diane Gallo (right in photo) is an award-winning writer and performance poet, as well as a master teacher. Her filmwork has received awards from American Women in Radio & Television and nominations from the American Film Institute. Gallo teaches creative writing and life-story workshops at universities and cultural institutes throughout the country and is a visiting poet with the Dodge Foundation Poetry Program, a humanist scholar with the National Endowment for the Humanities Poets in Person program, and co-founder of the newly formed Association of Teaching Artists.

Callahan and Gallo began working together in 1984 as a photographer/writer team for the Binghamton Press. As a result of many years of collaborative teaching, they became the first teaching artist team working with the Empire State Partnership project, jointly sponsored by the New York State Education Department and the New York State Council of the Arts. In 1996, they received fellowships to the Virginia Center for the Creative Arts, where they began working on a major project, which led to their selection by the Mid-Atlantic Foundation for their millennium project. Funded by the National Endowment for the Arts, the project—Artists & Communities: America Creates for the Millennium—named Callahan and Gallo as two of America's 250 most creative community artists.

MS: You've gained a lot of recognition for your recent text-based installations. Please describe *Storefront Stories*.

NC: Over the past two years we've had an extraordinary collaborative experience. As an extension of our writing, we developed a new type of text-based installation. One day as we worked on a story about ironing, we playfully hung a single wrinkled white shirt in the front window of our studio in Gilbertsville, New York. Below the shirt, we placed a small sign that said "No one irons anymore." As the lone shirt turned, it attracted attention, causing people on the sidewalk to stop, read

the window, and react. *Storefront Stories* was born.

DG: Objects became words; words transformed objects. Week by week, using storefront windows as a public stage, we wrote and presented installments of autobiographical stories. In one town, a single window was changed every 10 days, creating an ongoing narrative. In another, we used five windows in a row, like pages in a book. Bits of text and symbolic objects were used to tell stories about personal change. Stories and objects—combined with the unexpected street location—sparked curiosity and started a community dialogue.

MS: How did members of the community become participants?

NC: They just began telling us their stories. An elderly woman on her way to the post office stopped to tell us the story of how she had learned to type on an old Smith typewriter, just like the one in the window. Eleven-year-old boys on bicycles stopped by. A mother brought her children to the windows each week to read the story aloud. Couples strolling by in the evening asked, "What's coming next?"

DG: People talked to us easily, asking questions and encouraging us. Many times, we'd return to find handwritten stories, comments, and suggestions. We watched passersby examine the windows and heard them laughing and talking to each other as they pieced together the story. When a viewer made a good suggestion, we incorporated the idea into the next window. When community members saw their ideas so quickly incorporated, they realized they were more than passive viewers. They were now active participants, with a vital involvement in the artistic process. The collaboration which began between two artists quickly expanded, engaging the entire town.

MS: In your household installations you create complete environments to frame your stories. To create these environments, you spend many hours scouting thrift shops and garage sales, searching for just the right objects to evoke an exact time and place. Why are these objects so important?

NC: Household objects are the vocabulary of the everyday world. Everyone feels comfortable with them. The objects are a bridge—they allow the viewer to cross easily from everyday life into the world of our installations.

DG: After the object is safely in the viewer's mind, it becomes a psychic spark which triggers associations and amplifies memories. For example, while we were doing the ironing installation, a delivery man who stopped for a moment to watch us work said, "I don't know anything about art," and began talking deeply and at length about how, when he was a boy, his mother took in ironing to make extra money so that he could have a bicycle.

NC: His narrative then created another layer of collaboration.

MS: When you began creating the installations, did you expect this kind of public reaction?

NC: No. It was a shock. From the moment we hung that first wrinkled shirt in the studio window, people on the street were responsive. The immediate feedback was exhilarating.

Diane Gallo and Nancy Callahan, *Storefront Stories*, 1999. Mixed medium installation, 6 × 6 × 6 ft (1.83 × 1.83 × 1.83 m).

MS: What are the characteristics of a good collaboration?

DG: Quiet attention is crucial. We both have to really listen, not only to words but also to the implications.

NC: Always tell the truth. There can be no censoring. If something's bothering you, it's important to talk about it right away. Honesty and careful listening build trust. When you trust your partner, you can reveal more.

MS: When people first see your installations, many are almost overwhelmed. Why?

DG: We're balancing on a fine line between life and art, between the personal and the universal, the public and the private, the conscious and the unconscious. We're working on the edge of consciousness, looking for things you might only be half aware of under ordinary circumstances. It's like watching a horizon line in your mind, waiting for a thought or an answer to rise.

Problem Seeking
and Problem Solving

Artworks are generally experienced visually. By learning the basic elements of design and exploring many approaches to composition, you can increase the visual power of your work. Composition, however, is only part of the puzzle. With the increasing emphasis on visual communication around the world, the ideas being expressed by artists and designers have become more varied and complex. Conceptual invention is just as important as compositional strength. New ideas invite development of new types of artwork. When the concept is fresh and the composition is compelling, expression and communication expand.

PROBLEM SEEKING

The Design Process

In its most basic form, the design process can be distilled down to four basic steps. When beginning a project, the designer asks

1. What is needed?
2. What existing designs are similar to the design we need?
3. What is the difference between the existing designs and the new design?
4. How can we transform, combine, or expand these existing designs?

By studying the classic Eames chair, we can see this process clearly. Charles and Ray Eames were two of the most innovative and influential designers of the postwar era. Trained as an architect, Charles was a master of engineering and had a gift for design integration. Trained as a painter, Ray contributed a love of visual structure, a sense of adventure, and an understanding of marketing. Combining their strengths, this husband-and-wife team designed furniture, toys, exhibitions, and architecture and directed over 80 experimental films.

Their first breakthrough in furniture design came in 1940, when they entered a chair competition sponsored by the Museum of Modern Art. Many architects had designed furniture, and the Eameses were eager to explore this field. Many similar products existed. The most common was the overstuffed chair, which continues to dominate American living rooms. Extensive padding on a boxy framework supported the sitter. Another popular design

5.1 Marcel Breuer, Armchair, Dessau, Germany, 1925.
Tubular steel, canvas, 28¹¹⁄₁₆ in. h. × 30⁵⁄₁₆ in. w. × 26¾ in. d.
(72.8 × 77 × 68 cm).

5.2 Alvar Aalto, Paimio Lounge Chair, 1931–33. Laminated birch,
molded plywood, lacquered, 26 × 23¾ × 34⅞ in. (66 × 60.5 × 88.5 cm).

5.3 Overstuffed Chair

was the Adirondack chair, made from a series of flat wooden planes. Of greatest interest, however, were designs by architects such as Marcel Breuer (5.1) and Alvar Aalto (5.2). These designs used modern materials and clearly displayed their structure.

By comparing existing chairs with the chair they wanted, Charles and Ray could identify qualities they needed to retain and qualities that needed to be changed. The familiar overstuffed chair (5.3) was bulky and awkward, but it was comfortable. The Adirondack chair (5.4) was easy to mass-produce, but too large for interior use. The modern chairs were elegant and inventive but were expensive to produce and often uncomfortable. The Eameses wanted to create a modern chair that was comfortable, elegant, and inexpensive.

During World War II, the Eames team had designed and manufactured molded plywood splints, which were used by doctors in the U.S. Navy. After extensive research and experimentation, they had mastered the process of steaming and reshaping the sheets of plywood into complex curves. In developing their competition entry, they combined their knowledge of splints, love of modern chairs, understanding of painting, and mastery of architecture. Their plywood chair, designed in collaboration with architect Eero Saarinen, was awarded the first prize.

5.4 Adirondack Chair

5.5 **Charles and Ray Eames, Side Chair, Model DCM, 1946.**
Molded ash plywood, steel rod, and rubber shockmounts, 28¾ in. h.
× 19½ in. d. × 20 in. w. (73 × 49.5 × 50.8 cm).

5.6 **Frank Gehry, Cross Check Armchair, 1992.** Maple,
33⅜ in. h. × 28½ in. d. × 28½ in. w. (85.3 × 72.4 × 72.4 cm).

A series of Eames designs followed, including a metal and plywood version in 1946 (5.5) and several cast plastic versions. One popular chair was mass-produced by the thousands.

By addressing a need, visualizing existing designs, making comparisons, and combining the best characteristics of existing chairs, the Eames team produced a new kind of chair and thus firmly established themselves as leaders in the design field.

The Fine Art Process

For a designer, the problem-solving process begins when a client requests help or the designer identifies a specific need. With the Eames chair, the museum competition provided the impetus for an experiment that reshaped an industry. Design is generally utilitarian, and the problem is usually determined by a client.

Contemporary sculptors, printmakers, film-makers, and other fine artists generally invent their own aesthetic problems. Ideas often arise from personal experience and from the cultural context. Combining self-awareness with empathy for others,

many artists have transformed a specific event into a universal statement. For example, Picasso's *Guernica* (see figure 7.20, page 173) painted in response to the 1937 bombing of a specific Spanish village, is now revered as a universal statement about the horrors of war. Working more independently and with fewer deadlines, artists can explore ideas and issues of personal interest.

Sources of Ideas

Regardless of the initial motivation for their work, both artists and designers constantly scan their surroundings in an omnivorous search for images and ideas. As demonstrated by the profiles that appear throughout this book, the most improbable object or idea may provide inspiration. Memories of growing up in small-town America provide the stimulus for *Storefront Stories*, by Nancy Callahan and Diane Gallo. Biological systems inspire sculptor Heidi Lasher-Oakes. Ordinary vegetables and African vessels influence ceramicist David Mac-Donald. If you are at a loss for an idea, take a fresh look at your surroundings.

Transform a Common Object

Architect Frank Gehry based the exuberant armchair in figure 5.6 on the wood-strip bushel basket used by farmers (5.7). If you consider all the ideas that can be generated by a set of car keys, a pair of scissors, a baseball glove, or a compass, you will have more than enough to get a project started.

5.7 A Wood-Strip Bushel Basket

Study Nature

Ceramicist Ray Rogers is inspired by many natural forms, including mushrooms, stones, and aquatic life. His spherical pots (5.8) often suggest the colors, textures, and economy of nature. In figure 5.9, Vera Lisková used the fluidity and transparency of glass to create a humorous version of a prosaic porcupine. Through an inventive use of materials, both artists have reinterpreted nature.

5.8 Ray Rogers, Vessel, New Zealand, 1984. Large, pit-fired (porous and nonfunctional) with "fungoid" decorative treatment in relief. Diameter approximately 21⅝ in. (55 cm).

5.9 Vera Lisková, *Porcupine*, 1972–80. Flame-worked glass, 4¼ × 11 in. (10.8 × 28.2 cm).

Visit a Museum

Artists and designers frequently visit all kinds of museums. Carefully observed, the history and physical objects produced by any culture can be both instructive and inspirational. Looking at non-Western artwork is especially valuable. Unfamiliar concepts and compositions can suggest new ideas and fresh approaches. Beau Dick's *Mugamtl Mask* (5.10) is one example. First developed by a man who had revived from a deadly illness, it depicts the supernatural abilities (including flight) that he gained during his experience. His descendants now have the right to construct and wear this special mask. By understanding the story and studying the mask structure, you can more readily design a mask based on your own experiences.

5.10 Beau Dick, *Mugamtl Mask (Crooked Beak)*, 1993. Red cedar, cedar bark, paint, 24 × 26 × 16 in. (61 × 66 × 40.6 cm).

Characteristics of a Good Problem

Regardless of its source, the problem at hand must fully engage either the artist or the designer. By courageously confronting obstacles and seeking solutions, the artist or designer can develop increasingly ambitious work. Whether it is assigned or invented, a good problem includes many of the following characteristics.

Significant

When substantial amounts of time, effort, and money are being spent, it is wise to prioritize problems and focus on those of greatest consequence. Identifying and prioritizing your major goals can help you determine the significance of a job. Balancing this analysis with a sense of adventure can help you combine the best qualities of a risk-taker and a safe-keeper.

Socially Responsible

With the human population above 6 billion, it is unwise to pursue a project that squanders natural resources. In the past 20 years, designers have become increasingly aware of the environmental and social consequences of their actions. What natural resources will be required for a major project, and how will you dispose of resulting waste? Increasingly, designers consider the environmental as well as the economic implications of each project.

Comprehensible

It is almost impossible to solve a problem you don't understand. When working on a class assignment, ask questions if the assignment is unclear to you.

Open to Experimentation

It is important to distinguish between clear definition and restrictive limitations. Consider the following two assignment descriptions:

1. Organize at least 20 photocopies in such a way that they convey an idea or emotion.

2. Organize 20 photographs by American Civil War photographer Mathew Brady in order to tell a story about the life of Abraham Lincoln.

In the first case, the requirements of the project are clearly stated, but the solution remains open to invention. In the second case, the *solution* as well as the *problem* is described. For the inventive artist or designer, there are no "bad" problems, only bad solutions. Nonetheless, when limited to a narrow range of possible solutions, even the most inventive person will become ineffective. If you find yourself in a straitjacket, rethink the problem and try a new approach.

Ambitious yet Achievable

When the problem is too easy or the solution is too familiar, little is learned and nothing is gained. When the problem is too difficult or the solution is too time-consuming, completion is delayed and costs increase. Continued indefinitely, even the most exciting project can become a trap!

Authentic

Regardless of the source, every person approaches each problem on his or her own terms. Each of us has a unique perspective, and the connections, which are so important in design, will vary. Likewise, as a student, you will learn more when you really embrace each assignment and make it your own. Ask questions, so that you can understand the substance as well as the surface of each assignment. When you reframe the assignment in your own terms and plunge into the work wholeheartedly, the creative possibilities will expand and your imagination will soar.

CONVERGENT AND DIVERGENT THINKING

To see how it all works, let's work our way through an actual assignment, using two different problem-solving strategies.

> Problem: Organize up to 20 photocopies from the library so that they tell a story. Use any size and type of format as appropriate. Any image can be enlarged, reduced, cropped, or repeated.

Using Convergent Thinking

Convergent thinking involves the pursuit of a predetermined goal, usually in a linear progression and using a highly focused problem-solving technique. The word *prose* can help you remember the basic steps:

1. Define the *problem.*
2. Do *research.*
3. Determine your *objective.*
4. Devise a *strategy.*
5. *Execute* the strategy.
6. *Evaluate* the results.

In convergent thinking, the end determines the means. You know what you are seeking before you begin. For this reason, clear definition of the problem is essential: the most brilliant idea is useless if it doesn't solve the problem.

Convergent thinking is familiar to most of us through the scientific method, which follows the same basic procedure. It is orderly, logical, and empirical; there are clear boundaries and specific guidelines. Clearly focused on the final result, convergent thinking is a good way to achieve a goal and meet a deadline. Let's analyze each step.

Define the Problem

Determine the exact parameters of the assignment. Ask lots of questions, so that you understand the assignment objectives. Determine all of the physical and technical requirements and ask whether there are any stylistic limitations. Be sure that you understand the preliminary steps as well as the final due date.

Next, assess your strengths and weaknesses relative to the problem assigned, and determine your best work strategy. Let's consider the approaches taken by two hypothetical students, Jeremy (as a convergent thinker) and Angela (as a divergent thinker).

Jeremy begins by defining *story, images,* and *library.* From the dictionary, he finds that a *story* is shorter than a novel, that it may be true or fictitious, that a series of connected events is needed, and that it may take many forms, including a memoir, a play, or a newspaper article.

Next, he finds that an *image* is a representation of a person or thing, a visual impression produced by reflection in a mirror, or a mental picture of something: an idea or impression. This means that photographs from books or magazines and reproductions of paintings are fair game. Jeremy realizes that he can even include a mirror in the project, to reflect the viewer's own image.

Finally, by exploring the computer system in the *library,* he finds that Internet resources as well as books are available. He spends the first hour of class on brainstorming, then decides to develop a story about Irish immigration to America at the turn of the century.

Do Research

Creativity is highly dependent on seeking connections and making new combinations. The more information you have, the more connections you can make. Through research, you can collect and assess technical, visual, and conceptual information. For this assignment, Jeremy develops a plausible story based on immigrant diaries. He begins to collect images of ships, cities, and people.

Determine Your Objective

Jeremy now has the raw material needed to solve the problem. However, many questions remain unanswered, including

- What happens in this story? Is it fiction or nonfiction?

- Who is the storyteller? A 12-year-old boy will tell a very different story than a 20-year-old woman.

- What is the best format to use? A dozen letters, sent between fictitious brothers in Dublin and

Boston? A Website, describing actual families? A photo album?

At this point, Jeremy pauses to determine his objective, both as an artist and as a student. What does he really want to communicate? He considers:

- *Does it solve the problem?* He reviews the assignment parameters.

- *Is the solution conceptually inventive?* Is it really intriguing, or is it something we've all seen before, a cliché?

- *Is the planned solution visually compelling?*

- *Can this solution be completed by the due date?* To meet the due date, it may be necessary to distill a complex problem down to an essential statement. In this case, Jeremy decides to simplify his project by focusing on one main character.

Devise a Strategy

While some assignments can be done in an afternoon, three-dimensional projects and multiple-image works tend to take longer. Jeremy determines the supplies he needs and considers the best time and place to work on the project.

Execute the Strategy

Now, Jeremy just digs in and works. He has found it best to work with great concentration and determination at this point, rather than second-guessing himself.

Evaluate the Results

At the end of each work session, Jeremy considers the strengths and weaknesses of the work in progress. What areas in each composition seem timid or confusing? How can those areas be strengthened? He finally presents the project for a class critique.

Convergent Thinking Applications

Convergent thinking is most effective when

- The problem can be defined clearly.

- The problem can be solved rationally.

- The problem must be solved sequentially.
- Firm deadlines must be met.

Because many problems in science and industry fit these criteria, convergent thinking is widely used by scientists, businesspeople, and graphic designers.

Using Divergent Thinking

The advantages of convergent thinking are clarity, control, focus, and a strong sense of direction. For many tasks, convergent thinking is ideal. In some cases, however, convergent thinking can offer *too* much clarity and not enough chaos. Inspiration is elusive. Over-the-edge creativity is often messy and rarely occurs in an orderly progression. If you want to find something completely new, you will have to leave the beaten path.

In **divergent thinking,** the means determines the end. The process is more open-ended; specific results are hard to predict. Divergent thinking is a great way to generate ideas and move beyond preconceptions.

There are two major differences between convergent and divergent thinking. First, in divergent thinking, the problem is defined much more broadly, with less attention to "what the client wants." Research is more expansive and less tightly focused. Experimentation is open-ended: anything can happen. Second, because the convergent thinker discards weak ideas in the thumbnail stage, the final image is preplanned and predictable. The divergent thinker, on the other hand, generates many variables, is less methodical, and may have to produce multiple drafts of a composition in order to get the desired result.

While convergent thinking is usually more efficient, divergent thinking is often more inventive. It opens up unfamiliar lines of inquiry and can lead to a creative breakthrough. Divergent thinking is a high-risk/high-gain approach. By breaking traditional rules, the artist can explore unexpected connections and create new possibilities.

Let's try the same assignment again, now using Angela's divergent thinking.

> Problem: Organize up to 20 photocopies from the library so that they tell a story. Use any size and type of format as appropriate. Any image can be enlarged, reduced, cropped, or repeated.

Realizing that the strength of the source images is critical, Angela immediately heads for the section of the library devoted to photography. By leafing though a dozen books, she finds 30 great photographs, ranging from images of train stations to trapeze artists. She photocopies the photographs, enlarging and reducing pictures to provide more options. Laying them out on a table, she begins to move the images around, considering the stories that might be generated. Twenty of the images are soon discarded; they are unrelated to the circus story she begins to develop. She then finds 5 more images to flesh out her idea.

At this point, her process becomes similar to the final steps described in the preceeding section. Like Jeremy, she must clarify her objective, develop characters, decide on a format, and construct the final piece. However, because she started with such a disparate collection of images, her final story is more likely to be nonlinear. Like a dream, her images may suggest ideas rather than describe specific situations.

Divergent Thinking Applications

Divergent thinking is most effective when

- The problem definition is elusive or evolving.
- A rational solution is not required.
- A sequential work method is unnecessary.
- Deadlines are flexible.

Many creative people have used divergent thinking to explore the subconscious and reveal unexpected new patterns of thought. Surrealism, an art movement that flourished in Europe between the world wars, provides many notable examples of divergent thinking in art and literature. More interested in the essential substance of ideas and objects than in surface appearances, painter Yves Tanguy constructed *Multiplication of the Arcs* (5.11) from evocative abstract shapes. In *The Mystery and Melancholy of a Street* (5.12), Giorgio de Chirico used distorted perspective, relentless repetition, and threatening cast shadows to create a feeling of anxiety. More interested in stimulating the viewer's own response than in imposing a specific vision, the surrealists rejected rational thought.

Which is better—convergent or divergent thinking? A good problem-solving strategy is one

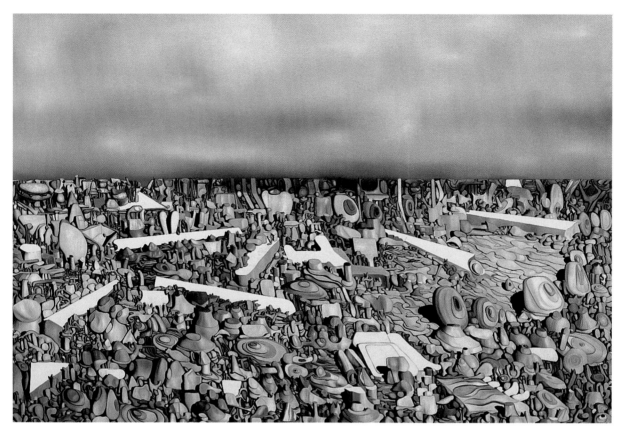

5.11 Yves Tanguy, *Multiplication of the Arcs*, 1954. Oil on canvas, 40 × 60 in. (101.6 × 152.4 cm).

5.12 Giorgio de Chirico, *The Mystery and Melancholy of a Street*, 1914. Oil on canvas, 24¼ × 28½ in. (62 × 72 cm).

that works. If five people are working on a Website design, a clear sense of direction, agreement on style, an understanding of individual responsibilities, and adherence to deadlines are essential. Such a design team will usually use convergent thinking. On the other hand, when an artist is working independently, the open-ended divergent approach can lead to a major breakthrough. By understanding both approaches, you can select the work method that is best for you.

BRAINSTORMING

Brainstorming plays an important role in both convergent and divergent thinking. It is a great way to expand ideas, see connections, and explore implications. The following are four common strategies.

Make a List

Let's say that the assignment involves visualizing an emotion. Start by listing every emotion you can, regardless of your interest in any specific area. Getting into the practice of opening up and actively exploring possibilities is crucial: just pour out ideas!

joy   sorrow   anger   passion   jealousy
sympathy   horror   exaltation

From the list of emotions, circle one that looks promising. To move from the intangible name of the emotion to a visual solution, develop a list of the *kinds, causes,* and *effects* of the emotion. Following is one example, using *anger* as a starting point.

KINDS	CAUSES	EFFECTS
annoyance	wrong-number phone call at 5 A.M.	slammed down phone
smoldering rage	friend gets award you want	argument with friend
desperate anger	fired from job	shouted at your child
anger at self	poor performance on test	major studying

By investigating specific kinds of anger and determining the causes and the effects, you now have some specific images to develop, rather than struggling with a vague, intangible emotion.

Use a Thesaurus

Another way to explore the potential of an idea is to use a thesaurus. Be sure to get a thesaurus that lists words conceptually rather than alphabetically. Use the index in the back to look up the specific word you need. For example, *The Concise Roget's International Thesaurus* has a section titled "Feelings," including everything from *acrimony* to *zeal.* Here is a listing of synonyms from the section on resentment and anger: *anger, wrath, ire, indignation, heat, more heat than light, dudgeon, fit of anger, tantrum, outburst, explosion, storm, scene, passion, fury, burn, vehemence, violence, vent one's anger, seethe, simmer,* and *sizzle!* Thinking about a wide range of implications and connections to other emotions can give you a new approach to a familiar word.

Explore Connections

By drawing a conceptual diagram, you can create your own thesaurus. Start with a central word. Then, branch out in all directions, pursuing connections and word associations as widely as possible. In a sense, this approach lets you visualize your thinking, as the branches show the patterns and connections that occurred as you explored the idea (5.13A).

In *Structure of the Visual Book,* Keith Smith demonstrates the value of verbal connections. Smith seeks immersion in his subject. He wants to know it

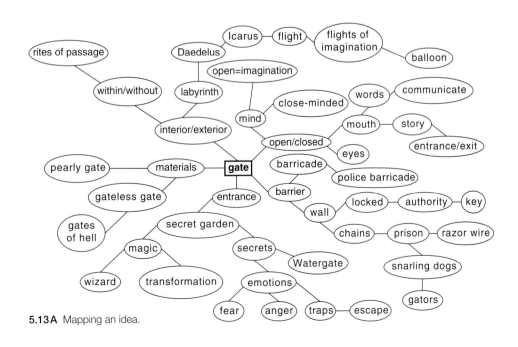

5.13A Mapping an idea.

If I am going to make drawings or photographs which include a bicycle, I might go for a bike ride, but more importantly I would fantasize about a bike. I would picture a bike in my mind. The most obvious depiction is the side view because this is the significant profile. I would then imagine a standing bicycle with no rider, looking from above, directly down on the bike, or from behind or in front of the standing bike with my eye-level midway between the ground and the handlebars. In these three positions the bicycle is seen from the least significant profile. It is a thin vertical line with horizontal protrusions of the pedals, seat and handlebars. The area viewed is so minimal that the bicycle almost disappears.

Before long in examining a bike I would become involved with circles. Looking at the tires, I think about the suspension of the rim and the tire, indeed, the entire vehicle and rider, by the thin spokes. It amazes me that everything is floating in space, connected only by thin lines. I imagine riding the bike through puddles and the trace of the linear journey from the congruent and diverging water marks left by the tread on the pavement. I might think about two friends together and separated. Symbolism.

I think about cycles of being with friends and apart. And again I would think literally of cycles, circles and tires.

I would think of the full moon as a circle and how in its cycle it turns into a line. I would see the tires from the significant profile and in my mind I would turn it in space and it would become an ellipse.

If I turned it further, until it was on an axis 90 degrees from the significant profile, it would no longer be a circle or an ellipse, but it would be a line. So again, line comes into my thoughts.

A circle is a line.

A circle is a straight line.[1]

5.13B

so well that, when he begins to work, he can pursue his images intuitively, with all the power and grace of a skillful cyclist. Try to follow the steps in figure 5.13B, as he explores the word *bicycle*.

Keep a Journal

Keeping a journal or sketchbook is an ideal way to record your ideas and create connections. In it, you can

- Classify, arrange, and record information.
- Brainstorm new ideas.
- Examine your current beliefs and analyze the beliefs of others.

- Record your responses to critiques.
- Make connections among your various classes.

Recording your ideas at the end of each class and reviewing them at the beginning of the next can help you construct your own learning process. Anything that expands your thinking is fair game, including

- Plans for projects, such as thumbnail sketches and rough drafts
- Comments on how your work can be improved
- Notes from textbook readings and clippings from magazines

- Notes on visiting artists or gallery visits
- Technical notes or information on materials used in class
- Questions you want to pose in the next class meeting

Your record keeping can take many forms, including

- Drawings and diagrams
- Written ideas, descriptions, and lists
- Poetry or other excerpts from literature and song lyrics

Ask yourself the following questions:

- What was the most compelling image I saw today? What made it compelling?
- What was the most memorable or most offensive idea I heard expressed today? Why was it memorable or offensive?
- What similarities and differences were there among my studio classes this week?
- What connections were there between my lecture classes and studios?
- What do I know today that I didn't know yesterday?
- What do I need to know in order to push my ideas further?

Viewing the journal as a record of your creative process is liberating. Just let your ideas flow. A random idea today can help you solve a visual problem tomorrow. Indeed, it is wise to review the journal as you move into upper-level classes. Many ideas that were too ambitious for a first-year class are perfectly suited to further development in an upper-level class.

VISUAL RESEARCH

Thumbnail Sketches

Library research played a major role in Angela's divergent thinking as well as Jeremy's convergent thinking. We will now consider various approaches to visual research.

Return to your original list of emotions you developed in the brainstorming exercise. Circle the most promising words or phrases you have generated and look for connections between them. Start working on thumbnail sketches, about 1.5 × 2 in. in size (5.14). Be sure to draw a clear boundary for the sketches. The edge of the frame is like an electric fence; by using the edge wisely, you can generate a lot of power!

As with the verbal brainstorming, move fast and stay loose at this point. It is better to generate 10 to 20 possibilities than to refine any single idea. You may find yourself producing very different solutions, or you may make a series of multiple solutions to the same idea: either approach is fine. Just keep moving. An open, nonjudgmental attitude is essential.

Model Making

When working two-dimensionally, it is often necessary to make one or more full-sized rough drafts to

5.15A Peter Forbes, Models for
Shelter/Surveillance Sculpture, 1994. Mixed
media, 10½ × 9½ × 9 in. (27 × 24 × 23 cm).

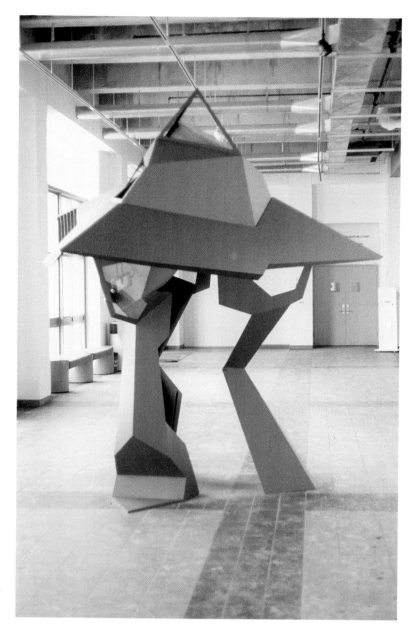

5.15B Peter Forbes,
Shelter/Surveillance Sculpture, 1994.
Mixed media, 11 ft 2 in. × 10 ft 4 in. ×
10 ft (3.4 × 3.2 × 3 m).

see how the design looks when enlarged. Refine-
ments made at this stage can make the difference between an adequate solution and an inspired solution.

Prototypes, models, and maquettes serve a
similar purpose when you are working three-
dimensionally. A **maquette** is a well-developed
three-dimensional sketch. Figure 5.15A shows Peter
Forbes' maquette for *Shelter/Surveillance Sculpture.*
In this chipboard "sketch," Forbes determined the
size of the sculpture relative to the viewer and developed a construction strategy. As a result, when
he constructed the final, 11-foot-tall sculpture,
Forbes was able to proceed with confidence. A
model is a technical experiment. A **prototype** can be

quite refined, as with the fully functional test cars
developed by automobile companies. In addition to
the aesthetic benefit of these preliminary studies, it
is often necessary to solve technical problems at this
stage. Is the cardboard you are using heavy enough
to stand vertically, or does it bow? Is your adhesive
strong enough? If there are moving parts, is the action fluid and easy, or does the mechanism consistently get stuck?

By completing these preliminary studies, you
can refine the idea, strengthen the composition, and
improve the craft of the final piece. As with a well-
rehearsed performance, the work you bring to the
critique is now really ready for discussion.

VARIATIONS ON A THEME

When we work creatively, the idea develops right along with the image. As the project evolves, we see other implications that go beyond our initial intention. By courageously pursuing these implications, we can exceed our original expectations. Just as the landscape appears to expand when we climb a mountain, so an image can expand when our conceptual understanding increases.

One way to get a lot of mileage out of an idea is through variations on a theme. Professional artists rarely do just one painting or sculpture of a given idea—most do many variations before moving to a new subject. *Thirty-Six Views of Mount Fuji* is one example. Printmaker Katsushika Hokusai was 70 years old when he began this series. The revered and beautiful Mount Fuji appeared in each of the designs in some way. Variations in the time of year and size of the mountain helped Hokusai produce very different images while retaining the same basic theme (5.16A–C).

5.16A Katsushika Hokusai, *Thirty-Six Views of Mount Fuji: Under the Mannen Bridge at Fukagawa,* Edo Period, c. 1830. Color woodblock print, 10¹⁄₁₆ × 14¹¹⁄₁₆ in. (25.7 × 37.5 cm).

5.16B Katsushika Hokusai, *Thirty-Six Views of Mount Fuji: The Great Wave off Kanagawa,* Edo Period, c. 1830. Color woodblock print, 10³⁄₁₆ × 14¹⁵⁄₁₆ in. (25.9 × 37.5 cm).

5.16C Katsushika Hokusai, *Thirty-Six Views of Mount Fuji: Near Umezawa in Sagami Province,* Edo Period, c. 1830. Color woodblock print, 10¹⁄₁₆ × 14⅞ in. (25.6 × 37.8 cm).

A very different series of variations is presented in figures 5.17 and 5.18. Here, the two artists offer very individual interpretations of the basic bracelet. Leslie Leupp's three bracelets present a playful dialogue between form and space. Lines, planes, and simple volumes dance around the wearer's wrist. In contrast, Lisa Gralnick's three bracelets are dark, massive, and threatening. The crisp angles, simple forms, and black acrylic are more suggestive of armor than of jewelry.

5.17 Leslie Leupp, Three Bracelets: Solidified Reality, Frivolous Vitality, Compound Simplicity, 1984. Steel, plastic, linoleum, laminate, aluminum. Constructed, each 3 × 4 × 3 in. (8 × 10 × 8 cm).

5.18 Lisa Gralnick, Three Bracelets, 1988. Black acrylic, gold, hollow construction, left to right: 3 × 3½ × 3½ in.; 4½ × 3½ × 3 in.; 3½ × 3½ × 3½ in. (7.6 × 8.9 × 8.9 cm; 11.4 × 8.9 × 7.6 cm; 8.9 × 8.9 × 8.9 cm).

AN OPEN MIND

As noted in Chapter Four, most creative people have a wide range of interests. The very best artists and designers are often accomplished in more than one field. For example, Michelangelo was acclaimed as a painter, sculptor, and poet, while da Vinci was a master of art, biology, and engineering. The study of philosophy has had a major impact on videographer Bill Viola and on installation artist Robert Irwin. Performer Laurie Anderson is equally an artist and a musician and derives many of her ideas from literature. Whenever the base of knowledge expands, the range of potential connections increases. When the islands of knowledge are widely scattered, as with interdisciplinary work, the imaginative leap is especially great.

The message is clear. The more you know, the more you can say. Read a book. Attend a lecture. Take a course in astronomy, archaeology, psychology, or poetry. Use ideas from academic courses to expand your studio work. Art and design require conceptual development as well as perceptual and technical skill. By engaging your heart, your eye, your hand, and your mind, you can fully use your emotional, perceptual, technical, and conceptual resources to create your very best work.

SUMMARY

- Concept and composition are equally important aspects of art and design.

- Designers usually solve problems presented by clients. Artists usually invent aesthetic problems for themselves.

- Ideas come from many sources, including common objects, nature, mythology, and history.

- Good problems are significant, socially responsible, comprehensible, achievable, and authentic. They provide basic parameters without inhibiting exploration.

- Convergent thinking is highly linear. The word *prose* can help you remember the steps.

- Divergent thinking is nonlinear and more open-ended than convergent thinking. It is less predictable and may lead to a creative breakthrough.

- Any idea can be expanded or enriched using brainstorming. Making lists, using a thesaurus, making a conceptual diagram, and creating connections are all common strategies.

- Visual and verbal research can provide the background information needed to create a truly inventive solution.

- Pursuing an idea through variations on a theme can help you realize its full potential.

Keywords

brainstorming
convergent thinking

divergent thinking
maquette

model

prototype

Profile:
Heidi Lasher-Oakes, Sculptor

The Infinite Journey: Exploring
Ideas in Art and Science

Heidi Lasher-Oakes is best known for her Biological Abstractions Series. Her exhibitions include "Seductive Matter, Sensual Form," which was installed in the Corcoran Art Gallery, and "In Three Dimensions: Women Sculptors of the 90's," which was held at the Snug Harbor Cultural Center. Educated at Reed College, the Pacific Northwest College of Art, and Syracuse University, Lasher-Oakes was awarded a residency at the Bemis Art Center in Omaha, Nebraska, and received a Pollock-Krasner Individual Artist Grant in 1997.

MS: What do art and science have in common?

HL: I have always believed that artistic and scientific methods are closely linked. A scientific experiment is aesthetically pleasing when it is simply and elegantly designed and takes into consideration all possible variables. On the other hand, the full exploration of an artistic idea requires the same rigor of inquiry and careful documentation as the exploration of a scientific hypothesis. In either discipline, if a process is aesthetically successful, it will lead to a coherent result. An aesthetic process requires that all components be ruthlessly considered and evaluated individually and as a unit. The aesthetic integrity of a process does not guarantee that the resulting artwork or experiment will be successful, but it does seem to guarantee that the subsequent work will not constitute a waste of time, either for the investigator or for the audience.

The Shakers have a philosophy of work that expresses this viewpoint simply: if you are going to do something, do it as well as you can.

MS: What is the connection between art and science in your work?

HL: The sculptures in my current Biological Abstraction Series are inspired by human anatomy and physiology, by the forms of cell and tissue structures as seen through an electron microscope, and by the relationships of these forms to manmade structures and objects. They also incorporate plant, animal, and rock forms. Science really provides the starting point for my artwork.

MS: Why are you a sculptor rather than a scientist?

HL: Art gives me a way to express my ideas and observations through the creation of physical objects. I am a haptic person, which means that I am as influenced by touch as I am by sight. I think this ties into a phrase common in our culture, "Let me see that!" which really means, "Give that to me: I want to hold it." To know a thing, I have to hold it, turn it over in my hands, take it apart, then put it back together.

MS: I'm intrigued by your strong emphasis on research, both in your own work and in the classes you teach. What is the value of research?

HL: Research is valuable for two reasons. It provides information for existing ideas and is a way of generating new ideas. Personally, I never know where research will take me. To my mind, the act of researching a subject is very much like exploring a hypertext site on the Internet — once you start clicking, you soon find that you have wandered far from your original reference point. While I understand the value of staying focused, it is the digressions and distractions that give me the best ideas, months or even years later.

Research is insurance. It provides context and fertilizes ideas. The more pieces of information you have, the more connections or associations you will be able to make. And associations are essential. Associative thinking is the ability to make original or unexpected connections. It is an essential part of creativity. Some people start out thinking this way, while for others it is a learned trait.

A wide range of interests seems to encourage associative thinking, so I keep my mind open. For example, I am currently reading a book on grasshoppers, two histories of military battle dress, a mystery novel by Antonia Fraser, three collections of American English proverbs, an introduction to chemistry, and a book by Jorge Luis Borges — and several others waiting in the wings!

MS: How do you get your ideas?

HL: Just about anything in my environment and experience can generate an idea — a book I read, a conversation, a walk in the woods.

MS: Your ideas are pretty complex. How do you communicate this information?

HL: Using association, I try to put as many ideas as possible into the forms I construct. For example, Biological Abstraction III, which depicts an ovary and associated seed structures, also embodies references to dandelion seeds, diving bells, and bomb casings. Each reference contains another piece of information which expands on a physical quality of the object and adds another layer of meaning. I'm not interested in making copies of the structures I study. Instead, I try to understand and express their essential forces and overriding themes.

MS: Please describe your working process.

HL: First, I identify a system for study. Since I am especially interested in human anatomy and physiology, I think of a system as an organ or group of organs in the human body. In this series, I have studied the female reproductive tract, the skin, the respiratory tract, and the inner ear.

Once I have chosen a system, I study it at microscopic and macroscopic levels to try to learn something about the relationship between its structure and function. Scale is really important: the microscopic view reveals an astonishing level of complexity in the simplest of structures! During this phase, I also look for materials that share the structural and functional properties of my system's cellular building blocks. I experiment by combining these materials to see how they might work together. At the same time, I begin to make plans and drawings for different aspects of the piece. When I have gathered enough information to give me a solid foundation, I begin construction.

MS: It sounds so orderly! My creative process is much more chaotic.

HL: Actually, my process is definitely *not* as linear as it sounds! The research, while extensive, is never complete: all art-making requires a balance between analysis and intuition. The materials always have something new to teach me if I am willing to learn. This element of unpredictability can be frustrating and uncomfortable, but it is absolutely essential. If I play it safe, if I'm inflexible, too insistent on sticking to a set plan, the resulting piece will be dull and lifeless. For me, learning comes from experimenting and making mistakes. It is the desire to learn about my materials, myself, and the world around me that keeps me actively engaged during many hours of physical work.

MS: I think we can appreciate the function of science in our culture. What is the function of art?

HL: For me, art helps to stimulate thought, encourage contemplation, increase understanding, and express emotion. Like science, it gives us a way to see beyond everyday experience and embrace the complexity and beauty of our world.

Detail

Heidi Lasher-Oakes, *Biological Abstraction III*, 1996. Wood, fiberglass, foam rubber, canvas, steel, dinghy anchors, rubber gasket material, fabricated and purchased hardware. Primary structure: 4 ft l. × 4 ft w. × 3½ ft h. (1.21 × 1.21 × 1.07 m), entire assembly approx. 15 ft l. (4.5 m).

Developing Critical Thinking

chapter six

Critical thinking combines

• Evaluation of all available information

• Analysis of visual relationships

• Exploration of alternative solutions

Never complacent, the best artists and designers continually seek to improve each image and expand each idea. Critical thinking is used to determine compositional strengths, develop concepts, and improve visual communication. Knowing what to keep and what to change is essential. By enhancing the best aspects of a design and deleting the weak areas, we can dramatically strengthen both communication and expression.

ESTABLISHING CRITERIA

Establishing the criteria on which judgments will be made is the first step. For example, if technical skills are being emphasized in an assignment, craftsmanship will be highly valued. Likewise, if the assignment must be done in analogous colors, a black-and-white painting will not meet the criteria, no matter how carefully it is composed. By determining the major questions being raised in each problem, we can understand the basis on which judgments will be reached. Consider the following questions:

• What is the purpose of the assignment? Does your teacher want you to learn any specific skills? What compositional and conceptual variables will you need to explore?

• What are the assignment parameters? Are there limitations in the size, style, or materials?

• When is the assignment due and in what form must it be presented?

It is important to distinguish between understanding assignment criteria and seeking the "right answer." In the first case, by determining the boundaries, you can fully focus your energy when you begin to work. Just as a magnifying glass can be used to focus sunlight into a powerful beam, so assignment parameters can help you focus creative energy. On the other hand, students who try to determine the "right answer" to a problem often simply want to know the teacher's solution. Such knowledge is rarely helpful. Any problem presented by a teacher simply sets a learning process in motion: you learn through your work. Since learning requires a personal process of investigation, finding your own answer is essential.

FORM, SUBJECT, AND CONTENT

The most effective compositions present a unified visualization of an idea or emotion. As a result, it is often difficult to dissect and analyze a design. Identifying three major aspects of an artwork can provide a beginning point for discussion.

Form may be defined as the physical manifestation of an idea or emotion. Two-dimensional forms are created using line, shape, texture, value, and color. The building blocks of three-dimensional forms are line, plane, volume, mass, space, texture, and color. Duration, tempo, intensity, scope, setting, and chronology are combined to create time-based art forms. For example, film is the form in which *Star Wars* was first presented.

The **subject,** or topic, of an artwork is most apparent when a person, an object, an event, or a setting is clearly represented. For example, the conflict between the rebels and the Empire provides the subject for *Star Wars.*

The emotional or intellectual message of an artwork provides its **content,** or underlying theme. The theme of *Star Wars* is the journey into the self. Luke Skywalker's gradual understanding of himself and acceptance of Darth Vader as his father provides an essential emotional undercurrent to the entire series.

STOP, LOOK, LISTEN, LEARN

Any of these three aspects of design can be discussed critically. A **critique** is the most common structure used. During the critique, the entire class analyzes the work completed at the end of an assignment. Many solutions are presented, demonstrating a wide range of possibilities. The strengths and weaknesses in each design are determined, and areas needing revision are revealed. These insights can be used to improve the current design or to generate possibilities for the next assignment.

Critiques can be extremely helpful, extremely destructive, or just plain boring, largely depending on the amount and type of student involvement. The main purpose of the critique is to determine which designs are most effective and why. Specific recommendations are most helpful: be sure to substantiate each judgment, so that your rationale is clear. Whether you are giving or receiving advice, come with your mind open, rather than your fists closed. A critique is not a combat zone! Listen carefully to any explanations offered and generously offer your insights to others. Likewise, receive their suggestions gracefully rather than defensively. You will make the final decision on any further actions needed to strengthen your design; if someone gives you bad advice, quietly discard it. An open, substantial, and supportive critique is the best way to determine the effect your design has on an audience, so speak thoughtfully and weigh seriously every suggestion you receive.

When beginning a critique, it is useful to distinguish between objective and subjective criticism. **Objective criticism** is used to assess how well a work of art or design utilizes the elements and principles of design. Discussion generally focuses on basic compositional concerns, such as

- The type of balance used in the composition and how it was created
- The spatial depth of a design and its compositional effect
- The degree of unity in a design and how it was achieved

Objective criticism is based on direct observation and a shared understanding of assignment parameters. Discussion is usually clear and straightforward. Alternative compositional solutions may be discussed in depth.

Subjective criticism is used to describe the personal impact of an image, the narrative implications of an idea, or the cultural ramifications of an action. Discussion generally focuses on the subject and content of the design, including

- The meaning of the artwork
- The feelings it evokes
- Its relationships to other cultural events
- The artist's intent

Because subjective criticism is not based on simple observation, it is more difficult for most groups to remain focused on the artwork itself or to reach any clear conclusions regarding possible improvements. The discussion may become more general and wide-ranging, as political or social questions raised by the works of art and design are analyzed. While these are important topics, because of the potential lack of clarity, subjective criticism may be used sparingly during the foundation year.

TYPES OF CRITIQUES

Description

The first step is to look carefully and report clearly. Without evaluating, telling stories, drawing conclusions, or making recommendations, simply describe the visual organization of the work presented. A **descriptive critique** can help you see details and heighten your understanding of the design. The student whose work you describe learns which aspects of the design are most eye-catching and readable and which areas are muddled and need work.

This is a particularly useful exercise when analyzing a complex piece, such as figure 6.1A. In an art history class you might write

Place de l'Europe on a Rainy Day is a rectangular painting depicting a street in Paris. A vertical lamppost and its shadow extend from the top edge to the bottom edge, neatly dividing the painting in half. A horizon line, extending from the left side and three-quarters of the way to the right, further divides the painting, creating four major quadrants. Because this horizon line is positioned just above center,

the bottom half of the composition is slightly larger than the top half.

A dozen pedestrians with umbrellas occupy the bottom half of the painting. At the right edge, a man strides into the painting, while next to him a couple moves out of the painting, toward the viewer. To the left of the lamppost, most of the movement is horizontal, as people cross the cobblestone streets.

When using description in a spoken critique, it is useful to consider the following compositional characteristics:

- What is the shape of the overall composition? A circle or sphere presents a very different compositional playing field than a square or a cube.
- What range of colors has been used? A black-and-white design is very different from a design in full color.
- What is the size of the project? Extremes are especially notable. A sculpture that is 10 feet tall or a painting that is 1-inch square will immediately attract attention.
- Is the visual information tightly packed, creating a very dense design, or is the design more spacious, with a lot of space between shapes or volumes?

6.1A Gustave Caillebotte, *Place de l'Europe on a Rainy Day,* Paris Street, 1877. Oil on canvas, 83½ × 108¾ in. (212.2 × 276.2 cm).

Cause and Effect

A descriptive critique helps us analyze the compositional choices made by the artist. A **cause-and-effect critique** builds on this description. In a simple description, you might say that the design is primarily composed of diagonals. Using cause and effect, you might conclude that, *because* of the many diagonals, the design is very dynamic. In a cause-and-effect critique, you discuss consequences as well as choices. Analyzing the same painting, you might write

> *Place de l'Europe on a Rainy Day* depicts a city street in Paris near the end of the nineteenth century. A lamppost, positioned near the center, vertically dissects the painting in half. The horizon line creates a second major division, with 45 percent of the space above and 55 percent below this line.
>
> A dozen pedestrians in dark clothing cross the cobblestone streets from left to right, creating a flowing movement. To the right of the post, the pedestrians move in and out of the painting, from background to foreground. Both types of movement add compositional energy. Two men and one woman are the most prominent figures. The man at the far right edge pulls us into the

painting, while the couple to his immediate left moves toward us, pushing out of their world and into our world. The movement that dominates each side of the painting is arrested by the lamppost. It is almost as if we are getting two paintings on one canvas.

As shown in figure 6.1B, a visual diagram can be used to support your written comments.

Compare and Contrast

In a **compare/contrast critique,** similarities and differences between two images are noted. We will use the Caillebotte painting one more time, now comparing the perspective used with the perspective in Raphael's *The School of Athens* (6.2).

> The city streets depicted in *The School of Athens* and *Place de l'Europe* demonstrate many differences between Renaissance and Impressionist perspective.
>
> The one-point perspective used in Raphael's painting leads our eyes to Plato and Aristotle, positioned just below the center of the composition. The other figures in the painting are massed in a

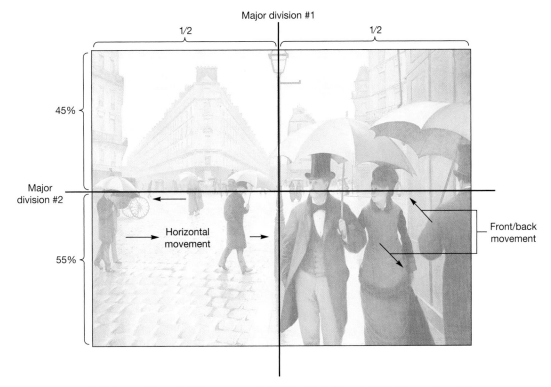

6.1B Gustave Caillebotte, *Place de l'Europe on a Rainy Day,* Paris Street, 1877. Compositional diagram.

6.2 Raphael, *The School of Athens*, 1509–11. Fresco, 26 × 18 ft (7.92 × 5.49 m). Stanza della Segnatura, Vatican, Rome.

horizontal band from the far right to the far left side and in two lower groups, to the right and left of the central figures. Our eyes are led back to the philosophers by a man sprawled on the steps to the right and by the scribes' tables on the left. Like a proscenium arch in a theater, a broad arch in the foreground frames the scene. Overlapping arches add to the depth of the painting. This composition combines the stability of one-point perspective with a powerful illusion of space.

In the Caillebotte painting, a lamppost occupies center stage, rather than a philosopher. The perspective in the cobblestone street and in the buildings on the right is complicated by the perspective used for a large background building on the left. This unusual illusion of space, combined with the movement of the pedestrians, creates a feeling of instability.

Compare and contrast essays are often used in art history classes. This form of analysis helps demonstrate differences in historical periods or artistic styles. The same approach, however, may be used in the studio, for either spoken or written critiques. The following is an example, written by two students in a basic design class. The assignment was to complete an 18 × 24 in. design, transforming the music building (Crouse College) into a labyrinth.

Looking at Cally's design (6.3), Trish wrote

Cally's piece uses strong black-and-white contrast, with both negative and positive space clearly developed. On the other hand, my design is brightly colored, representing a kaleidoscope based on the stained glass windows in the building.

We both use the staircase as a major element. Cally's stair leads you in and around the building, creating a way to explore the space. My stair becomes part of the overall pattern.

I thought of the labyrinth as an abstract puzzle, a design you could draw your pencil through to find the ending. I wanted my design to be playful. Cally's design focuses on the psychological, creating an entry into the human mind. Cally's design is mysterious. Her staircases seem to lead nowhere.

We both use lines very deliberately. Where one line ends, another begins. Without lines in a labyrinth, it wouldn't be as puzzling or mysterious. It would just be another design, rather than a puzzle to solve or a fun house to explore.

6.3 Cally Iden, *Transforming Crouse College into a Labyrinth.* Student work, 18 × 24 in.

6.4 Tricia Tripp, *Transforming Crouse College into a Labyrinth.* Student work, 24 × 18 in.

Looking at Trish's design (6.4), Cally wrote

The first difference I notice is that my labyrinth uses black and white to form a high-contrast composition, whereas Trish uses color to transform the building into a complex pattern. My vertical format helps suggest the height of the building, which is dominated by two amazing staircases. Trish's horizontal format contains a design that is as abstract as a computer circuit board.

Next, I notice conceptual differences between our solutions. My drawing is representational, depicting a psychological labyrinth, whereas Trish's turns the labyrinth into a puzzle. The space is essentially flat in her design: color is used to create a balanced composition rather than being used to create any illusion of space. On the other hand, because my design is representational, I used the illusion of space to create a convincing interior space.

One similarity between our drawings is in the inclusion of the staircase. Trish used the stairs as a *background* shape that adds dynamism to the composition. I used the stair as a primary motif, a means by which people using the building can explore their own minds.

For me, Trish's design creates a sense of alienation. There is no evidence of human experience here — it is a purely visual world, made up of complex shapes. It produces no strong emotion for me, no sense of mystery. It is purely visual.

On the other hand, there are hints of "the human" in my composition, but it is lost within the maze of repetitive stairs: only traces remain. I want to convey the feeling of being caught in a labyrinth, solving mysteries, and finding one's self.

Both critiques are honest without being abusive and offer a discussion of both concept and composition. While they are very different, each of the students clearly respects the approach taken by the other.

Greatest Strength/ Unrealized Potential

Many projects have one notable strength and one glaring weakness. To create a positive atmosphere, start by pointing out the strength in the work. Begin by looking for

- The level of unity in the design and how was it achieved

- The amount of variety in the design and how much energy it generates

- The visual rhythms used and their emotional effect
- The attention to detail. This could include craftsmanship, conceptual nuance, or compositional economy.
- A conceptual spark. We all love to see an unexpected solution that redefines the imaginative potential of a project.

Using figure 6.5A as an example, you could say,

> The primary strength of this project is unity. The use of black marker throughout gives the design a simple, clean, and consistent look. The repetition of the arches helps tie it all together. Vertical and horizontal lines dominate, creating a type of grid.

Next, consider ways to improve the project. Mentally arm yourself with a magic wand. If you could instantly transform the design, what single aspect would you change? How can the potential of the project be more fully realized? Some basic questions follow.

- Is it big enough? Is it small enough?
- Is it bold enough? Is it subtle enough?
- How rich is the concept? Can it be expanded?
- How can the concept be communicated more clearly? How can the concept be communicated more fully?

The assignment was to create a labyrinth. Figure 6.5A is spatially shallow. To strengthen the composition, you might suggest

> When I think about a labyrinth, I think of it as a mysterious place that I can enter and explore. As it now stands, this design is spatially flat: it gives me no place to go, so you might try increasing the illusion of space. Greater size variation in the arches, with larger ones in the front and smaller ones in the back, could help. Overlapping some of the arches could increase the space and add rhythm to the work. And have you considered

6.5A Design variation.

6.5B Design variation.

using gray marker for the background shapes? This would reduce the contrast and push those shapes back in space.

The resulting design (6.5B) is more spatially complex.

DEVELOPING A LONG-TERM PROJECT

Critical thinking is useful at many points in a project, not just at the end. When working on a project for 10 hours or more, it is useful to assess progress at the beginning or the end of each work period. This may be done in a large-group critique, in small teams, in discussion with your teacher, or on your own. Several effective strategies follow.

Week One Assessment

Determine Essential Concept

As a project begins to evolve from brainstorming, to thumbnails, to rough drafts, the concept may also evolve. Your initial idea may expand or shift during the translation from the mind to the hand to the page. Stopping to reconsider your central concept and refine your image can bring great clarity and purpose to the work. What is the design *really* about? You can speak more forcefully when you know what you want to say.

Explore Polarities

Sometimes, the best way to strengthen an idea is to present the exact opposite. For example, if you want to show the *joy* a political prisoner feels on being released from jail, you may need to show the *despair* she felt before her release. To increase the *dynamism* in a design, add some emphatically *static* elements. The contrast created by polarities can heighten communication.

Move from General to Specific

"Be specific!" demands your writing teacher. Just as vague generalities weaken your writing, so vague generalities can weaken your designs. Details are important. "A bird watched people walk down the street" is far less compelling than "Two vultures hovered over University Avenue, hungrily watching the two hapless students stagger from bar to bar." Specifying the kind of bird, type of people, and exact location makes the image come alive.

Move from Personal to Universal

Autobiography is a particularly rich source for images and ideas. The authenticity of personal experience is extremely powerful. However, if you focus too tightly on your own family, friends, and experience, the viewer must know you personally in order to appreciate your design. Try expanding your field of vision. Use a story about your high school graduation to say something about *all* rites of passage from childhood to adulthood.

Week Two Assessment

A well-developed rough or a full-scale model may be presented at this stage. The purpose of this critique is to help the artist or designer determine ways to increase the visual and conceptual impact of an existing idea. Following are three major strategies.

Develop Alternatives

By helping someone else solve a problem, we can often solve our own problem. Organize a team of four or five classmates. Working individually, design 5 to 10 possible solutions to a visual problem using 3×4 in. thumbnail sketches. Then, have one person present his or her ideas verbally and visually. Each team member must then propose an alternative way to solve the problem. This can be done verbally; however, once you get going, it is more effective and stimulating if everyone (including the artist) draws alternative solutions. This process helps the artist see the unrealized potential in his or her idea. And, because of the number of alternatives presented, the artist rarely adopts any single suggestion. Instead, the exercise simply becomes a means of demonstrating ways to clarify, expand, and strengthen intentions already formed. Continue until everyone has made a presentation.

Edit Out Nonessentials

Have you ever found it difficult to determine the real point of a lengthy lecture and thus lost interest? In our zeal to communicate, teachers sometimes provide so many examples and side issues that students get lost. Likewise, if your design is overloaded with peripheral detail or if a secondary visual element is given the starring role, the result will be cluttered and impact will be lost. Look carefully at your design, focusing on visual relationships. Are there any extra shapes or volumes that can be deleted?

Amplify Essentials

Just as it is necessary to delete extraneous information, it is equally important to strengthen the essential information. Review the section on emphasis in Chapter Three and consider ways to increase your compositional power. Try "going too far," wildly exaggerating the size, color, or texture of an important visual element. The only way to get an extraordinary image is to make extraordinary compositional choices.

Developing a Self-Assignment

In the following two pages, Jason Chin describes the development of a month-long self-assignment he completed near the end of his freshman year. The original project proposal is given at the top of the first page. The rest of the text is devoted to Jason's analysis of his actual work process. This type of personal assessment can bring an extended project to a memorable conclusion.

Self-Assignment:
Jason Chin
The Mythological Alphabet

Original Proposal

Description: I plan to make an illustrated alphabet book with 32 pages and a cover. The theme of the book will be myths and heroes. I am interested in illustrating the essence of each hero's story. Specifically, how can I visually communicate the story of a tragic hero versus a triumphant one? Further concerns with the book will be making it work as a whole. That means keeping it balanced and making it flow: I don't want the images to become disjointed.

Primary Concerns

1. How do I communicate the individual nature of the characters?

2. How do I connect each hero to all the others?

3. How will the book affect the reader? I want to get the reader fully involved in the book.

4. How can I best use the unique characteristics of the book format?

Time Management

Week 1:   Research myths and heroes. Identify possible characters for the book.

Week 2:   Bring at least 20 thumbnail sketches to the first team meeting.

Week 3:   Bring finalized design/layout for book. Each page must have a final design in the form of thumbnails.

Week 4:   Complete half of the pages.

Week 5:   Finish remaining pages and present at the critique.

Commentary

The independent project was both a blessing and a curse. Given the freedom to do what I chose was liberating, but the burden of what to do with that freedom was great. Ultimately, it became one of the best learning experiences of my freshman year.

I had decided to pursue illustration as my major, because of my interest in storytelling. This interest in stories led me to choose to make a book for my project. The next step was to find a story to tell. To limit my workload, I looked for a story that had already been told, one that I could reinterpret, as opposed to writing my own story. At this point, I came across two books, one of Greek myths, and an alphabet book illustrated by Norman Rockwell, and my initial concept was born.

Once the idea was initiated, I set to work researching Greek myths. The idea was to find one character for each letter of the alphabet. It proved more difficult than I had first thought. I found about 20 names with no problem, but I soon realized that several letters in our alphabet did not exist in the Greek alphabet. To overcome this hurdle, I took some liberties on the original problem and did not limit myself strictly to characters from myths (for example, I included the White Island for the letter W). Once the subject of each illustration was chosen, I set about the task of doing the images and designing the format of the book.

Doing the illustrations and designing the format of the book all came together at about the same time.

As I was working out the drawings I made several key decisions that heavily influenced the outcome of the project. First, I decided that each picture would have to be black and white if I was going to pull this whole thing off. Second, I knew that they would have to be relatively small. Through my art history class, I gained a strong interest in Japanese woodblock prints and was especially attracted to their strong compositional sensibility. This became the focus of my attention while working out the illustrations. Finally, the decision to make the illustrations small helped determine the way I used text in the book, because it all but eliminated the possibility of overlaying text on image.

I designed each image in my sketchbook, doing thumbnails and comp sketches of all sizes and shapes, until I found the image that I felt best represented the character. For example, Zeus has the biggest and busiest frame in the book because he is the king of the gods, while the image of the White Island is quite serene because it is a burial ground.

When I had each individual image worked out, I redrew them in order in the pages of my sketch book as if they were in the real book. I could now see how each image would work as a double-page spread, as well as how well the book could flow visually. With this mockup of the book in front of me it was very easy to see obvious mistakes and correct them before going to final art.

I did the final illustrations in pen and ink, on illustration board, and when they were finished, it was time to drop in the text. My first concept for the text was to be very minimal; each page would read, "A is for," "B is for," and so on. However, I soon real-ized that making each page rhyme would drastically increase the reader's interest in the book. So I wrote a more extensive text and put the rhyming parts on opposite pages in order to give the reader one more incentive to turn the page.

The final touch for the book was putting the colored paper down. The decision to do this came when I went to place the type. The only means I had to get good type was to print it out on the computer, but I had no way to print it on the illustration board. So I had to put it on printer paper and cut and paste it. No matter how carefully I cut the paper and pasted it on, it just didn't look right. I came up with two solutions: one, print the words on colored paper and paste it on, or two, cut frames of colored paper to cover over the entire page except for the image and the text. I chose the latter and was pleased to discover that the local art store had a vast selection of handmade and colored papers.

Today I look back on this project as a pivotal experience in my art education, because I had free range to pursue storytelling, something that has since become an essential aspect of my art. In the professional world, bookmaking is rarely an individual process. It is a collaborative process, involving editors, artists, and writers, so for me to be able to pursue it on my own was in fact a blessing. I got to make a book the way that I thought it should be done, and pursue my own personal vision of what a Mythological Alphabet should be. By making this book, I discovered something that I love to do, and want to make a career of doing, and to me the vision that I have gained from this experience is invaluable.

Jason Chin, *A Is for Apollo* (left) and *U Is for Urania* (right). Student work.

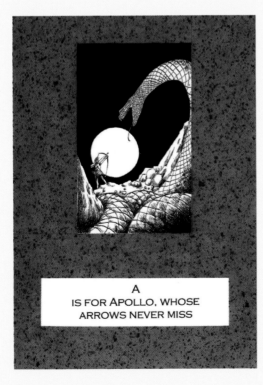

A
IS FOR APOLLO, WHOSE
ARROWS NEVER MISS

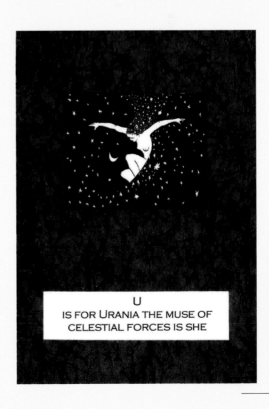

U
IS FOR URANIA THE MUSE OF
CELESTIAL FORCES IS SHE

TURN UP THE HEAT: PUSHING YOUR PROJECT'S POTENTIAL

Some compositions are so bold that they seem to explode off the page. Other compositions have all the right ingredients but never really take off. By asking the following questions you can more fully realize the potential of any assignment.

Basic Arithmetic

1. Should anything be *added* to the design? If your composition lacks energy, consider adding another layer of information or increasing the illusion of space. Notice how texture changes the composition in figures 6.6A and 6.6B.

2. Should anything be *subtracted?* If the composition is cluttered, try discarding 25 percent of the visual information. Then, use the remaining shapes more deliberately (6.7A–B). Get as much as possible from every visual element. Economy is a virtue.

3. What happens when any component is *multiplied?* As shown in figures 6.8A and 6.8B, repetition can unify a design, add rhythm, and increase the illusion of space.

4. Can the design be *divided* into two or more separate compositions? When a design is too complicated, it may become impossible to resolve. Packing 20 ideas into a single design can diminish rather than improve communication. In figures 6.9A and 6.9B, a complicated source image has been separated into several different designs, creating a series of stronger images.

6.6A Linear design.

6.6B Adding invented texture.

6.7A Visual clutter.

6.7B Visual clarity.

6.8A Basic composition.

6.8B Elaborated composition.

6.9A Completed labyrinth design.

6.9B Divided labyrinth design.

Transformation

Works of art and design present ideas in physical form. Each composition is strongly influenced by the materials used, the relationships created, and the viewing context chosen. Consider the following alternatives:

1. What happens when the material is changed? Even when the shapes stay the same, a silver teapot is very different from a glass, steel, or ceramic teapot. Sculptor Claes Oldenburg has used transformations in material extensively, often changing hard, reflective materials into soft vinyl. This form of transformation is especially effective when the new material brings structural qualities and conceptual connotations that challenge our expectations.

2. What is the relationship of the piece to the viewer? What is the relationship between the artwork and its surroundings? What happens

6.10 Claes Oldenburg and Coosje van Bruggen, *Shuttlecocks*, 1994. South facade of the Nelson-Atkins Museum of Art and the Kansas City Sculpture Park. Aluminum, fiberglass-reinforced plastic, urethane paint, approx. 19 ft 2⅜ in. h. × 16 ft diameter (5.9 × 4.9 m).

when a chair is reduced to the size of a salt shaker? Or when a 20-foot-tall badminton shuttlecock (6.10) is placed in front of a museum? How does any image change, both visually and conceptually, when size is dramatically reduced or increased?

3. Can a change in proportion increase impact? Working with the same basic information, a seemingly endless number of solutions can be produced through variations in proportion (6.11).

4. Is a physical object compelling from all points of view? Does the composition of the artwork encourage the viewer to view it from other angles?

5. Will a change in viewing context increase meaning? The context in which a composition is seen can dramatically alter its meaning. For example, a side of beef has a very different meaning when it is hung in a gallery rather than staying in a slaughterhouse. Likewise, pop artists, such as Andy Warhol and Roy Lichtenstein, brought new meaning to soup cans and comic books by using them as subject matter in their paintings.

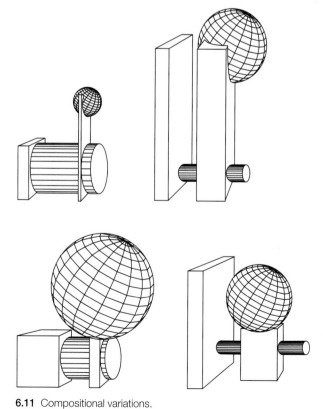

6.11 Compositional variations.

Reorganization

Time-based work, such as visual books, comic books, film, and video, is generally constructed from multiple images. Changing the organization of the parts of the puzzle can completely alter the meaning of the piece. For example, Angela contemplates entering the building in the sequence shown in figure 6.12. Using a different organization of the same three images, Angela now wonders what will happen when she opens the door at the top of the stairs (6.13). By repeating the image of Angela, we can present a dilemma: she is now in a labyrinth — which route should she take (6.14)?

6.12

6.13

6.14

CONCEPT AND COMPOSITION

Any compositional change affects the conceptual impact of an artwork. Henry M. Sayre provides a striking example in *A World of Art.*[1] A distilled version of his ideas follows.

Robert Rauschenberg's Monogram (6.15) is constructed from a stuffed goat, an automobile tire, and a painted plywood base. Seeking to combine painting and sculpture, Rauschenberg created three different versions of this piece. In the first version (6.16), he placed the goat on a shelf that extended from the center of a 6-foot-tall painting. This created a connection between the painting and the goat but diminished its sculptural

6.15 Robert Rauschenberg, *Monogram,* 1955–59. Freestanding combine, 42 × 63¼ × 64½ in. (106.7 × 160.7 × 163.8 cm).

6.16 Robert Rauschenberg, *Monogram,* 1st State, c. 1955.
Combine painting: oil, paper, fabric, wood on canvas, plus stuffed Angora goat and three electric light fixtures, approximately 75 × 46 × 12 in. (190.5 × 114.3 × 30.5 cm). No longer in existence.

6.17 Robert Rauschenberg, *Monogram, 2nd State,* c. 1956.
Combine: oil, paper, fabric, wood, plus rubber tire and stuffed Angora goat on wood, 115 × 32 × 44 in. (292 × 81.3 × 111.8 cm).

impact. In the second version, Rauschenberg placed a tire around the goat's midsection and moved the animal in front of the painting (6.17). This enhanced its three dimensionality but created too much of a separation between the animal and the painting. He finally hit on the right combination when he placed the painting on the floor and positioned the goat in the center. The painting retained its integrity as a two-dimensional surface, the goat retained its physical presence, and a highly unified combination of the two elements was achieved. The addition of the tire enhanced the goat's sculptural form and gave the artwork a humorous twist.

ACCEPTING RESPONSIBILITY

We have explored only a few of the many approaches to critical thinking in this chapter. Every assignment presents new possibilities for critiques, and each teacher invents his or her own way to address the needs of a specific class.

Regardless of the specifics, however, two facts are inescapable. First, you will learn only what you want to learn. If you reject out-of-hand the alternatives suggested, or if you avoid responsibility for your conceptual and compositional choices, you will gain nothing from the critique, no matter what strategy is used. Second, there are no free rides. Everyone in the class is responsible for the success of the session. It is often difficult to sustain your attention or honestly assess your work or the work of others. When you get a superficial response to a project, insisting on further clarification is not easy. Every critique demands sincere and sustained attention from each participant. And, when the responses are supportive and substantial, remarkable improvements in works of art and design can be made.

SUMMARY

- Using critical thinking, an artist or a designer can identify strengths and weaknesses in a project and determine the improvements that need to be made.

- Understanding the criteria on which a project will be judged helps focus critical thinking.

- Many artworks can be analyzed in terms of three basic aspects: form, subject, and content.

- Objective critiques focus on observable facts. Subjective critiques focus on feelings, intentions, and implications.

- Four common critique methods are description, cause and effect, compare and contrast, and greatest strength/unrealized potential.

- Many critique methods may be used when you are working on a long-term project. In every case, there are three primary objectives: explore alternatives, delete nonessentials, and strengthen essentials.

- It is only by pushing a project to the limit that its potential will be fulfilled. Basic arithmetic, transformation, and reorganization can be used to increase compositional power.

- Responsibility for the success of a critique rests with each participant. Come with your mind open rather than your fists closed.

Keywords

cause-and-effect critique	critique	objective criticism
compare/contrast critique	descriptive critique	subject
content	form	subjective criticism

Profile:
Bob Dacey, Illustrator

Tell Me a Story: Illustrating *Miriam's Cup*

Bob Dacey is an internationally renowned artist whose drawings and paintings have been published as limited- and multiple-edition prints, as well as in a wide range of books and periodicals, including *McCall's,* Ballantine Books, Book-of-the-Month Club, *Playboy,* and Scholastic Publications. His commercial clients include The White House, ABC, CBS, NBC, PBS, Mobil Oil, Sony, the U.S. Post Office, Air Japan, and many others. Dacey has recently received a Silver Medal from the Society of Illustrators in New York for 1 of the 16 paintings he produced for Scholastic Publications illustrating a 32-page book, *Miriam's Cup,* which is themed on the Exodus of the Israelites from Egypt. The book tells the story of Miriam, the older sister of the prophet Moses. Dacey collected an extensive library of books on Egypt and spent almost a year on research. From costumes to musical instruments, Dacey insisted on getting all the details just right.

MS: Give me a bit of background on *Miriam's Cup.* What was the significance of this project, and what aspects of the story did you want to emphasize in the illustrations?

BD: *Miriam's Cup* gave me a chance to expand on my single-image work. I've always approached each illustration as a moment in time, as if it had a "before" and an "after." This book gave me a chance to push that much further. I started every painting by focusing on the emotion in the moment being depicted. I always ask myself: "What is the essence of this moment?" The composition follows. Shapes and values serve the emotional content, while movement is used to unify the composition.

MS: You have said that 75 percent of your work on this project was devoted to research. Can you describe your research and tell me why it was so important?

BD: For *Miriam's Cup,* I had to understand the culture of Egypt and the Jewish culture of the time. Fortunately, I've always had an extensive interest in both. My personal library contains more books on Egypt than the local library system. Research helped open new ideas, leading in some unexpected directions. Those bullrushes are one example. I looked up the word in three dictionaries and

two encyclopedias. One of these sources mentioned that the bullrushes of ancient Egypt are papyrus, those beautiful fan-shaped reeds that can be fashioned into a kind of paper. Without that knowledge, the image I arrived at would have been impossible.

MS: I understand that you have a seven-step process by which you refine and expand your ideas. Can you describe this process as it applies to the cover image for *Miriam's Cup?*

BD: I first consider the intent of each painting: what must this piece communicate? In this painting, I focused on Miriam's exuberance as she celebrates her escape from Egypt. Second, the composition must support my intent. The circular movement of the tambourine and flowers dominates this painting. The movement from the raised hand holding the tambourine, to Miriam's hair, to her face, and on to her cupped hand provides a secondary pattern. And that cupped hand repeats the curve of the flowers. Third, the shapes depend on both the intent and the composition. If I am painting a very stoic character, I use a lot of verticals. Diagonals are used when the character or event is very dynamic. Value is fourth on my checklist. I assign value according to the mood of the painting.

Lighter values are used for celebratory images, like this one; darker values dominate when the mood is somber. A mix of light and dark value is best. I base my compositions on the Golden Section [a classic use of proportion], and I often use a 60/40 proportion between light and dark values. Texture, step five, often results from the placement of shape and value — but it really deserves a place of its own, due to its importance as a constructive or destructive factor. When everything else works but the image still suffers, textural discord is usually the culprit! Color comes next. I really have to have the other questions resolved first. Color without composition, value, or intent just doesn't cut it. This painting is dominated by rich pastel colors, which help convey the exuberant emotion.

All of this contributes to the overall image, the final step. If all of the preceding factors serve my intent, the image can emerge naturally and effectively.

MS: In addition to the extensive research you did for *Miriam's Cup*, it seems that you have a very wide range of interests in general.

BD: Well, everything feeds into my work — and I've always been interested in everything! My under-graduate majors included theater and anthropology before I settled on ad design as the field in which I finally got my degree. Now, my readings range from archaeology to philosophy to psychology to paleontology, and more. I'm also developing my interest in writing and plan to pursue a master's in writing in order to increase my understanding of narrative.

MS: One of the questions my students often have is this: how do I get from where I am as a student to where you are as a professional?

BD: Focus on your goals and research the field. Talk to professionals you admire. Set high standards for yourself and be realistic about the level of professionalism and quality required.

MS: Any final bits of advice?

BD: Don't limit yourself. We all have great potential that serves the higher purpose of society. Pursue your goals with the knowledge that you can succeed. And remain flexible and open-minded, so that you can redirect your efforts as opportunities present themselves. Read everything! Draw everything!

Bob Dacey, Cover of *Miriam's Cup*, by Fran Manushkin, 1988. Scholastic Press.

Constructing Meaning

Cultivating creativity, seeking and solving visual problems, and developing critical judgment all require hours of hard work. Why are these skills so highly valued by artists and designers and so strongly emphasized by college teachers?

The answer is simple. At a professional level, art and graphic design projects are done in order to communicate ideas and express emotions. Turning elusive concepts into effective communication is not easy. Clay, ink, metal, fabric, and other physical materials must somehow stimulate an audience to see, understand, and respond to a visual message. In this chapter, we will explore the essentials of visual communication and identify some of the strategies artists and designers use to construct meaning.

BUILDING BRIDGES

Shared Language

A shared language is the basis on which all communication is built. For example, if you are fluent in English and I am effective as a writer, the ideas I want to communicate in this chapter should make sense to you. On the other hand, if English is your second language, some of the vocabulary may be unfamiliar. In that case, you may have to strengthen the bridge between us by looking up words in a dictionary.

Figure 7.1 demonstrates the importance of shared language. For a reader of Chinese, the flowing brushstrokes form characters that communicate specific ideas. For those of us who know only English, the calligraphy is visually

7.1 Huai-su, Detail of Autobiography, Tang dynasty, 7th – 10th centuries. Ink on paper.

enticing but conveys no specific message. We cannot understand the characters.

Iconography

Many visual images rely on cultural references to build meaning. **Iconography** (literally, "describing images") is the study of symbolic visual systems. Iconography plays a major role in all forms of visual communication.

Deborah Haylor-McDowell's *The Serpent Didn't Lie* (7.2) is loaded with cultural references. An anatomical diagram copied from Leonardo da Vinci's notebooks appears in the upper left corner, while the nude couple near the center is based on *The Kiss,* a sculpture by August Rodin. In the upper right corner, Haylor-McDowell has reproduced Einstein's computations for the theory of relativity, and, in the foreground, a baby takes his first steps. A snakeskin border surrounds the image. What does it all mean? Haylor-McDowell says:

> Ignorance may spare us the pain of difficult decisions. However, the price we pay is high. Can humankind's greatest gifts, emotion and intellect, mature in a world that is free of suffering? In the absence of adversity, will our humanness be lost?
>
> *The Serpent Didn't Lie* is based on a biblical text dealing with good and evil in the Garden of Eden. What is the price we pay for knowledge? The images I used in the composition deal with the complexities and responsibilities of our pursuit of knowledge.

Through a sophisticated use of iconography, the artist created a puzzle that is filled with ideas for us to unravel and explore. For those who understand the cultural references, this print presents a survey of types of knowledge in a compelling visual form. For those who do not understand the references, the print is simply a beautifully crafted collection of architectural and figurative fragments.

Graphic designers are especially aware of the importance of iconography. On a purely visual level, Milton Glaser's 1996 poster for the School of Visual Arts (7.3) is intriguing and evocative in itself. The hovering hat, shadowy figure, and curious text raise all sorts of questions. When we compare the poster with surrealist René Magritte's *Golconde* (7.4),

7.2 Deborah Haylor-McDowell, *The Serpent Didn't Lie,* **1997.** Etching, 15 × 23 in. (38.1 × 58.42 cm).

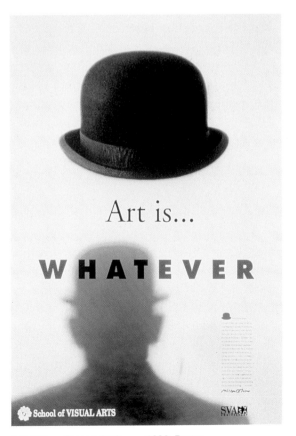

7.3 Milton Glaser, *Art is . . .,* **1996.** Poster.

7.4 René Magritte, *Golconde*, **1953.** Oil on canvas, 31¾ × 38⅝ in. (80.65 × 98.11 cm).

6.1A, page 148) presents yet another approach. It captures a quiet moment in time and space. There is minimal action, just the movement of groups of people within an architectural setting. This painting is compelling to a mature viewer yet lacks the action and excitement sought by a younger audience. To engage children, many museums use storytelling or other bridge-building activities when presenting paintings of this kind to school groups.

Immediacy

When the bridge between the image and the audience is explicit, communication can occur almost instantaneously. When the iconography is elusive or complex, communication takes longer and is more varied. Each approach can be effective in the right time and place. When driving a car, our lives depend on the immediate message we receive when a traffic light turns red. When visiting a museum, we often seek greater complexity and emotional resonance.

Graphic designers generally seek a combination of immediacy, clarity, and resonance. For them, an effective poster or billboard can be understood at a glance. Figure 7.7 is an excellent example. The bold, white hangman immediately attracts attention, and the book title itself is simple and direct. The position of the figure's head adds an additional layer of meaning to this critique of capital punishment.

By comparison, *Solstice Greetings* (7.8) by Georgiana Nehl and David Browne requires extended viewer involvement. The collage includes a map, international postage stamps showing birds in flight, various pieces of patterned paper, a color chart, and butterflies, both dimensional and drawn. A tiny watch, two insects, three globes, two cubes, a child's jack, a circle, and a spiral orbit around the egg at the center of the composition. The message here is neither explicit nor immediate. As with Haylor-McDowell's work, the viewer must piece together a complex set of

the ideas expand much further. In this and other paintings by Magritte, the man in the bowler hat represents anyone who is courageously navigating through the chaos of contemporary life. When we make the connection between Glaser and Magritte, the School of Visual Arts poster becomes poignant as well as provocative. Like the man in the bowler hat, each art student must find a path through the complexities of contemporary life in order to develop a meaningful approach to art and design.

Audience

Just as films are targeted and rated for specific audiences, so many forms of visual communication are designed for a particular type of viewer. Illustrator Kenny Kiernan specializes in cartoons for preteens (7.5). The subject matter is light-hearted; the icongraphy is simple; the drawing style is exuberant. A very different approach was used for figure 7.6. Realizing that disfigurement is of greater concern than death for many teenagers, the designers have focused on the scarred face of a traffic accident survivor. Seeking to discourage drunk driving, they have targeted the teenager's greatest fear in order to drive home their message. Caillebotte's *Place de L'Europe on a Rainy Day* (see figure

7.5 Kenny Kiernan, *Rock Stars*. Vector art created in illustrator.

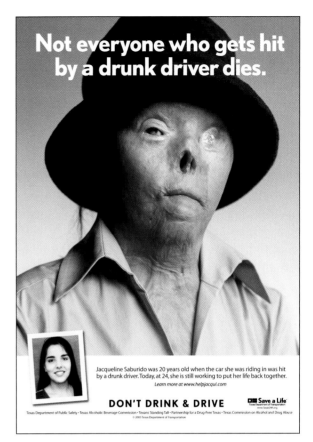

7.6 **Sherry Matthews & Associates,** photography, poster.

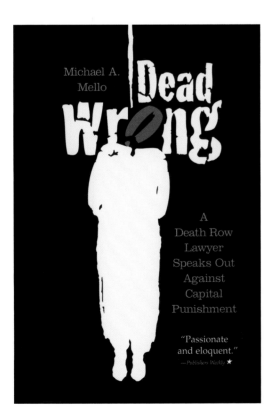

7.7 Mark Maccaulay, book jacket.

7.8 **Georgiana Nehl and David Browne, *Solstice Greetings*, 1998.** Color photograph of constructed assemblage, 5 × 5 in. (12.7 × 12.7 cm).

clues, then reach his or her own conclusions about journeys, the passage of time, and the transience of life. The message is conveyed using layers of iconography.

Stereotypes

A **stereotype** is a fixed generalization based on a preconception. On a benign level, when we use a stereotype, we ignore individual characteristics and emphasize group characteristics. For example, the broken wine glass in figure 7.9 is widely used on shipping crates to communicate fragility. Glass is actually a very versatile material that can be cast as bricks, spun into fiberoptic cables, and polished to create lenses. However, we are most familiar with fragile wine glasses and bottles. Relying on this *general* perception, the shipping label designer used a stereotype to communicate fragility.

Racial stereotyping, which is never benign, tends to exaggerate negative generalizations. Even when a positive assumption is made (such as "Asian-Americans are brainy overachievers"), the overall effect is demeaning. Rather than learning about an individual person, we make judgments based on our preconceptions.

Stereotypes are often used to create the bridge on which communication depends. Because they are based on preconceptions, stereotypes require little thought. The viewer responds automatically. In some situations, an automatic response is ideal. Four airport pictograms are shown in figure 7.10. Can you determine the meaning of each? If the designer is successful, even an exhausted traveler from New Zealand will be able to determine at a glance where to find a baggage locker, an elevator, or a toilet. Especially notice the use of the male and female stereotypes for the toilet pictograms. Despite the wide range of clothing worn by female travelers, the designer used a dress to create a stereotypical female.

Clichés

A **cliché** is an overused expression or a predictable treatment of an idea. Phrases such as "Let's level the playing field" and "Think outside the box" are powerful the first time we hear them. However, when we hear them repeatedly, they lose their impact and become clichés. Visual clichés are equally predictable. Skulls representing death and seagulls representing tranquility may be effective at first but tend to become worn out when used repeatedly.

Surprise

A shift in a stereotype or cliché upsets our expectations and challenges our assumptions. The resulting shock can surprise or delight an audience, making the message more memorable. Originally based on the cowboy stereotype, the Marlboro Man has been reinterpreted in figure 7.11. This ad, which begins like an ordinary cigarette commercial, quickly shifts from the heroic cowboy to a man with a hacking cough. At this point, the narrator suggests that "cowboys are a dying breed" because of the cancer caused by smoking. By breaking the stereotype, the designers attract the viewers' attention, challenge the conventional cigarette ad, and strengthen their nonsmoking message.

7.9 Fragile pictogram.

Baggage lockers
Elevator
Toilets, men
Toilets, women

7.10 Roger Cook and Don Shanosky, images from a poster introducing the signage symbol system develped for the U.S. Department of Transportation, 1974.

NARRATOR: No wonder cowboys are a dying breed. If

you need help quitting, tune into project QUIT, and take   control of your life.

7.11 Agency: Ruhr/Paragon, Minneapolis. Production: Lotter, Minneapolis. Details: TV, 30 seconds, color. First appearance: February 1988. Account Supervisor: Anne Bologna. Creative Director/Art Director: Doug Lew. Associate Creative Director/Copywriter: Bill Johnson. Agency Producer: Arleen Kulis. Production Company Director: Jim Lotter.

Key Questions

- Are there any symbolic meanings embedded in your composition? Are these meanings consistent with the message you want to convey?
- Have you used a stereotype or a cliché? Does this strengthen or weaken your message?
- What audience do you want to reach? Is the form and content of your design appropriate for that audience?

PURPOSE AND INTENT

Any number of approaches to visual communication can be effective. We simply choose the style, iconography, and composition best suited to our purpose.

Let's consider three very different approaches to human anatomy. *Arterial Fibrillation* (7.12) was developed for the cover of a medical journal. With equal training in art and science, medical illustrator Kim Martens combined anatomical accuracy with

7.12 Kim Martens, *Arterial Fibrillation*, 2000. Photoshop.

7.13 A page from *Understanding Healthcare* by Richard Soul Wurman. Design Firm: Pentagram Design.

7.14 Robert Rauschenberg, *Booster*, 1967. Lithograph and serigraph, printed in color, composition 71 9/16 × 35 1/8 in. (181.7 × 89.1 cm).

artistic imagination to create this design. Intent on sales, the art director for the magazine requested an image that was both physically correct and visually enticing. Designed as an anatomical roadmap, *Understanding Healthcare* (7.13) had to present complex information in a clear and concise way. To make the text accessible to a general audience, the designers used a loose grid, dominated by vertical columns at the top and a strong horizontal band at the bottom. Arrows and other visual cues increase visual impact and help the reader navigate from page to page. *Booster* (7.14) is dominated by series of X-rays of the artist's body. In this unconventional self-portrait, Robert Rauchenberg combined a collection of personal X-rays with various examples of technological notation, including an astronomer's chart, diagrams analyzing the movement of drills and arrows, graphs, and an empty chair. The title adds further meaning, suggesting a connection to booster shots, booster rockets, and booster seats, which increase the height of an ordinary chair so that young children can sit at a table comfortably. Reduced to an X-ray image and surrounded by fragments of technological information, the artist becomes a cog in the machinery of mass culture.

CONTEXT

The compositional context in which any image appears profoundly influences meaning. In figure 7.15, the juxtaposition of a quiet line of hungry people with a propagandistic billboard makes us rethink the phrase "There's no way like the American way."

The social context in which an image appears is equally important. In figure 7.16, Winston Churchill, the prime minister most responsible for British victory during World War II, extends two fingers to create the "V for victory" gesture he used throughout the war. If we are familiar with Churchill and know about the desperate struggle of the British people during the war, we immediately make the correct connection. In figure 7.17, the same gesture communicates a very different idea. As part

7.15 Margaret Bourke-White, *At the Time of the Louisville Flood*, 1937. Getalin silver print.

7.16 Alfred Eisenstadt, *Winston Churchill, Liverpool*, 1957. Getalin silver print.

of the signage for the Minnesota Children's Museum, the extended fingers now communicate the number two. Realizing that many young visitors to the museum may not be able to read, the designers used both a number and a gesture to communicate location. Finally, in Sean O'Meallie's *Out-Boxed Finger Puppets Perform the Numbers 1 Through 5 in No Particular Order* (7.18), the same gesture becomes a playful piece of sculpture as well as an indication of the number two. We now see the extended fingers in the context of a series of whimsical forms. In each of these three cases, the meaning of the two fingers depends on context.

CONNECTIONS

Analogies, similes, and metaphors are figures of speech that link one thing to another. An **analogy** creates a general connection between unrelated objects or ideas, while a **simile** creates the connection using the words *as* or *like*, as in "She has a heart as big as Texas." A **metaphor** is more explicit: speaking

7.17 Minnesota Children's Museum, Pentagram design, NY, NY. Tracy Cameron and Michael Beirut, Designers.

7.18 Sean O'Meallie, *Out-Boxed Finger Puppets Perform the Numbers 1 Through 5 in No Particular Order*, 1999. Polychromed wood.

Y2K's coming.
Don't just sit there.

Safely move your information from this millennium to the next.™

Y2K is headed your way and how much damage it does to your important files and applications is up to you.
So be smart and get prepared. With Iomega's Y2K Software Suite, getting help is as easy as 1-2-3.

1. Back Up Before anything else, use   **2. Update** Use the Y2K Software   **3. Protect** Now that you're on your way,
Iomega disks, drives, and software to   Suite to diagnose potential problems   Iomega software automatically protects
make copies of everything on your PC.   and either fix or update your PC.   your files well into the next millennium.

Get some help with the Iomega® Y2K Software Suite and drives.

Iomega Y2K Software Suite
Back up your files, update, and protect
your PC well into the next millennium
with Iomega's new software bundle.

Iomega drives and disks
With the help of Y2K software,
protect your important files
with Zip and Jaz drives.

Look for free software in specially marked packages of Zip® and Jaz® disks at your
computer retailer or visit www.iomegadirect.com. For more Y2K help, visit: www.iomega.com/y2k

iomega

7.19 Iomega Corporation, "Y2K's coming. Don't just sit there."

metaphorically, we would say "Her heart *is* Texas." As you can see, the shift in meaning can be substantial when a metaphor is used.

In all cases, the original word is given the qualities of the linked word. For example, when Robert Burns wrote the simile "My love is like a red red rose," he gave the abstract concept of "love" the attributes of a glorious, colorful, fragrant, thorny, and transient rose.

Metaphorical thinking can be used to connect an image and an idea. Take the phrase, "I have butterflies in my stomach." This phrase is widely used to describe nervousness. Substitute other insects for butterflies, such as bees or wasps. How does this change the meaning? To push it even further, start with the phrase "My mind was full of clouds." What happens when "clouds" is replaced by mice on treadmills, rats in mazes, shadowy staircases, beating drums, screaming children — or even butterflies? When my mind is full of butterflies, I am happy, but butterflies in my stomach indicate fear. In addition to expanding your ideas, metaphors can help provide specific images for elusive emotions.

Metaphorical thinking and symbolism have always been used by artists and designers to strengthen communication. Exaggerated metaphors

are often used in advertising design. The massive wave that threatens the computer user in figure 7.19 is a metaphor for the destructive power of the Y2K computer bug that once seemed likely to create massive computer failures on January 1, 2000.

Picasso's *Guernica* (7.20) is also loaded with metaphors. In *A World of Art,* Henry Sayre offers the following description:

The horse, at the center left, speared and dying in anguish, represents the fate of the dreamer's creativity. The entire scene is surveyed by a bull, which represents at once Spain itself, the simultaneous heroism and tragedy of the bullfight, and the Minotaur, the bull-man who for the Surrealists stood for the irrational forces of the human psyche. The significance of the electric light bulb at the top center of the painting, and the oil lamp, held by the woman reaching out the window, has been much debated, but they represent, at least, old and new ways of seeing.[1]

Rather than showing exploding bombs or collapsing buildings, Picasso filled his painting with abstracted animals, screaming humans, and various light sources. In so doing, he focused on the meaning and emotion of the event, rather than the appearance.

7.20 Pablo Picasso, *Guernica*, 1937. Oil on canvas, 11 ft 5½ in. × 25 ft 5¼ in. (3.5 × 7.8 m).

DRAMA

Regardless of the medium used or the message conveyed, all communication can be strengthened through dramatic delivery. Even Martin Luther King's "I Have a Dream" speech loses much of its power when delivered in a flat, monotonous tone of voice. Just as a playwright sets the stage for the story he or she seeks to tell, so an artist can set the stage for visual communication.

All of the elements and principles of design described in this book can be used to increase compositional drama. To increase conceptual drama, we can:

- *Personify the idea.* When we identify with a character in a play, we become more empathetic and involved in the story. Likewise, when we identify with a character in a painting or a poster, we are much more likely to remember the idea or emotion being conveyed. For example, the shattered face of the woman in figure 7.6 makes an immediate connection. We look her in the eye and feel her sorrow.

- *Focus on essentials.* It has often been said that theater is "life with the boring parts left out." To be meaningful to an audience, the characters and events in a play must have a strong relationship to direct experience. However, a playwright rarely shows a character flossing his or her teeth. Too much detail clutters the composition, confuses the audience, and muddles the message. Including the right amount of information in just the right way can add drama to even the simplest idea.

- *Seek significance.* Any event, character, or time period can be used to create an effective play. Likewise, any object, event, or idea can be used in our quest for visual communication. A unique approach to a familiar subject or an insightful interpretation of personal and political events can add significance and increase impact.

AESTHETICS AND ANESTHETICS

In *Design in the Visual Arts*, Roy Behrens notes the difference between the words anesthetic and aesthetic (or esthetic). An *anesthetic* is used to induce insensitivity or unconsciousness. In an anesthetic state, we are numbed and disoriented. We may not be able to determine the size or location of objects or the sequence of events. On the other hand, *aesthetics* is the study of human responses to beauty. In an aesthetic experience, our feelings are enhanced and our understanding is expanded.

SUMMARY

- A shared language is the basis on which all communication is built.

- Iconography (the study of symbolic visual systems) provides us with a way to analyze the meaning of images and objects.

- Immediacy is often highly valued in graphic design. By comparison, many paintings require extended viewer involvement and longer viewing time.

- A stereotype is a fixed generalization based on a preconception. Stereotypes can easily create a bridge between the image and the audience.

- A cliché is an overused expression or predictable treatment of an idea. Even the most interesting image will lose its power if overused.

- A shift in a stereotype or cliché challenges our assumptions and can increase impact.

- Artists and designers choose the style, iconography, and composition best suited to their purpose. A mismatch between the type of image and its purpose creates confusion.

- The visual and social context in which an image appears will profoundly affect its meaning.

- Analogies, similes, and metaphors are figures of speech that link one thing to another. Metaphors are especially widely used in visual communication.

- Dramatic delivery of a message can enhance meaning.

Keywords

aesthetics	**cliché**	**metaphor**	**simile**
analogy	**iconography**	**metaphorical thinking**	**stereotype**

Profile:
Ken Botnick,
Graphic Designer

Landscape of the Page:
Conceiving and Composing Books

Ken Botnick has been making books for over 25 years. From 1979 to 1988, he and Steve Miller ran Red Ozier Press in New York City, producing over 50 limited-edition titles of contemporary poetry and fiction. From 1988 to 1993, Botnick was production and design manager of the art books at Yale University Press, with three of his book designs winning medals from the American Association of University Presses. He has also designed books for Princeton Architectural Press, Harry N. Abrams, Princeton School of Architecture, and the University of Alabama Press. Professor Botnick was Executive Director of the Penland School of Crafts in North Carolina for four years, has taught extensively.

MS: Some artists pursue a very linear career path. Other artists, who are equally or even more interesting, come to art and design through a more circuitous route. Please describe your path.

KB: My origin is in landscape design. I trained in this field and worked on a whole range of projects, from community gardens to artist-designed parks. I was fascinated by the relationship of the parts to the whole and love physical materials, such as plants, soil, and stone.

MS: How, and why, did you shift to book design?

KB: For me, landscape design became more and more about proposals and paperwork and less and less about the actual designs and the doing.

Since I had been involved with books since my undergraduate years at the University of Wisconsin, joining my friend Steve Miller at Red Ozier Press seemed like the right move. I began to think of the words as the soil and the paper, the type and ink as the plants that grow from it. In quick order, Steve and I were partners and publishers running a very active press in New York City, working with the most amazing writers and artists. We took our jobs very seriously and made careful choices as to whom we would publish. When you are setting type or printing 150 copies of a book, you see the text differently. You get to read in a way that you would never do ordinarily.

MS: "Landscape" is an unusual word to associate with book design. What is the meaning of this title?

KB: Like a landscape, a well-designed book is full of nuances and complex relationships. The page size, the weight and texture of the paper, the size and style of the type, and the layout of information on the page all contribute to the reading experience. For me, the page is a construct that you move through, literally and figuratively. Like the window on a train, the frame remains constant, while the landscape continually changes.

MS: Please talk us through your design process for *The Bicycle Rider*, a novel in 100 sections by Guy Davenport. which was produced as a limited edition at Red Ozier Press.

KB: In designing typography for a text, I first ask "What are my emotional responses to the content of the story?" Throughout *The Bicycle Rider*, Davenport refers to Dutch painter Piet Mondrian and the primary colors he used in his mature work. Like the bicycle rider, Mondrian was a master of proportion, balance, and daring. Reds and blues pop up throughout the text. So, instead of using illustration, I used various typographic embellishments and created a title page inspired by Mondrian's paintings. The book was bound in a subtle brown handmade paper, with simple typography and color in order to play off the idea of the plain wrappers of not-so-plain books. This brown text paper is filled with red and blue fibers that echo the color of the ink.

Next, I assess my current visual surroundings, including other design books, painting, sculpture, and so on. When working on *The Bicycle Rider,* I was looking at a pamphlet of poems by Kenneth Patchen that had been printed during World War II, with big red numbers in the margins of each poem. This book seems to do everything "wrong" typographically, yet because of its great energy, it is one of my favorite books. To emulate Patchen, I selected a clear and classic-looking typeface, then adapted his bold red numbers for the section numbers. Combined with the classic typeface, these numbers added a syncopated beat to the pages.

MS: It seems that a lot of planning is required and that everything in your design is intentional.
KB: The planning has to be there to support the spontaneity. I especially enjoy working with students who are planning their projects. Making the dummies of a book, exploring alternatives, and giving shape to the ideas are the most enjoyable part of the process. Most people are surprised at how much planning happens before production, yet that is where the magic really happens.

The beauty of craft is that there are all these repetitive functions one must go through in the studio: cutting paper, setting type, cleaning the presses, printing. These hours are vital to the creative process because they place you into direct contact with the materials, physically and sensually. That is the fertile time when many of the best ideas are formed. Creativity is not segmented out into "big-idea time" versus "boring production time"—it is all part of a fluid process. Ideas are elusive. The more you try to trap them, the more they escape.

MS: From whom did you learn the most?
KB: Even though I never took a book course, I worked closely with book artist Walter Hamady during my last year at the University of Wisconsin. I went to his house to plant trees, then stayed on to cook a meal and talk. It was really about building a life. I learned that a personal investment in life and a willingness to pour all of your energy into an activity is crucial.

My collaboration with Steve Miller was also pivotal. When it is working well, a partnership can be a wonderful mirror, reflecting what you do especially well and what your partner does especially well. It also taught me a great deal about transforming a vision into reality.

MS: What advice do you have for my students?
KB: First, keep your eyes open: don't limit yourself through rigid self-definitions. If I had limited myself to architecture, I would never have become a graphic designer. Mindless careerism can be the path to ruin. Be willing to take side trips: they may change your life. Second, read, read, and read some more! The opportunities for learning are endless and through books, you can access the wisdom of the masters in all fields.

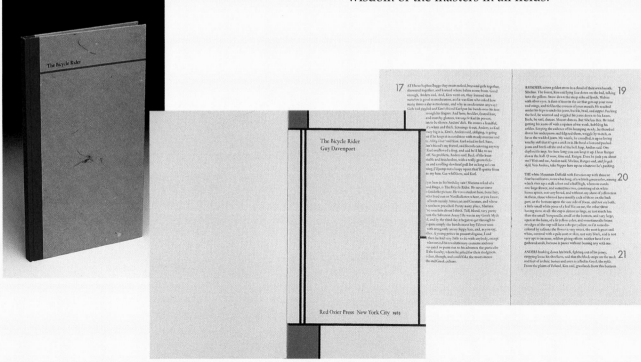

Ken Botnick, *The Bicycle Rider,* **1985.** Guy Davenport, author. Letterpress printing, 5½ × 9½ in. (14 × 24 cm).

Part Two
Multimedia Resources

Take advantage of the multimedia resources for Part Two in order to expand your understanding of how to generate ideas and manage your projects.

Resources

www.mhhe.com/launching2

Student Center
Chapter 4
Chapter 5
Chapter 6
Chapter 7

Core Concepts in Art CD-ROM

Contents

Learning objectives for each chapter
Study outlines for each chapter
Quizzes with instant feedback
Flashcards for studying art vocabulary
Internet exercises for developing critical viewing skills
Book suggestions for your personal library and research projects

An Internet guide to help you maximize connectivity and avoid problems
A study skills primer to help you make the most of your courses

Studio projects for Part Two are described and illustrated for teachers on the Web and on a CD-ROM.

Resources

www.mhhe.com/launching2

Instructor Center
IM Part Two

Instructor's Resource CD-ROM

Part Two

Projects

Limited/Unlimited: Pushing beyond apparent limitations
Microcosmo/Macrocosmos: Connecting simple and complex forms
Poster Design: Integrating words and images; the importance of research
Collaborative Compositions: Digitally creating a collaborative collage
Expanding Escher: An exercise in collaborative creativity
Word/Image Synergy: Exploring juxtaposition
Build a Concept Generator: A basic cube turns into a conceptual toy
Capstone Assignment: Expanding creativity through in-depth exploration

Katherine Wetzel (photograph), Elizabeth King (sculpture), *Pupil* **from** *Attention's Loop* **(detail), 1987–90.** Installation at the Bunting Institute, Radcliffe College, 1997. Porcelain, glass eyes, carved wood, brass. One-half life size.

Three-Dimensional Design

As we begin our investigation of three-dimensional design, it is useful to consider both the similarities and differences between flat compositions and physical constructions. In both cases, basic design elements are organized to communicate ideas, express emotions, and create functional objects. The basic principles of design are used to create images and objects that offer an effective balance between unity and variety. And, in both two- and three-dimensional design, concept development and critical thinking are essential aspects of the creative process.

However, in two-dimensional design, we use our technical, perceptual, and conceptual skills to create flat visual patterns and convincing illusions. It is the viewer's *mental* response that gives the artwork meaning. By contrast, our experience in the three-dimensional world is physical and direct. As we traverse an architectural space, we alter our perception with each step we take. When we circle a sculpture, we encounter new information on each side. The materials used in the construction of a three-dimensional object determine its structural strength as well as its aesthetic appeal.

This physical connection gives three-dimensional design an inherent power. When we shift from an illusory world to a tangible world, a substantial shift in communication occurs. Confronted by the physical presence of a three-dimensional object, the viewer responds viscerally as well as visually.

This section is devoted to the elements, organization, and implications of three-dimensional design. The basic building blocks of three-dimensional design are discussed in Chapter Eight. In Chapter Nine, the principles of three-dimensional design are described. The unique characteristics of various materials are considered in Chapter Ten. Chapter Eleven is devoted to the ways in which artists have transformed their ideas into physical objects and to a discussion of differences between traditional and contemporary sculpture.

Elements of Three-Dimensional Design

When we paint a realistic seascape, we use our technical, perceptual, and conceptual skills to create a convincing illusion. In the painting, lines, shapes, colors, and textures are combined to represent a three-dimensional world. Based on these clues, each viewer mentally reconstructs the setting. Those who have walked on a beach can create a detailed mental image of sea, sand, and sky. Those who have never seen the sea may create a more fanciful world. For both viewers, however, it is the imagination that constructs the cosmos.

Our experience in the three-dimensional world is more direct. When we walk on an actual beach, we feel the wind, hear the waves, and smell the air. We can examine the marvelous creatures in a tidal pool and create castles in the sand. Tangible evidence of three-dimensional design surrounds and supports us. We use a cooler to transport a picnic lunch, recline in a folding chair, and construct a tent for shelter.

Line, plane, volume, mass, space, texture, light, color, and time are the basic building blocks from which three-dimensional designs are made. Just as oxygen and hydrogen are powerful both individually and when combined as H_2O, so these visual **elements** are powerful both individually and in combination. In this chapter, we will consider the unique characteristics of three-dimensional design and explore the primary uses of each of the basic elements.

DEFINING FORM

As noted in Chapter Six, **form** can be defined as the physical manifestation of an idea. **Content** refers to the idea itself, including the subject matter plus its emotional, intellectual, spiritual, and symbolic implications.

Form has an additional definition in three-dimensional design. In this context, *form* can refer to three-dimensionality itself. For example, a circle, a square, and a triangle are two-dimensional shapes, while a sphere, a cube, and a pyramid are three-dimensional forms.

To build a deeper understanding of three-dimensional design, we can expand this basic definition even further. Consider the following types of form.

• An empty three-dimensional form is generally defined as a **volume,** while a solid form is generally defined as a **mass.**

8.1 Jean-Baptiste Carpeaux, *The Dance* (after restoration), **1868–69.** Marble, 7 ft 6½ in. (2.3 m).

8.2 Jean Tinguely, *Chaos 1*, **1973–74.** Metal construction with moving balls on tracks, electric motors, 30 × 28 × 15 ft (915 × 854 × 458 cm).

- An effective three-dimensional composition balances **positive forms** (areas of substance) with **negative space.**

- **Organic forms** (forms that visually suggest nature or natural forces) create a very different effect than **geometric forms,** which are typically based on cubes, spheres, and other simple volumes.

- The degree of actual or implied movement in a form can expand our vocabulary even further. **Static forms** appear stable and unmoving. Designed to last forever, the Great Pyramids at Giza exemplify stability and repose. **Dynamic forms** imply movement. *The Dance* (8.1), by Jean-Baptiste Carpeaux, is a highly dynamic form. Dominated by rotating figures and curving lines, this sculpture swirls with energy.

Kinetic forms actually move. In Jean Tinguely's *Chaos 1* (8.2), a bowling ball on a track trips a series of movements in a massive metal mechanism.

As noted in Chapter Seven, determining the best form for our expressive content is one of the major challenges we face.

FORM AND FUNCTION

An artist seeks to express concepts and evoke emotions. For example, a sculptor explores an idea, chooses materials, and develops a composition based on his or her aesthetic intention. Public art projects, such as Eero Saarinen's *Jefferson National*

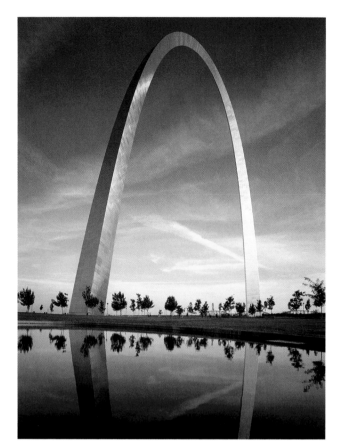

8.3 Eero Saarinen, *Jefferson National Expansion Memorial (Gateway Arch)*, St. Louis, 1966. 1868–69.

A Force Fin

B Multi Force Fin

C Excellerating Force Fin

8.4 A–C Bob Evans, *Force Fin Variations*, 1990–present. Molded polyurethane, size variable.

Expansion Memorial (8.3) and ritual objects, such as the Mugamtl mask (see page 132), often commemorate historical events or express social values.

A designer uses the same mastery of concept, composition, and materials to create an object that is functional as well as beautiful. For example, when designing aquatic gear, designer Bob Evans carefully analyzes the needs of swimmers and then creates equipment to best meet those needs. The basic *Force Fin* (8.4A) provides the maneuverability needed for snorkeling. The *Multi Force Fin* was designed as a training device to strengthen a swimmer's legs (8.4B), while the *Excellerating Force Fin* (8.4C) provides the extended power needed by scuba divers. For any designer, the form must fulfill a specific **function,** or purpose.

While the industrial designer has a different purpose than the sculptor, both use the same basic elements and principles of design. Both must organize line, plane, volume, mass, space, texture, and color into coherent form. The structural integrity of a sculpture is just as important as the structural integrity of a wheelchair, and a teapot that is both beautiful and functional is ideal. By thoroughly understanding the elements of three-dimensional design, both the artist and the designer can create compelling compositions.

ORTHOGRAPHIC PROJECTION

Height, width, and depth are the three dimensions in three-dimensional design. In computer-aided design, these three dimensions are defined using the x, y, and z axes used in geometry (8.5). Using the cube as a basic building block, we can create many variations on these basic dimensions (8.6A–C).

There are many methods of depicting three-dimensional form on a two-dimensional surface. **Orthographic projection** is one of the most useful. Unlike perspective drawing, which relies on vanishing points to create the illusion of space,

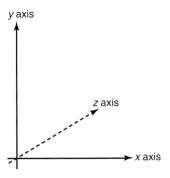

8.5 The three dimensions are defined through height, width, and depth.

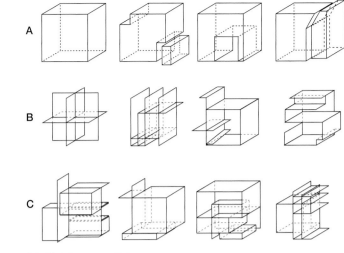

8.6 Variations on a Cube

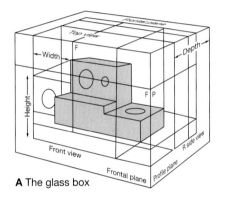

A The glass box

8.7A–C Orthographic projection can be used to define structural details.

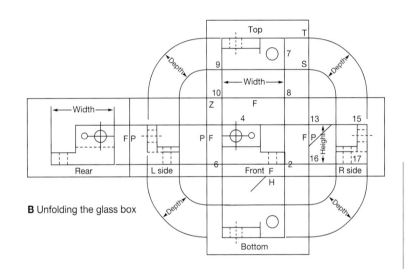

B Unfolding the glass box

C The three dimensions

orthographic projection uses parallel lines to define structural details.

An orthographic projection represents six views of a three-dimensional form. Imagine that your project is enclosed in a glass box (8.7A). As you look through the top, bottom, front, and back, then at the right and left sides, you can see six distinctive views. In effect, an orthographic drawing is created when you unfold and flatten this imaginary box (8.7B). Using orthographic projection, we can examine and record various surfaces of a three-dimensional object (8.7C).

DEGREES OF DIMENSIONALITY

Our experience of a three-dimensional artwork is very different from our experience of a flat print or painting. We tend to construct an imaginary world when looking at a two-dimensional image, while our response to a three-dimensional object is generally more physical and direct. As a result, the degree of our physical involvement strongly affects our understanding of both the form and the content of the artwork. Four variations on dimensionality are described in this section.

8.8 Robert Longo, *Corporate Wars* (detail), 1982. Cast aluminum, lacquer on wood relief, 7 × 9 × 3 ft (2.1 × 2.7 × .9 m).

Relief

When working in **relief,** the artist uses a flat backing (such as a wall or ceiling) as a base for three-dimensional forms. For example, Robert Longo's *Corporate Wars* (8.8) is like a sculptural painting. Using the boundaries created by the supporting wall and the four outer edges, it presents a group of white-collar warriors engaged in hand-to-hand combat. The figures are trapped, bound both to the backing and by their struggle for money.

Three-Quarter Works

A **three-quarter work,** such as Jean-Baptiste Carpeaux's *The Dance* (see figure 8.1) is more three-dimensional. We can walk around this piece, examining the front and two sides. As a result, the dancing figures create a vortex of implied motion.

Freestanding Works

Freestanding works are designed to be seen from all sides. When we circle August Rodin's *The Kiss* (8.9A–B), we capture every nuance in the movement of the two figures. Details (such as the man's stroking hand and the woman's raised heel) add energy to the inanimate marble.

Environmental Works

An **environmental work** (or **environment**) presents a space that can be physically entered. **Installations** (which are usually presented indoors) and **earthworks** (which are usually presented outdoors) are two major types of environments. Such works often require active audience participation and may present a series of images, ideas, and experiences that unfold over time.

Installations

Typically, an installation is an ensemble of images and objects that are presented within a three-dimensional environment. Surrounded by information, we become emotionally and physically involved in the artwork. For example, on entering Antoni Muntadas' *The Board Room* (8.10), the viewer confronts 13 chairs facing a long table. In a reference to the Last Supper described in the Bible, these chairs are accompanied by photographs of religious leaders, from the Ayatollah Khomeini to Billy Graham. Inserted in the mouth of each man, a small video monitor plays a film clip showing him in action. In this installation, religion becomes an extension of both business and politics.

The Board Room presents a series of clearly defined figures in a dramatic setting. In Christian

8.9A Auguste Rodin, *The Kiss,* 1886–98. Marble, over life size. Dramatic lighting accentuates form and can heighten emotion.

8.9B Auguste Rodin, *The Kiss,* 1886–98. Marble, over life size. A slight change in the viewer's position substantially changes the orientation of the two figures.

8.10 Antoni Muntadas, *The Board Room,* 1987. Installation at North Hall Gallery at Massachusetts College of Art, Boston. Thirteen chairs placed around a boardroom table. Behind each chair is a photo of a religious leader, in whose mouth a small video monitor shows the leader speaking. Subjects include Ayatolla Khomeini, Billy Graham, Sun Myung Moon, and Pope John Paul II.

Marclay's *Amplification* (8.11), a series of translucent figures shift, merge, and divide, depending on the viewer's position within the room. Surrounded by images and enticed, enchanted, or assaulted by audio information, the viewer can become part of the artwork.

Earthworks

An earthwork is a large-scale outdoor installation. Often extending over great distances in time and space, earthworks may require substantial physical engagement by the artist, audience, and inhabitants of the site. Robert Smithson's *Spiral Jetty* (8.12) is an excellent example. This 1,500-foot-long coil of rock and earth extends from the shore into the water of the Great Salt Lake in Utah. For Smithson, the spiral created "a dot in the vast infinity of universes, an imperceptible point in a cosmic immensity, a speck in an impenetrable nowhere."[1] Remote and mysterious, this artwork evokes a cosmic connection that extends far beyond the walls of a museum or gallery.

8.11 Christian Marclay, *Amplification*, 1995. Mixed media with six found prints and six photographic enlargements on cotton scrim. Dimensions variable. Installation at the Chiesa di San Stae, Venice, Italy.

8.12 Robert Smithson, *Spiral Jetty*, Great Salt Lake, Utah, 1970. Rock, salt crystals, earth, algae, coil, 1,500 ft (457 m).

8.13 Todd Slaughter, *Mano y Balo* (details), 1997. Aluminum and steel, hand 27 × 40 × 4 ft (8.2 × 12.2 × 1.2 m), ball 20 ft (6 m) diameter. Overlooking the Straits of Gibraltar.

Site-Specific Artwork

A **site-specific** artwork is specifically designed and installed in a particular place. Commissioned by the port city of Algeciras in Spain, *Mano y Balo* (8.13) rests on a bluff overlooking the Straits of Gibraltar. The 40-foot-long hand may be catching or throwing the 20-foot-tall ball positioned roughly 50 feet away. Sculptor Todd Slaughter notes that "the implied action of the hand metaphorically alludes to the history of exchange of religion, art, power and conflict between the European and African continents." To heighten the metaphor, the hand has been designed to disappear when the wind blows. One thousand movable panels were covered with a photographic image of a hand, on the front and back. A strong wind shifts the panels from their vertical position to a horizontal position, causing the image to dissolve visually into the surrounding sky. In site-specific works such as *Mano y Balo*, the idea and the environment are inextricably intertwined. If moved to another location, this sculpture would lose much of its meaning.

LINE

In three-dimensional design, **line** can be created through

- *A series of adjacent points.* The cars that make up Ant Farm's *Cadillac Ranch* (8.14) are distinct objects in themselves as well as the points that create a line of cars. Commissioned by a rancher in Texas, this sculpture has been described as a requiem for the gas-guzzling American automobile.[2]

- *A connection between points. Free Ride Home,* by Kenneth Snelson (8.15) was constructed using two types of line. The aluminum tubes provide

8.14 Ant Farm (Chip Lord, Hudson Marquez, Doug Michels), *Cadillac Ranch,* 1974. Ten Cadillacs. Amarillo, TX.

8.15 Kenneth Snelson, *Free Ride Home,* 1974. Aluminum and stainless steel, 30 × 30 × 60 ft (9.1 × 9.1 × 18.2 m). Storm King Art Center, Mountainville, NY.

8.16 Moira North and Rudi Stern, *Neon Skates,* 1986. Battery-operated neon skates for performance by The Ice Theater of New York, Moira North, director.

a linear skeleton which becomes elevated when the connecting lines are attached. The resulting sculpture is compositionally dominated by diagonal lines that seem to defy gravity.

- *A point in motion.* When a skater wears the *Neon Skates* by Moira North and Rudi Stern, he or she can literally create lines from a moving point of light (8.16).

Line Quality

Each line has its own distinctive quality. This quality is largely determined by the line's orientation, direction, and degree of continuity, as well as the material used.

Orientation refers to the horizontal, vertical, or diagonal position of the line. Based on our experience in the natural world, we tend to associate horizontals with stability and diagonal lines with movement. Vertical lines tend to accentuate height and can make an object or interior appear more formidable and imposing.

All three types of line are used in Mark di Suvero's *Ik Ook Eindhoven* (8.17) and Peter Pierobon's *Ladderback Chair* (8.18). The di Suvero sculpture is

dominated by two horizontal I beams suspended from a vertical support. The diagonal lines that are connected to this primary structure emphasize the weight of the artwork and add visual movement. On the other hand, it is the tall vertical back that transforms Pierobon's chair into a whimsical sculpture. Its exaggerated height pulls our eyes upward and provides a support for the nine jagged lines that create the rungs of the ladder.

Curved lines can carve out more complex patterns in space and may encompass an object to create a harmonious whole. In José de Riviera's *Brussels Construction* (8.19), a single line of steel slices through space. As the sculpture slowly rotates on its motorized base, the movement suggested by the line is accentuated by its physical rotation.

Direction refers to the implied movement of a line. A line of consistent width tends to suggest equal movement in both directions. Varying line width can create a more specific sense of direction. For example, in *Jefferson National Expansion Memorial* (see figure 8.3, page 182), the massive lines at the bottom drive downward into the earth, while the tapered arch at the top lifts our eyes skyward.

Continuity, or linear flow, can increase movement and accentuate form. In *Brussels Construction,*

8.17 Mark di Suvero, *Ik Ook Eindhoven,* **1971–72.** Painted steel, 24 × 24 × 33 ft (7.3 × 7.3 × 10 m).
In the background: *Are Years What?* **(For Marianne Moore), 1967.** Painted steel, 40 × 40 × 30 ft (12.2 × 12.2 × 9.1 m).

8.19 José de Riviera, *Brussels Construction,* **1958.** Stainless steel, 46½ × 79 in. (118.1 × 200.6 cm).

8.18 Peter Pierobon, *Ladderback Chair.*
Firm & Manufacturer: Snyderman Gallery.

8.20 Chris Burden, *Medusa's Head*, 1989–92. Cement, wood, train tracks, 16 ft. diameter, 5 tons.

the smooth steel line is as elegant and as energetic as a calligrapher's mark. The diagonal sections firmly position us in space, while the horizontal section accelerates our eye movement across the midsection of the piece. Continuity plays a very different role in Chris Burden's *Medusa's Head* (8.20). Here, a mad tangle of toy train tracks flows around and through the mass of rock, plywood, and cement. Representing the snakes that crowned the head of a mythical monster, these writhing lines accentuate the spherical mass and give us a fresh interpretation of an ancient Greek myth.

Actual Lines

Through their physical presence, **actual lines** can connect, define, or divide a design. *Laocoön and His Two Sons* (8.21) depicts a scene from the Trojan War. When the Greeks offer a large, hollow wooden horse to the Trojans, Laocoön warns against accepting the gift. The Greek goddess Athena then sends two serpents to attack and kill the seer, thus gaining entry into Troy for the soldiers hidden in the horse. The writhing serpent compositionally connects the terrified men while adding emotional intensity to this tale of Athena's wrath. In figure 8.22, dancers from the Nikolais Dance Theatre push against the elastic lines that define their space. The interaction between the lines and the dancers provides choreographic tension as well as visual energy. The line dividing Gordon Matta-Clark's *Splitting: Exterior* (8.23) changes an abandoned house into an evocative sculpture. Combining his background in architecture with a propensity for anarchy, Matta-Clark often sought to "undo" a building and thus challenge the social conditions that led to its construction.[3]

8.22 **The Nikolais Dance Theatre Performing** *Sanctum.* With Amy Broussard, Phyllis Lambat, and Murray Louis.

8.21 **Laocoön and His Two Sons.** Marble, 7 ft (2.13 cm).

8.23 **Gordon Matta–Clark,** *Splitting: Exterior,* **1974.** Black-and-white photograph.

Implied Lines

Implied lines are created through mental rather than physical connections. *The Rape of the Sabine Women*, by Giovanni da Bologna (8.24), relies on a series of implied lines for its impact. Starting at the bottom and exploding upward, the repeated diagonals in the sculpture create a visual vortex as powerful as a tornado. At the bottom is the husband of the captured woman. In the center, a standing Roman soldier is intent on stealing a wife for himself. The agitated movement culminates at the top with the extended arm of the embattled woman.

A **sight line** activates Nancy Holt's *Sun Tunnels* (8.25). At first glance, the four 22-ton concrete tunnels seem static. Upon entering each tunnel, the viewer discovers a series of holes that duplicate the size and position of the stars in four major constellations. The light pouring in through these holes shifts as the sun rises and travels across the sky. During the winter and summer solstices, the sculpture is further transformed as light from the rising and setting sun is framed by an alignment in the circular tunnels. Like a telescope, the massive cylinders are more important for the visions they create than as objects in themselves.

Line Networks

Both artists and designers use linear networks in many different ways. In figure 8.26, interlocking metal lines form the woven mesh used on a fencer's mask. Due to its linear construction, it is light

8.24 Giovanni da Bologna, *The Rape of the Sabine Women,* completed 1583. Marble, 13 ft 6 in. (4.1 m).

8.25 Nancy Holt, *Sun Tunnels,* 1973–76. Great Basin Desert, UT. Four tunnels, each 18 ft long × 9 ft 4 in. diameter (5.5 × 2.8 m), each axis 86 ft long (26.2 m). Aligned with sunrises and sunsets on the solstices.

8.26 Steve McAkkuster. Photograph.

in weight and protects the athlete's face without blocking vision. As shown in Claire Zeigler's *Red Forest* (8.27), most fiber works are created through the organization of multiple lines of thread, yarn, or other materials. Single lines can bring a simple eloquence to a design, while multiple lines can be used to create strong, complex, and versatile forms.

Key Questions

- Vertical, horizontal, diagonal, and curving lines all have unique strengths. How can each type of line be used in your design most effectively?

- What can line continuity or discontinuity contribute to your design?

- What happens to your design when you increase or decrease the number of lines?

8.27 Claire Zeisler, *Red Forest*, 1968.
Dyed jute, 8 ft 2 in. h. × 7 ft 4 in. w. × 2 ft d. (249 × 224 × 61 cm).

8.28 Antoine Pevsner, *Torso*, 1924–26. Construction in plastic and copper, 29½ × 11⅝ × 15¼ in. (74.9 × 29.4 × 38.7 cm).

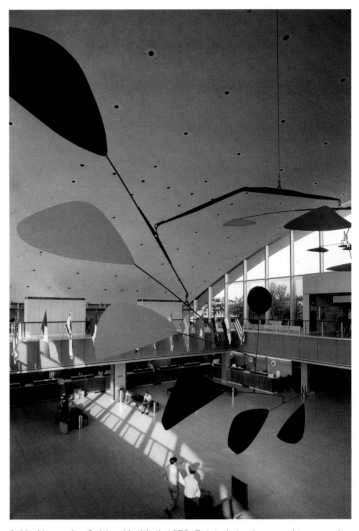

8.29 Alexander Calder, *Untitled*, 1976. Painted aluminum and tempered steel, 29 ft 10½ in. × 76 ft (9.1 × 23.2 m). National Gallery of Art, Washington, DC.

PLANE

A **plane** is a three-dimensional form that has length and width but minimal thickness. Depending on the material used, planes can be transparent or opaque, rigid or flexible. Complex surfaces and enclosures can be constructed using folded or bent planes, and when slotted together, planes can be used to create a variety of sturdy forms.

Antoine Pevsner used all of these variables in *Torso* (8.28), one of the first major sculptures made using plastic. More interested in space than in mass, he essentially built the figure from the inside out. Cut and folded planes define anatomical details simply and clearly.

Alexander Calder was also a master of planar construction. In his famous mobiles (8.29), he put simple planes in motion. Inspired by the delicate weights and balances he saw in the paintings of Piet Mondrian, (see figure 3.34, page 76), Calder used these structures to represent the movement of heavenly bodies within the universe. Exquisitely balanced, the flat planes and curving lines can be activated by the slightest flow of air.

When slotted together, planes can create large-scale structures that are remarkably strong. With outdoor sculptures, such as Alexander Calder's *La Grande Vitesse* (8.30), structural integrity is especially important. Located in a public plaza, the sculpture must withstand wind, rain, and snow while presenting minimal risk to pedestrians. Intersecting planes, combined with a ribbed reinforcement at stress points, create this durable structure.

8.30 **Alexander Calder, *La Grande Vitesse*, 1969.** Painted steel plate, 43 × 55 ft (13.1 × 16.8 m). Calder Plaza, Vandenberg Center, Grand Rapids, MI.

Key Questions

- Consider the limitations of the material you are using. Can it be cut or scored and folded to create curving planes?

- What are the structural and compositional advantages of curved or twisted planes versus flat planes?

- What happens to your design when you pierce or slot together any or all of the planes?

VOLUME

In general terms, volume is the amount of space an object occupies. In three-dimensional design, **volume** refers to an enclosed area of three-dimensional space.

Industrial designers often create functional objects using **polyhedra,** or multifaceted volumes (8.31). Such volumes can be surprisingly strong. In an assignment at Ohio State University (8.32), students used a variety of polyhedra to construct lightweight bristol board helmets.

Octahedron Net

Hexahedron Net

Dodecahedron Net

Octahedron

Hexahedron (cube)

Dodecahedron

8.31 A variety of polyhedra

8.32 OSU students used a variety of polyhedra to construct bristol board helmets. Charles Wallschlaeger, professor emeritus, The Ohio State University, Department of Industrial, Interior, and Visual Communication Design.

8.33 Ettore Sottsass, *Ginevra Carafe,* 1997. Manufactured by Alessi, Crusinallo, Italy.

The specific amount of enclosed space is essential when we create any kind of container, from architecture to glassware. *The Ginevra Carafe,* by Ettore Sottsass (8.33), easily holds a liter of wine. This narrow cylinder requires little table space, and an extra disk of glass at the base increases weight and stability. An additional glass cylinder at the top ensures that the lid will remain firmly in place.

Weaving, folding, and slotting are a few of the strategies artists and designers use when creating volume. Defining an enclosed space while maintaining structural integrity is essential. If the structure fails, the volume will collapse and the space will be lost.

Each strategy has its advantages. As demonstrated by the fencer's mask on page 193, woven structures can be elegant, light in weight, and remarkably strong. Package designers generally create volume through folding. The heavy paper used for this purpose can be printed while flat, then scored, cut, and folded. The patterns used are mathematically specific and often structurally complex (8.34). And surprisingly strong volumes can be created using slotted planes. "Egg-crate" slotted structures (8.35) can be used to protect and separate fragile contents (such as wine bottles) and to hold them in a specific position.

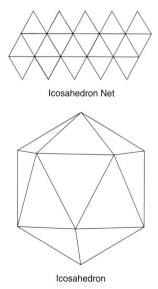

Icosahedron Net

Icosahedron

8.34 Package design pattern.

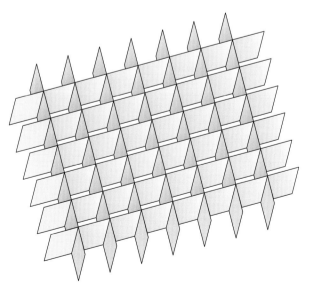

8.35 Example of "egg-crate" slotted structure.

MASS

A **mass** is a solid three-dimensional form. A massive object can be as dense and heavy as a bar of gold or as light and porous as a sponge.

Massive sculptures are often carved from a solid block of plaster, clay, or stone or are cast using bronze, glass, or other materials. Solid and imposing, they tend to dominate the environment in which they are placed.

Just as Alexander Calder took advantage of the buoyancy of a thin plane to create his mobiles, so Henry Moore took advantage of the power of mass when he created *Locking Piece* (8.36A). In such structures, the **primary contours** (or outer edges) are complemented by the **secondary contours** created by internal edges (8.36B). As the viewer circles the form, these contours visually alternate, as the primary contours become the secondary contours and the secondary contours become the primary contours.

Massive forms tend to suggest stability, power, and permanence. A series of colossal heads produced by the Olmec people of ancient Mexico combine the abstract power of a sphere with the specific power of a human head (8.37). The pyramids at Giza present an even more extreme example of permanence and stability. Built almost 5,000 years ago to memorialize and protect a deceased pharaoh, they continue to dominate the landscape and the human imagination.

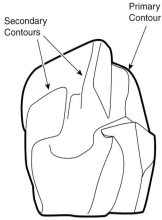

8.36A-B Henry Moore, *Locking Piece*, 1963–64. Bronze, 115 × 110¼ × 90½ in. (292 × 280 × 230 cm).

Key Questions

- Experiment with various ways of creating volume, including folding, weaving, and using slotted structures. Which is most effective for your design?

- When should a closed volume (such as a cube) be used and when is an open, "eggcrate" structure preferable?

- What is the relationship between line, plane, volume, and mass in your design?

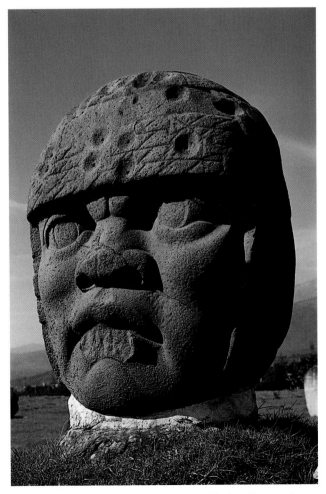

8.37 Colossal Head, 1300–800 B.C. Stone. Mexico, Olmec culture, Jalapa, Veracruz, Mexico.

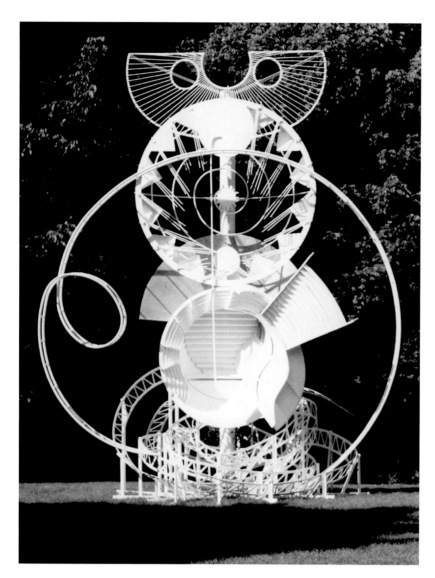

8.38 Alice Aycock, *Tree of Life Fantasy,*
Synopsis of the Book of Questions Concerning
the World Order and/or the Order of Worlds,
1990–92. Painted steel, fiberglass, and wood,
20 × 15 × 8 ft (6.1 × 4.6 × 2.4 m).

SPACE

In three-dimensional design, **space** is the area within
or around an area of substance. A dialogue between
a form and its surroundings is created as soon as an
artist positions an object in space. Space is the partner
to substance. Without it, line, plane, volume, and
mass lose both visual impact and functional purpose.

The proportion of space to substance triggers an
immediate response. The space in Alice Aycock's
Tree of Life Fantasy (8.38) is defined by a filigree of
delicate lines and planes. Inspired by the double-
helix structure of DNA and by medieval illustrations showing people entering paradise through a
spinning hole in the sky, Aycock combined a linear
structure with a series of circular planes. The resulting sculpture is as open and playful as a roller

coaster. By comparison, Burden's *Medusa's Head* (see
figure 8.20, page 190) presents a relatively solid
mass of tangled cement, wood, and metal. With
sculptures of this kind, the *surrounding* space becomes more important than any enclosed space.
Like a stone placed in a glass of water, the large,
solid mass seems to displace the surrounding space,
pushing it into the edges of the room.

Positive and Negative

The interrelationship between space and substance
is demonstrated in every area of three-dimensional
design. David Smith's *Cubi XXVII* (8.39) is dominated by a central void. The 10 gleaming geometric
volumes are activated by the space they enclose.

Space plays an equally important role in representational work. The open mouth in *Model of a Trophy Head* (8.40) really animates the mask. No facial expression, however extreme, would be as lively if this mouth were closed.

Negative space is especially noticeable in designs that are dominated by positive form. Karen Karnes' *Vessel* (8.41) is a functional pot, with its internal bottom placed just above the vertical slit. In effect, the lower half of the design serves as a pedestal for the functional container at the top. This narrow slit of negative space presents a strong contrast to the solidity of the cylindrical form and helps energize the simple form.

8.39 David Smith, *Cubi XXVII,* March 1965. Stainless steel, 111⅜ × 87¾ × 34 in. (282.9 × 222.9 cm).

8.40 *Model of a Trophy Head,* Ecuador, La Tolita, 600 B.C.–A.D. 400. Ceramic.

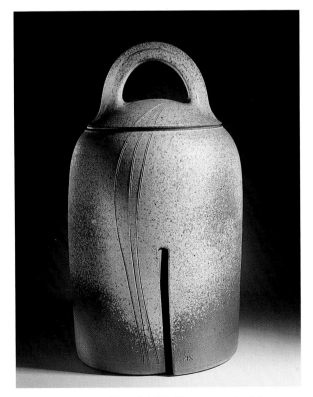

8.41 Karen Karnes, *Vessel,* 1987. Stoneware, wheel-thrown, glazed, and wood-fired, 16½ in. h. × 10½ in. d. (41.9 × 26.7 cm).

8.42 Richard Serra, *Torqued Ellipse VI,* **1998–99.** Weatherproof steel, 13 ft 8 in. × 33 ft 5½ in. × 19 ft 8¼ in. © FMGB Guggenheim Bilbao Museoa. All Right Reserved.

8.43 Walter de Maria, *The Lightning Field,* **1977.** Near Quemado, NM. Stainless steel poles, average height 20 ft 7½ in. (6.1 m), overall 5,280 × 3,300 ft (1,609.34 × 1,005.84 m).

Compression and Expansion

Space is never passive or meaningless. It is just as important as the surrounding substance, and it can be manipulated very deliberately. The tangibility of space is especially apparent in the works of Richard Serra and Walter de Maria. Using four enormous steel plates, Serra created a sense of spatial compression in figure 8.42. Upon entering the piece, the viewer immediately becomes aware of the weight of the tilted planes and of the support the compressed space seems to provide. The space in de Maria's *Lightning Field* (8.43) is equally clearly defined yet is wonderfully expansive. Arranged in a grid over nearly 1 square mile of desert, 400 steel poles act as a collection of lightning rods. Impressive even in daylight, the site becomes awe-inspiring during a thunderstorm. Lightning jumps from pole to pole and from the sky to earth, creating a pyrotechnic display.

Activated Space

The space in an artwork may be contemplative, agitated, or even threatening. For example, a Japanese Zen garden is usually made from an enclosure containing several large rocks surrounded by carefully raked white sand. A few simple objects are used to create a contemplative space. By contrast, the space in Anish Kapoor's sculptures is often unsettling. Placed in the floor of a large, empty room, *Turning the World Inside Out II* (8.44) creates a sculptural whirlpool that seems to drain space, light, and energy from the surrounding room. Such activity becomes even more noticeable when the space itself is animated, as in *Lightning Field* during a thunderstorm.

8.44 Anish Kapoor, ***Turning the World Inside Out II,*** **1995.** Installed Fondazione Prada, Milan.
Chromium-plated bronze, 57 × 73 × 73 in. (145 × 185 × 185 cm).

8.45 **Lucas Samaras,** *Mirrored Room,* **1966.** Mirrors on wooden frame, 8 × 8 × 10 ft (2.44 × 2.44 × 3 m).

8.46 Donna Dennis, *Subway with Silver Girders,* 1981–82. Wood, masonite, acrylic, enamel, cellulose compound, glass, electrical fixtures, and metal, 12 ft 2½ in. w. × 14 ft 3½ in. d. (31 × 36 cm).

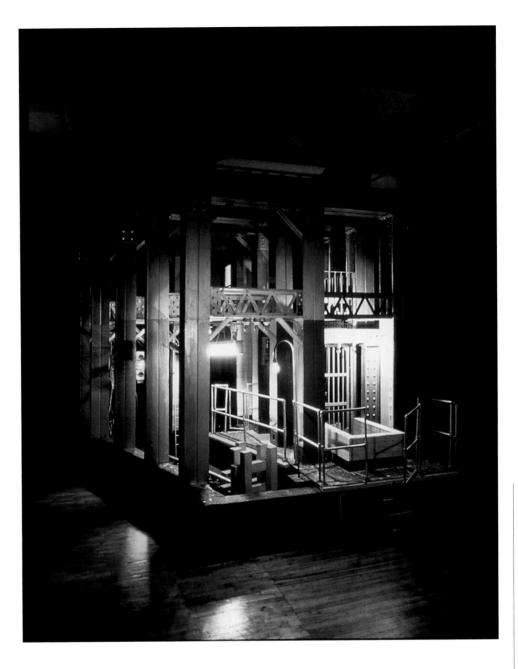

Entering Space

Some sculptures are designed to be entered physically. Lucas Samaras' *Mirrored Room* (8.45) multiplies and divides the reflection of each visitor who enters. Other sculptures can only be entered mentally. *Subway with Silver Girders* (8.46), by Donna Dennis, recreates in great detail the architecture and lighting we find in a subway station. Constructed at two-thirds the scale of an actual station, the sculpture presents a magical entry into a prosaic place. This subway station provides transportation for the mind, rather than the body.

Key Questions

- What is the relationship between substance and space in your design?

- What would happen if you substantially increased or decreased the amount of space? For example, would 70% space and 30% mass strengthen or weaken your design?

- How can the space play a stronger role in your design?

TEXTURE

Texture refers to the visual or tactile quality of a form. The increased surface area of a three-dimensional form heightens the impact of texture. The surface shifts and turns, presenting many opportunities for textural elaboration.

Degrees of Texture

Variations in the surface of a volume may be subtle or pronounced. In *Blackware Storage Jar,* by Maria Montoya Martinez and Julian Martinez (8.47), a burnished, shiny surface was combined with a subtle matte surface. The visual effect is dramatic despite the minimal textural variation. The geometric patterns enhance the surface of the jar but never compete with the purity of the graceful form. Gertrud and Otto Natzler used a very different approach for *Pilgrim Bottle* (8.48). The volume as well as the textural surface is exaggerated. Between the narrow neck and compressed base, the jar bulges out in a circular shape, as magical and as pockmarked as the surface of the moon. The unusual union between volume and surface, combined with the intriguing title, invites intellectual speculation. Who is the pilgrim, and what might this bottle contain?

Characteristic and Contradictory Textures

Every material has its own inherent textural properties. Clay, glass, and metal can be poured, cast, or pressed to create a wide variety of textures. Gold, which may occur in nature as dust, in nuggets, or in veins, can be cast, hammered, enameled, and soldered. Despite the adaptability of most materials, however, we are accustomed to their use in specific ways. The reflective surface of

8.47 Maria Montoya Martinez and Julian Martinez, *Blackware Storage Jar,* **1942.** Hopi, from San Ildefonso Pueblo, NM. Ceramic, 18¾ in. h. × 22½ in. d. (47.6 × 57.1 cm).

8.48 Gertrud Natzler and Otto Natzler, *Pilgrim Bottle,* **1956.** Earthenware, wheel-thrown, and glazed, 17 × 13 × 5 in. (43.2 × 33 × 12.7 cm).

8.49 Richard Notkin, *Vain Imaginings,* **1978.** White earthenware, glaze, brass, redwood, white cedarwood, 16 × 13½ × 16½ in. (40.6 × 34.3 × 41.9 cm).

a steel teapot, the transparency of glass, and the earthy functionality of clay fulfill our expectations.

When a material is used in an uncharacteristic way, or when strange textures are added to familiar forms, we must reappraise both the material and the object it represents. Except for the wooden platform and brass screws, Robert Notkin's *Vain Imaginings* (8.49) is made of clay. The textures of wood, plastic, glass, and bone have been skillfully imitated. Clay is very unlike any of these materials, and a purist may argue that such mimicry violates its inherent nature. On closer examination, however, we can see a perfect match between the image and the idea. The table, which symbolizes the world, supports a chess set, suggesting risk, and a television set, which presents an illusion. The ceramic skull is placed on top of four books titled *The Shallow Life, Moth and Rust, Vain Imaginings,* and *By Bread Alone.* The image on the screen repeats the skull. The clay itself suggests impermanence (as in "he has feet of clay") and mortality (as in "earth to earth, dust to dust," which is often said during funerals). In this masterwork of imitation, ceramicist Robert Notkin has created a "fake" sculpture for a false world.

Doormat, by Mona Hatoum (8.50), offers an even more disorienting interpretation of a familiar object. Constructed from steel pins, this mat is part of a series of political art projects by this Palestinian artist.

8.50 Mona Hatoum, *Doormat*, 1996. Stainless steel and nickel-plated pins, glue, and canvas, 1 × 28 × 16 in. (2.5 × 71 × 40.6 cm).

Commenting on the realities of racism, Hatoum suggests that for African-Americans, the opportunities offered by the Civil Rights movement may seem as illusory as a welcome mat made of pins.

The Implications of Texture

On a compositional level, texture can enhance or defy our understanding of a physical form. In figure 8.51, the lines carved into the surface of the vessel increase our awareness of its dimensionality. Concentric circles surrounding the knobs at the base of each handle create a series of visual targets that circle the globe, while additional grooves accentuate the surface of the sturdy handles. On a conceptual level, texture can add layers of meaning to art and design. In *Rock Bible* (8.52), Takako Araki used three kinds of

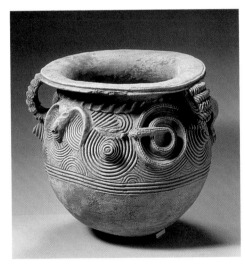

8.51 Globular Vessel with Inverted Rim, Tenth Century, Igbo, Nigeria. Terra-cotta, 16 in. (40.6 cm).

8.52 Takako Araki, *Rock Bible*, 1995. Ceramic, silkscreen, 8¼ × 23⅝ × 16½ in. (21 × 60 × 42 cm).

texture to animate an artwork and expand its meaning. The words on the pages of the Bible provide one texture, the rough surface of the disintegrating book provides a second, and the inherent texture of the clay provides a third.

In summary, texture can increase the surface area of an object, add contrast, and enrich our understanding of the physical and conceptual qualities of any three-dimensional object.

Key Questions

- How many textures can be created with the material you are using?
- What happens when a surface gradually shifts from a polished, smooth texture to a very rough texture?
- Can contradictory texture enhance or expand the idea you want to convey?

LIGHT

Light can enhance or obscure our perception of form. It can affect our emotions, entice us to enter a room, and create a mystery. It can even become a sculptural medium in its own right. Often overlooked, light is actually an essential aspect of three-dimensional design.

Value and Volume

A gradated series of highlights and shadows is produced whenever light pours across a surface. These **values,** or variations in light and dark, are our primary means of perceiving space. As demonstrated by two views of Daniel Chester French's *Head of Abraham Lincoln* (8.53), a surface that appears flat when lit from the front can become spatially rich when lit from the top or sides. Product designers are equally aware of the importance of light. A badly lit form will lack definition and impact, while even the simplest form will attract attention when it is dramatically lit. In figure 8.54, highlights, gradations and shadows give definition to each of Stan Rickel's *Teapot Sketches.*

8.53 Daniel Chester French, *Head of Abraham Lincoln* (Detail of Seated Figure), 1911–22. Full-size plaster model of head of marble statue, Lincoln Memorial, Washington, DC, 1917–18. Head 50½ in. h. (128.3 cm), total figure 19 ft h. (5.8 m).

Striking a Surface

Light is strongly affected by the substance it strikes. As demonstrated by the teapots in figure 8.54, light creates a continuous series of values when it strikes an opaque surface. Light behaves very differently when it strikes a transparent surface, such as clear plastic or glass. It is often refracted (or bent), creating a complex network of luminous shapes. Reflective surfaces can bounce light back into space. As a result, objects that are made from polished steel, mirrors, and other reflective materials can appear to emit their own light. A translucent surface is partially transparent. Neither fully opaque nor fully transparent, translucent surfaces can be mysterious and evocative.

Each type of surface can be used expressively. *The Dance* (figure 8.1) is dominated by the movement of seven opaque figures in and out of space. Light and shadow accentuate the action of the exuberant marble dancers. The same composition would dissolve into visual chaos if it were cast in transparent glass. On the other hand, the energy in Larry Bell's *The Iceberg and Its Shadow* (8.55) comes from the effects of light on a transparent and reflective surface. Multiple plates of glass create reflections, which continually shift, separate, and surround the viewer. Like a house of mirrors, the sculpture is both tangible and transient.

8.54 A

8.54 B

8.54 C

8.54 D

8.54 E

8.54 F

8.54 Stan Rickel, *Teapot Sketches*, **1991.** Mixed medium, 12 × 12 × 12 in. (30.5 × 30.5 × 30.5 cm).

8.55 Larry Bell, *The Iceberg and Its Shadow,* 1977. Clear and gray glass coated with inconel, 60 in. w. (152.4 cm), 57 in. to 100 in. h. (144.8 to 254 cm). Busch Lobby, MIT Permanent Collection.

8.56 Robert Irwin, *Part II: Excursus: Homage to the Square*[3]. Installation at Dia Center for the Arts, New York. September 1998–June 1999.

Translucent materials can create even more complex effects. Robert Irwin's *Part II: Excursus: Homage to the Square*[3] (8.56) was installed at the Dia Center for the arts in New York in 1998–1999. This structure consisted of nine cubic rooms, defined by delicate walls of translucent cloth. The translucency of the fabric varied, depending on the amount and location of the light. Two vertical fluorescent lights illuminated each cube, creating subtle changes in color from room to room.

Entering the installation was both inviting and disorienting. From any point, all of the rooms were visible yet veiled. The layers of fabric and the variations in light made the most distant rooms appear to dissolve. The vertical fluorescent lights, which always remained visible, read first as individual, then as mirror, images, creating a hallucinatory experience similar to a carnival funhouse. All activity within the space was created by the visitors themselves, who entered, explored, and left the installation like ghostly silhouettes.

Ambient and Directed light

Ambient light encompasses an entire space or setting. For example, when we enter an open courtyard on a sunny summer afternoon, we are surrounded by warm ambient sunlight. Everything we see is colorful and brightly lit. **Directed light** is localized and focused, like a spotlight on a singer.

Exhibition designers are masters of light. They use directed light to focus the viewer's attention and increase visual drama. They use ambient light to create the underlying feeling. For example, the designers of a 1989 NASA exhibition used low ambient light to suggest the mystery of space travel. Bright pools of directed light were then used to emphasize individual displays (8.57).

Light as Sculpture

Many types of sculptural light are used by contemporary artists and designers. Some shape neon tubes into sculptural forms.

8.57 **NASA Exhibit at the 1989 Paris Air Show.** Designers: Bill Cannan, Tony Ortiz, H. Kurt Heinz. Design Firm: Bill Cannan & Co.

Others use commercial lighting fixtures and illuminated signs to convey aesthetic meaning. Still others project light onto various shapes and surfaces, creating effects that range from the humorous to the bizarre.

Projection and containment are two common ways to create sculptural light. James Turrell's *Afrum-Proto* (8.58) was created when a powerful beam of projected light struck the corner of an empty room. The resulting form was a complete illusion yet totally convincing: viewers *saw* a cube. Bill Parker's *Jewel of Enlightenment (Hashi-no Toma)* (8.59) demonstrates the power of containment. Measuring 40 inches in diameter, the transparent globe is both a container for electricity and a compelling volume in itself. Standing 5 feet from the floor, the sphere is slightly above ordinary eye level, making it even more awe-inspiring.

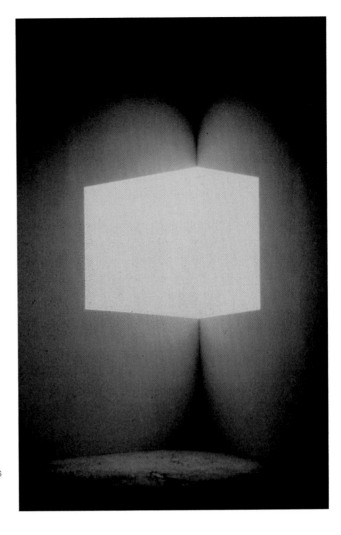

8.58 James Turrell, *Afrum-Proto*, 1966. Quartz-halogen projection, as installed at the Whitney Museum of American Art, New York, 1980.

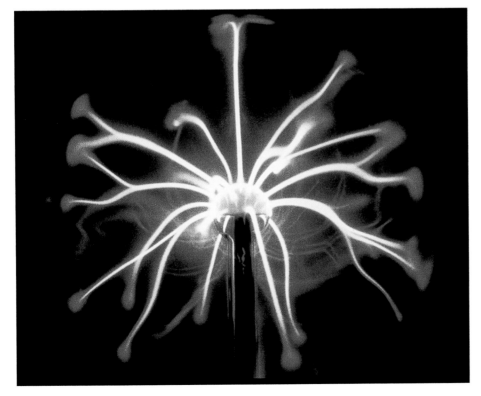

8.59 Bill Parker, *Jewel of Enlightenment (Hashi-no Toma)*, 1989. 40 in. (101.6 cm) diameter sphere standing 5 ft (1.5 m) from the floor, glass sphere, gas mixture, high voltage at high frequency.

8.60 Bill Viola, *The Veiling*, 1995. Video/Sound Installation.

With the increasing use of new media, light has become an eloquent and versatile addition to the elements of three-dimensional design. In addition to its traditional role in accentuating form, it has now become a sculptural medium in itself. For example, in *The Veiling* (8.60), Bill Viola hung thin sheets of translucent fabric on parallel lines across the center of a darkened room. An image of a man was projected from one end, while an image of a woman was projected from the opposite end. These projections became increasingly diffused as they passed through the multiple layers of cloth. Finally, the two figures merged on a central veil as pure presences of light.

Key Questions

- How can lighting direction diminish or accentuate the dimensionality of your artwork?

- Does your object require special illumination, such as an internal light source, fiberoptics, or a video screen?

- How can light enhance the expressive content of your artwork?

- Can your object be redesigned to use light more effectively? If so, how?

8.61 A. Hue

8.61 B. Value

8.61 C. Intensity

8.61 D. Temperature

8.62 *Smartronics Learning System* **by Fisher-Price**

8.63 Toshiyuki Kita, *Kita Collection* of chairs with removable seats for Stendig International Inc. Beechwood frame and upholstered seat.

COLOR

Color definitions remain the same whether we are creating a three-dimensional or a two-dimensional composition. Each color has a specific **hue** (8.61A), which is determined by its wavelength. **Value** (8.61B), the lightness or darkness of a color, helps determine legibility. **Intensity,** or **saturation** (8.61C), refers to the purity of a color. **Temperature** (8.61D) refers to the psychological characteristics attributed to a color.

Degrees of Harmony

Selecting the right colors for a product and determining the degree of color **harmony** can make or break a design. The triadic harmony used in *Smartronics Learning System* by Fisher-Price (8.62) creates an attractive educational toy for young children. The large red, yellow, and blue buttons are easy to push and invite even the most skeptical child to play. A very different type of harmony is offered in *Kita Collection,* by Toshiyuki Kita (8.63).

These simple chairs with their removable seats can be color-customized to fit into any interior. The buyer can create his or her own sense of harmony.

Disharmony can also be used effectively. In figure 8.64, Keith Edmier portrays his pregnant mother on the day President Kennedy was assassinated. She is wearing the same Chanel suit pattern that Jackie Kennedy wore, and she pensively rubs her glowing belly. The orange-reds and purple-reds suggest traditional monochromatic harmony but seem skewed and off-key. While the surface of normalcy remained intact, the substance of American politics shifted after Kennedy's death. Likewise, while the artist's mother seems calm, the colors and materials used suggest an undercurrent of anxiety.

8.64 Keith Edmier, *Beverly Edmier*, 1967. Cast resin, silicone, acrylic paint, fabric.

8.65 Michael Graves, *Alessi Coffee Set.* Glass, silver, mock ivory, and Bakelite.

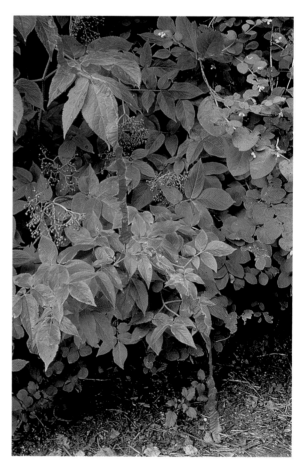

8.66 Andy Goldsworthy, *Poppy Petals*, August 1994. Leaves and flowers.

Contrast

Artists and designers often use contrasting colors to accentuate the function of a product or to create a distinctive image. Contrasting colors and contrasting materials distinguish Michael Graves' *Alessi Coffee Set* (8.65). The fragile, transparent glass is protected by metallic armor. These metal bands accentuate the cylindrical forms, while the blue handles and bright red accents further animate the set. Using natural materials in natural settings, Andy Goldsworthy often creates intense areas of red, green, or gold to alert the viewer to junctions, boundaries, or unusual configurations between objects in the landscape. These accents of color are especially powerful when the surrounding colors are subdued. The scarlet poppy petals in figure 8.66 create a glowing line, which cascades down the leaves of the host tree.

Color and Emotion

The emotional implications of color can be demonstrated by a visit to any car dealership. Bright red, black, or silver sports cars are often marketed as

8.67 Adele Linarducci, *Slingshot Wheelchair,* 1989. Polystyrene, vinyl, PVC, and other materials, a nonworking model created while artist was a student at Rochester Institute of Technology.

8.68 George Segal, *Walk, Don't Walk,* 1976. Museum installation, with viewer. Plaster, cement, metal, painted wood, and electric light, 104 × 72 × 72 in. (264.2 × 182.9 × 182.9 cm).

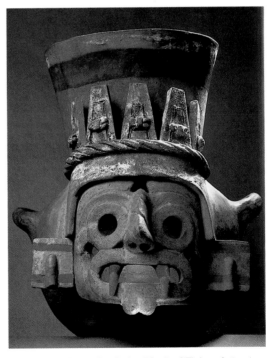

8.69 Ritual Vessel Depicting Mask of Tlaloc, Aztec, Mexico, Tenochtitlan, 1400–1521. Ceramic.

oversized toys for single drivers, while more subdued colors are often used for the minivans and station wagons favored by families. In figure 8.67, color is used to add a sporty look to quite a different vehicle. This manual wheelchair, designed by Adele Linarducci for children ages 6 to 11, gives the user a psychological boost while encouraging the development of physical strength and dexterity.

On the other hand, it is the absence of color that brings power to the life-size figures in George Segal's installations. Despite their proximity to the viewer and their large scale, the white figures in *Walk, Don't Walk* (8.68) are drained of color and emotionally distant. Here, an antiseptic white is used to suggest alienation.

Symbolic Color

Symbolic color is culturally based. Because each culture is unique, color associations vary widely. For example, yellow signifies the direction north in Tibet but the qualities of light, life, truth, and immortality to Hindus.[4] Blue represents mourning in Borneo, while in New Mexico it is painted on window frames to block entrance by evil spirits. In ancient times, blue represented faith and truth to the Egyptians yet was the color worn by slaves in Gaul.[5]

The blue face that dominates the mask of the Aztec god Tlaloc in figure 8.69 is both symbolically and visually appropriate. Symbolically, the blue represents sky and the rain that Tlaloc calls forth to nourish the crops. Visually, the contrast between the warm, reddish clay and the sky-blue paint increases the impact of the ferocious face.

8.70 George Rickey, *Five Lines in Parallel Planes*, 1965. Stainless steel, 228 × 24 × 24 in.

Key Questions

- Which will work better in your design, a limited range of hues or a wide range of hues?

- Are all of the colors in your design similar in intensity? What would happen if you combined low-intensity colors with high-intensity colors?

- What is the proportion of warm and cool colors in your design — is it around 50/50, 70/30, 20/80? What would happen if these proportions were changed?

TIME

Every object occupies a position in time as well as space. In some cases, the specific temporal location is of minor importance. For example, *Locking Piece* (see figure 8.36, page 197) is as meaningful now as it was when constructed in 1963. Formalist in approach, it makes no specific reference to social or political events. Constructed from durable bronze, it has effectively withstood the effects of time. In other cases, temporal location gives the object its meaning. As noted on page 192, Nancy Holt's *Sun Tunnels* creates a kind of celestial observatory. Light pours through the holes in the curving walls, creating projections that mark the movement of the planets. If the element of time were removed, the concrete tunnels would have no more meaning than drainage pipes at a construction site.

Two aspects of time are of particular importance to sculptors. **Actual time** refers to the location and duration of an actual temporal event. For example, it takes less than a minute for the bowling ball to roll down the ramps in Tinguely's *Chaos 1* (see figure

8.2, page 181). By contrast, **implied time** is the suggested location or duration of an event. The traffic light in Segal's *Walk, Don't Walk* changes, but the sculptural figures never move.

Actual motion and implied motion are equally important. The long metal lines in George Rickey's *Five Lines in Parallel Planes* (8.70) actually move, creating a seemingly endless variety of compositions over time. By contrast, all of the motion in Erwin Hauer's *Project California Condor* (8.71) is implied. We can almost hear the flapping wings, but the sculptural birds remain still.

Viewing time is a final basic consideration. The multiple surfaces presented by any three-dimensional object require extended analysis. We walk around Rodin's *The Kiss*, noting every nuance in form and texture; we rotate a ceramic vessel in our hands, savoring every detail. *The Board Room* (see figure 8.10, page 185), *Part II: Excursus* (see figure 8.56, page 208) and other installations require even more viewing time. To understand the artwork, the viewer must enter and fully explore the site.

8.71 Erwin Hauer, *Project California Condor*, 1978–83. Plastic laminate, wingtip to wingtip 9 to 10 ft (2.75 to 3.05 m).

THE COMPLEXITY OF THREE-DIMENSIONAL DESIGN

Completing a new project every week or so is quite common in a basic two-dimensional design class. By contrast, a month of work may be devoted to a major project in a three-dimensional design class. The materials are less familiar, the construction methods are more time-consuming, and the multiple surfaces of a physical object present a particular challenge. Used poorly, the elements of three-dimensional design can become adversarial, resulting in a disjointed composition. Used well, each design element contributes to a wonderfully complex and compelling artwork.

SUMMARY

- *Form* may be defined as the physical manifestation of an idea. *Content* refers to the idea itself, including the subject matter plus its emotional, intellectual, spiritual, and symbolic implications.

- In three-dimensional design, *form* also refers to dimensionality itself. Thus, a circle is a shape; a sphere is a form.

- The first step in creating a design is to understand its purpose. A sculptor seeks to convey ideas and express emotions. A craftsperson or designer is equally concerned with the function and the beauty of an object.

- Height, width, and depth are the three dimensions in three-dimensional design. Orthographic projection provides a means of clearly drawing these dimensions.

- Artworks can vary in dimensionality from relief, which uses a flat backing to support dimensional forms, to environmental works that the viewer can enter and physically explore.

- A line can connect, define, or divide a design. It can be static or dynamic, increasing or decreasing the stability of the form.

- A plane is a three-dimensional form that has length and width but minimal thickness.

- In three-dimensional design, *volume* refers to an enclosed area of three-dimensional space.

- A mass is a solid three-dimensional form. A massive object can be as dense and heavy as a bar of gold or as light and porous as a sponge.

- Space is the area within or around an area of substance. Space is the partner to substance. Without it, line, plane, volume, and mass lose both visual impact and functional purpose.

- *Texture* refers to the visual or tactile quality of a form. The increased surface area of a three-dimensional form heightens the impact of texture.

- Light can enhance our perception of a three-dimensional form, attract an audience, or be used as a material in itself.

- Hue, value, intensity, and temperature are the major characteristics of color.

- Every object occupies a position in time as well as space. Actual time, implied time, actual space, and implied space can be combined to create compelling objects of great complexity.

Keywords

actual line	freestanding work	mass	secondary contour
actual time	function	negative space	sight line
ambient light	geometric form	organic form	site specific
continuity	harmony	orientation	space
contrast	hue	orthographic projection	static form
directed light	implied line	plane	symbolic color
direction	implied time	polyhedra	temperature
dynamic form	installation	positive form	texture
environmental work	intensity	primary contour	three-quarter work
earthwork	kinetic form	relief	value
form	line	saturation	volume

Profile:
Rodger Mack, Sculptor

The Oracle's Tears: Conception, Composition, and Construction

Rodger Mack was best known for his work in bronze and steel. His work is included in the collections of the Museum of Modern Art in Barcelona, Spain; the Grand Hotel in Guayaquil, Ecuador; the Arkansas Arts Center Museum, Little Rock; the Albrecht-Kemper Museum of Art in St. Joseph, Missouri; the Munson-Williams-Proctor Institute in Utica, New York; and the Everson Museum in Syracuse, New York. Mack, who always used travel as a major inspiration for his imagery, was the recipient of a Fulbright grant for study in Italy, grants from the National Endowment for the Arts and the New York State Council on the Arts, and workshop grants for projects in England, Barcelona, and South Africa.

My meeting with Mack in 2000 was delayed for almost a year, due to his many commissions and elaborate projects. We got together over lunch just before he left for Italy. I had always admired Mack's abstract sculptures that so elegantly combine power and grace. Indeed, I expected our conversation to focus on the elements and principles of design. As you will see, the conversation that actually developed was equally devoted to concepts and composition.

MS: One of the biggest questions my students have is this: how do I get from where I am, as a beginner to where you are, as a professional? Can you describe that path briefly?

RM: I always knew that I wanted to study art, and I began my undergraduate work at the Cleveland Institute of Art, planning to become an automotive designer. In the fourth year of the five-year BFA program, I had the good fortune of being picked by General Motors to participate in an experimental summer internship. It was an exciting time: I was well paid and directly involved in my intended career.

I realized, though, that automotive design limited my possibilities as an artist, and I turned instead to a major in sculpture, with a minor in ceramics. At Cleveland, ceramicist Toshiko Takaezu was a great influence. She taught me a level of professionalism and an understanding of a new level of quality, both in concept and in craft. I was further influenced by Toshiko's teacher, Maija Grotell, who had developed the ceramics program at Cranbrook, where I did my graduate work. At the age of 70,

she was continuing to do pioneering work with ceramic glazes.

Finally, as an apprentice to William McBey, I learned about working on commissions and the realities of day-to-day work in the studio. With sculpture, cleaning up is important: if you don't control your work space, it will control you!

MS: How do you get started on a sculpture?

RM: I don't have to get started, because I never stop! I'm always watching, listening, and thinking. When I do stop the merry-go-round long enough, I record my ideas in a notebook. I always carry this notebook on the plane: while others read, I draw. I always have many more ideas than I can handle: I wish I could build them as fast as I can think them up.

Whenever I stop generating new material, I just visualize the inventory of sculptural parts I already have in the studio. Putting them together in new ways provides even more possibilities: an idea gets me working with the metal, which then generates more ideas. I always try to have something ready for casting each month, if only to add to this inventory of parts.

I only make maquettes when they are required for a commission. The small scale of a maquette is so different from the actual scale of the piece, especially for a major project. I remember one maquette I made for a commission in North Little Rock, Arkansas. It was made of bronze, and I charged them $200 for the maquette. Before the meeting to review the project, one of the city councilors put a box of multi-colored sticks of plasticine in front of me and said, "Next time, make it out of this." He was annoyed that I had made the maquette in bronze. In fact, the city council was against the project — they just didn't want to spend the money — but a grassroots civic group saw the importance of the work, and the commission was approved.

MS: How do you choose which of the drawings to make into sculptures?
RM: I might choose a drawing because I can't see the other side. I get curious. There is something in the drawn side that compels me to spend the time and money on the sculpture, so that I can see the other side. Drawings that I really finish are the sculptures that I never make.

MS: It seems that you actually "draw" with the metal; that is, you approach it with the same openness with which I approach a sheet of paper. How malleable is it?
RM: Just malleable enough! I like it because it is NOT easy. It is hard, and you have to really commit yourself to the piece. I am most intuitive when I am working with existing fragments from my inventory, essentially collaging parts together. Starting with a collection of parts, I create connections, often heating a bar of bronze to just the right temperature and bending it to form a bridge or activate a space. I see the space around each volume as much as I see the volume itself.

MS: Please describe your latest piece, The *Oracle's Tears*.
RM: I've always been drawn to ancient cities and architectural forms and have been working with mythological themes for the past six years, with a series of maidens, a minotaur, a Trojan horse, and several oracles completed so far. When I visit these ancient civilizations, it saddens me that they are gone, destroyed to make way for new civilizations.

This sculpture is made from six major parts. The column is the dominant feature, structurally and conceptually. Just above it, I have placed a form which has reappeared in my work for 30 years, the Oracle. It is like an image on a tarot card, the hanging man, perhaps. A smaller piece, based on a shape I found in a market in Athens, connects the oracle and the column. On the top, the "capitol" repeats the triangular spaces seen throughout the sculpture. The tears are created by the three descending lines. The base is the final element. It provides a stable support and adds a sense of completion.

MS: How was the sculpture made?
RM: I used a combination of fabrication and casting. The oracle form was made by cutting out shapes from a sheet of 1/8-inch bronze and welding them together. The tears and the column were cast in sections, then welded. A potassium dichloride patina, applied using a blowtorch, gives the piece its golden color.

MS: This is an especially important piece for you, I think.
RM: You always hope your latest piece is the best! But yes, it combines ideas I've been working on for three years, with an overall theme, which first appeared in my work when I was in undergraduate school.

MS: What advice do you have for a beginning student?
RM: There's the old cliché: learn the rules before you break them. Always worked for me.

Rodger Mack died in September 2003. Hundreds of friends and former students from around the world attended his memorial service.

Rodger Mack, *The Oracle's Tears,* **1999.** Cast and welded bronze, 17 × 6 × 4 ft (5.18 × 1.83 × 1.22 m).

Principles of Three-Dimensional Design

Composition can be defined as the combination of multiple parts into a unified whole. In a well-composed design, all of the elements work together, as a team. As one element becomes dominant, another element becomes subordinate. A dialogue is created between positive and negative forms, and opposing forces add vitality rather than causing confusion.

Each compositional part makes a positive contribution to an effective design. Graceful metal lines have been combined with a series of contoured masses to create the elegant and utilitarian form of Niels Diffrient's *Freedom Chair* (9.1). In Alice Aycock's *Tree of Life Fantasy* (see figure 9.9, page 224), line, plane, and space have been combined to create an exuberant dance. Every element is both dependent on and supportive of every other element. Martin Puryear's *Seer* (9.2) consists of a closed volume at the top and an open volume

9.1 Niels Diffrient, *Freedom Chair*, 1999. Die-cast aluminum frame with fused plastic coating; four-way stretch black fabric.

9.2 Martin Puryear, *Seer*, 1984. Water-based paint on wood and wire, 78 × 52¼ × 45 in. (198.2 × 132.6 × 114.3 cm).

at the bottom. The horn-shaped top piece is powerful and imposing, while the open construction at the bottom invites us to enter and visually explore the structure. A series of curving vertical "ribs" unifies the top and bottom sections, while the contrast between open and closed forms adds a touch of mystery. In both 9.1 and 9.2, the compositional parts work together to create a compelling whole.

The elements of design are the building blocks from which compositions are made. The principles of design describe ways in which these building blocks can be combined. Unity and variety are the overriding principles of three-dimensional design. Any composition gains when unity and variety are appropriately balanced. Balance, scale, proportion, emphasis, and rhythm are commonly listed as the other essential principles of design. These design principles can be used to create unity and variety.

UNITY AND VARIETY

Unity can be defined as similarity, oneness, togetherness, or cohesion. **Variety** can be defined as difference. Unity and variety are the cornerstones of composition.

Increasing Unity

We tend to scan an entire composition, then analyze the specific parts. A composition composed of units that are unrelated tends to appear random and unresolved. Evidence of deliberation and order tends to increase unity. Grouping, containment, proximity, continuity, repetition, and closure are six common strategies for increasing order.

Grouping

When presented with a collection of separate visual units, we immediately try to create order and make connections. **Grouping** is one of the first steps in this process. As noted in the discussion of Gestalt psychology in Chapter Three, we generally group visual units by location, orientation, shape, and color. *Many Times* (9.3), by Juan Muñoz, clearly demonstrates grouping by location. We first see a complete composition, comprised of seven figures. It is roughly triangular in shape, starting with the single seated figure on the right and extending to the standing figure at the far left. The division between the two sets of bleachers creates two subgroups, comprised of two figures on the right and five figures on the left. We can further group the three figures positioned on the top bleachers and the three figures on the bottom, with the single standing figure providing a visual exclamation point for the sculpture as a whole.

9.3 Juan Muñoz, *Towards the Corner*, **1998.** Seven figures, wood, resin and mixed media.

9.4 Roni Horn, *How Dickinson Stayed Home,* **1993.** Installation. Solid aluminum and plastic. 25 cubes, each 5 × 5 × variable lengths.

9.5A Louise Nevelson, *Wedding Chapel IV,* **1960.** Painted wood, height c. 9 ft. Private collection.

9.5B Line drawing of Figure 9.5A, showing containers in red and overall continuity in black.

9.6 Aaron Macsai, *Panels of Movement.* Bracelet, 18K gold, sterling, copper, ⅞ × 7 in. (2 × 18 cm).

9.7 Mona Hatoum, *Doormat,* 1996. Stainless steel and nickel-plated pins, glue and canvas, 1 × 28 × 16 in. (2.5 × 71 × 40.6 cm).

Containment

Containment is a unifying force created by the outer edge of a composition or by a boundary within a composition. A container encourages us to seek connections among visual units and adds definition to the negative space around each positive form. The room itself provides the container for Roni Horn's *How Dickinson Stayed Home* (9.4). Letters from the alphabet are presented on 25 small cubes. Like Emily Dickinson's poetry, the installation is both economical and expansive. A minimal amount of information evokes a wide range of interpretations. Contained by the white walls and dark floor of the room itself, the blocks create a unified statement, despite their seeming random distribution.

Proximity

In design, the distance between visual units is called **proximity.** Even the most disparate forms can become unified when they are placed in close proximity. For example, Louise Nevelson constructed *Wedding Chapel IV* (9.5A) from an improbable collection of wooden crates, staircase railings, dowels, chair legs, and other scrap. Organized into 14 rectilinear containers and placed in close proximity, the various pieces have become unified into a lively whole.

Continuity

Continuity can be defined as a fluid connection among compositional parts. When objects are placed in close proximity, continuity often happens naturally. As demonstrated by figure 9.5B, each form in

Wedding Chapel IV touches several other forms. As a result, our eyes move easily from section to section, increasing connections among the parts.

Repetition

Repetition occurs when we use the same visual element or effect any number of times within a composition. In Aaron Macsai's *Panels of Movement* (9.6), similar lines, shapes, textures, and colors were used in each of the 10 panels from which the bracelet was constructed. A spiral shape, a wavy line, a sphere, and at least one triangular shape appear repeatedly. Despite their variations in size, texture, and location, these repeated forms create a strong connection from panel to panel.

Closure

Closure is the mind's inclination to connect fragmentary information to produce a completed form. In Mona Hatoum's *Doormat* (9.7), we must visually connect hundreds of steel pins to create the word *welcome.* Closure makes it possible to communicate using implication. Freed of the necessity to provide every detail, the artist or designer can convey an idea

9.8 *Tower of Photos* from Ejszyszki, Completed in 1993, United States Holocaust Memorial Museum, Washington, DC. James Ingo Freed, lead designer.

9.9 Alice Aycock, *Tree of Life Fantasy,* Synopsis of the Book of Questions Concerning the World Order and/or the Order of Worlds, 1990–92. Painted steel, fiberglass and wood, 20 × 15 × 8 ft (6.1 × 4.6 × 2.4 m).

through suggestion, rather than description. When the viewer completes the image in his or her mind, it is often more memorable than an explicit image.

Combining Unifying Forces

James Ingo Freed used all of these unifying forces to create the *Tower of Photos* in the Holocaust Museum in Washington, DC (9.8). His design team wanted to demonstrate the number of lives lost in one Polish village while honoring the individuality of the inhabitants. They collected and framed thousands of photographs, including groups of schoolchildren, weddings, and family snapshots. Placed in close proximity and relentlessly repetitive, the photographs personalized the victims while emphasizing their connection to the lost community. Based on the chimneys used to burn the bodies of the dead, the tower itself provides the dominant structure for the exhibition, both structurally and emotionally.

Increasing Variety

Difference in any aspect of a design increases variety. By reviewing the elements of design described in Chapter Eight and the principles of design described in this chapter, you can quickly create a checklist of areas for variation, such as

- *Line variation.* Lines of different diameter were combined with double linear "train tracks" in Aycock's *Tree of Life Fantasy* (9.9).

- *Variation in texture.* Combining smooth and textured surfaces can add energy and interest to even the simplest form.

- *Variation in pattern.* The Pacific island mask shown in figure 9.10 is unified through symmetrical balance. This underlying order freed the artist to experiment with many colors and patterns.

Degrees of Unity

Creating an effective partnership between unity and variety is essential. Excessive unity can be monotonous, while excessive variety can be chaotic. As noted in Chapter Seven, our compositional choices must support our conceptual intentions. Some

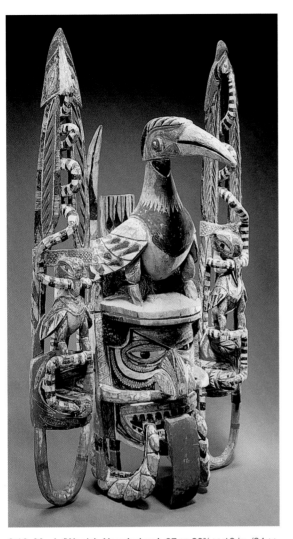

9.10 Mask (Wanis), New Ireland. 37 × 20⅞ × 19 in. (94 × 53 × 48.3 cm).

9.11 Sol LeWitt, *Wall/Floor Piece #4*, 1976. White painted wood, 43¼ × 43¼ × 43¼ in. (109.9 × 109.9 × 109.9 cm).

designs require a high level of unity. Based on a grid, Sol Lewitt's *Wall/Floor Piece #4* (9.11) provides a methodical transition from the horizontal floor to the vertical wall. Other designs require a high level of variety. The lines, shapes, volumes, and masses in Judy Pfaff's *Rock/Paper/Scissor* (9.12) ricochet off the floor, walls and ceiling with an almost chaotic energy.

9.12 Judy Pfaff, *Rock/Paper/Scissor,* 1982. Mixed media installation at the Albright-Knox Art Gallery, Buffalo, NY, September 1982.

9.13 **Leonardo Drew, *Number 56,* 1996.** Rust, plastic, wood, 113 × 113 in. (287 × 287 cm).

Grid and Matrix

A **grid** is created through a series of intersecting lines. A **matrix** is a three-dimensional grid. Both can unify a design by creating containment, continuity, and proximity.

In *Number 56* (9.13), Leonardo Drew poured rust into hundreds of plastic bags, which were then connected to a wooden support. The rust and the relentlessly numbered plastic specimen bags create a dialogue between the orderly grid and the decaying metal. The resulting combination of order and disorder balances monotony and mystery.

Daniel Buren's *The Two Plateaus* (9.14) offers another variant on the grid. This public art project, located in the Palais Royal in Paris, covers a 1,000-square-foot plaza. The striped cylinders range in height from about 2 to 6 feet. Mimicking the columns in the building and organized on the pavement like players on a checkerboard, they bring both energy and humor to the site.

In *Current Disturbance* (9.15), Mona Hatoum used a matrix for unity and a sequence of lights for variety. A single clear lightbulb has been placed in each compartment within the structure. Controlled by a computer, these lights flicker in various patterns, from near darkness to a crescendo of illumination when all are lit. A single lit bulb in the center of the piece and the matrix itself are the only constants.

Key Questions

- What strategies have you used to unify your composition?
- What gives your composition variety?
- Is the balance between unity and variety appropriate for the ideas you want to express?
- What would happen if your composition were constructed using a pattern or grid?

9.14 **Daniel Buren, *The Two Plateaus,* 1985–86.** 1,000-square-foot sculpture for the Cour d'Honneur, Palais Royal, Paris. Black marble, granite, iron, cement, electricity, water.

9.15 Mona Hatoum, *Current Disturbance,*
1996. Wood, wire mesh, lightbulbs, timed
dimmer unit, amplifier, four speakers,
9 ft 2 in. × 18 ft × 16 ft 6 in. (279 × 550.5 ×
504 cm).

BALANCE

In design, **balance** refers to the distribution of
weight or force among visual units. For the architect, sculptor, and industrial designer, physical
balance is a structural necessity, while a degree of
visual balance is an aesthetic necessity. As with
physical balance, visual balance requires equilibrium, or equality in size, visual weight, and force.
Especially in three-dimensional design, visual balance can be created through the absence as well as
the presence of form.

There are three major types of balance.

In **symmetrical balance,** forms are mirrored on
either side of a central axis. The resulting form is
generally physically and visually stable. The central
face in figure 9.16A is an example of symmetrical
balance.

With **radial symmetry,** design elements extend
out from a central point, as with the spokes of a
wheel. Radiating in all directions while remaining
anchored at the center, this type of balance tends to
generate a great deal of energy while retaining a
high level of unity. The outer ring in figure 9.16 is an
example of radial balance. Diagram 9.16B shows
both of these forms of symmetry.

Asymmetrical balance creates equilibrium
among visual elements that do *not* mirror each other

**9.16A Bella Coola Mask Representing the
Sun, from British Columbia, before 1897.**
Wood, diameter 24¾ in. (63 cm).

9.16B Diagram of Bella Coola mask. The
central face is an example of symmetrical
balance. The outer ring is an example of
radial symmetry.

9.17 Examples of Asymmetrical Balance

on either side of an axis. Depending on the degree of asymmetry, the resulting design may be quite stable, very dynamic, or nearly chaotic. Many strategies can be used to create asymmetrical balance:

- A large form is placed close to the fulcrum, while a small form is placed farther away. Just as a child at the end of a seesaw can balance an adult near the center, so large and small forms can be balanced in a design (9.17A).

- Multiple small forms can balance a single large form (9.17B).

- A small, solid form can balance a large, open form. The solidity and stability of the square give it visual weight as well as physical weight (9.17C).

9.18 Theodore Gall, *Plaza Facets*, 2001. Cast bronze, 6 × 6 × 6 in. (15.2 × 15.2 × 15.2 cm).

Most artworks are constructed from multiple parts. Size variations among the parts affect both the physical balance and expressive impact. A **dominant,** or primary, form is often balanced by one or more **subordinate,** or secondary, forms. For example, in Theodore Gall's *Plaza Facets* (9.18), the large head on the left is balanced by the column and fragmentary heads on the right. The seven smaller figures create yet a third compositional level. Using these compositional hierarchies, artists and designers can create unified designs using distinctly individual parts.

Two contrasting interpretations of a single figure further demonstrate the expressive power of balance. Figures 9.19 and 9.20 both represent St. Bruno, an eleventh-century Catholic saint who founded an austere, contemplative religious group known as the Carthusian Order. Members lived in caves and devoted their time to manuscript transcription, meditation, and prayer.

The first statue, completed by Michel-Ange Slodtz in 1744, dramatizes a pivotal moment in Bruno's life. Preferring his contemplative existence to the power and prestige of a more public life, Bruno rejects promotion to the office of bishop. Slodtz used asymmetrical balance to express this dramatic moment. The small bishop's hat, proffered by the angel in the lower right corner is the focal point of the entire sculpture. The much larger figure of St. Bruno recoils when confronted by this symbol of authority. As a result, the small hat matches the power of the saint.

A very different interpretation of the life of St. Bruno is given in the second sculpture. Completed by Jean-Antoine Houdon in 1766, it emphasizes the contemplative nature of the Carthusian Order and its founder. Using symmetrical balance, Houdon presents a dignified, introspective man. If we divide the figure in half from top to bottom, the two sides basically mirror each other. This saint is a philosopher, very much at peace with the choices he has made. Just as asymmetrical balance is appropriate for the dramatic moment represented by Slodtz, so symmetrical balance is ideal for the serenity shown by Houdon.

Exaggerated weight or buoyancy can shift the balance in an artwork and enhance meaning. In Chuichi Fujii's *Untitled* (9.21), a cedar log seems to have been crushed by the weight of a second log.

9.19 Michel-Ange Slodtz, *St. Bruno*, 1744. Marble.

9.20 Jean-Antoine Houdon, *St. Bruno of Cologne*, 1766. Stucco.

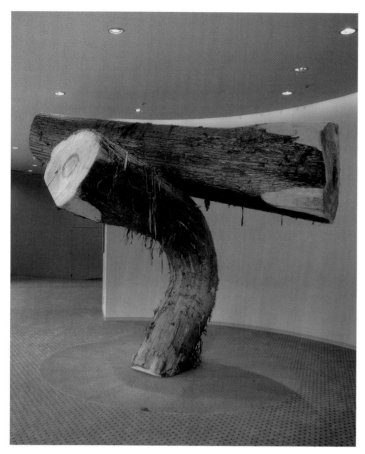

The combination of the rough logs and the exaggerated weight seems to bring a powerful natural force into the pristine gallery. At the other extreme, Patricia A. Renick's *Life Boats/Boats About Life* (9.22) seems to float on air, as weightless as a dream. Dramatic lighting and cast shadows heighten the magical effect. This artwork derives its power from the denial of gravity.

Key Questions

- Which form of balance is most effective for the ideas you want to express?

- Which is the dominant form in your design? Is its dominance conceptually justified?

- What happens when an unexpected part of the design plays the dominant role?

9.21 Chuichi Fujii, *Untitled,* **1987.** Japanese cedar, 10 ft 6 in. × 13 ft ½ in. × 11 ft 6 in. (320 × 400 × 350 cm).

9.22 Patricia A. Renick, *Life Boats/Boats About Life,* **1979–80.** 1 to 1½ ft high × 5 to 6½ ft long × 1 to 1½ ft deep (30.5 to 45.7 cm high × 152.4 to 198.1 cm long × 30.5 to 45.7 cm deep).

SCALE

Scale commonly refers to the size of a form when compared with human size. Using our bodies as a constant, we can identify three major types of scale relationships. Small-scale objects can be **hand-held,** while **human scale** refers to designs that are roughly our size. Very large objects and installations are **monumental** in scale.

Returning to Thomas Gall's sculpture, we can explore the implications of each scale type. The actual artwork is roughly 6 × 6 × 6 in. and can be hand-held. At this scale, we are invited to enter and explore the artwork mentally rather than physically (9.23A). At triple this size (18 × 18 × 18 in.), the dominant head in the design would be about the size of our own head (9.23B). This would create a very different dialogue between the audience and the artwork. Expanded to monumental scale — say, 32 × 32 × 32 feet — the artwork would invite physical entry (9.23C). We could now stand beside the sculptural figures in the piece. Simply by changing the scale, the artist could create three very different responses to the same composition.

PROPORTION

Proportion refers to the relative size of visual elements *within* an image. When we compare the width of the head with its height, or divide a composition into thirds, we are establishing a proportional relationship.

In industrial design, changes in proportion can enhance or diminish function. The five gardening tools in figure 9.24 are all based on the same basic combination of handle, blades, and a simple pivot. Variations in proportion determine their use. The short-handled pruner in the lower left corner is used to trim twigs and small branches from shrubs. It must fit comfortably in a single hand. The proportions of the lopper in the opposite corner are much different. Its 20-inch-long handle provides the leverage needed to cut heavier branches from small trees. For the industrial designer, function often determines proportion.

In sculpture, variations in proportion can increase aesthetic impact. Three proportional variations

A

B

C

9.23A–C Scale variations, from hand-held to monumental.

9.24 Home Pro Garden Tool Line. Designers: James E. Grove, John Cook, Jim Holtorf, Fernando Pardo, Mike Botich. Design Firm: Designworks/USA.

9.25 Constantin Brancusi, *Maiastra*, 1912. Polished brass, 29⅞ × 7¼ × 7½ in. (75.7 × 18.5 × 19 cm).

9.26 Constantin Brancusi, *Golden Bird*, 1919, Pedestal c. 1922. Bronze, stone, and wood, 37¾ in. h. (95.9 cm), base 48 in. h. (121.9 cm).

9.27 Constantin Brancusi, *Bird in Space*, 1928. Bronze (unique cast), 54 × 8½ × 6½ in. (137.2 × 21.6 × 16.5 cm).

of Constantin Brancusi's *Bird in Space* are shown in figures 9.25 through 9.27. In *Maiastra* (9.25), the abstract bird form is dominated by the egg-shaped torso, which tapers into the folded wings at the bottom and the raised head at the top. This bird is approximately 3 times taller than it is wide. Brancusi further abstracted *Golden Bird* (9.26) and elongated the body. The bird is now 7 times taller than it is wide, and an elaborate base adds even more height to the sculpture. With *Bird in Space* (9.27), Brancusi elongated the form even more and added an expanding "foot" below the folded wings. This bird is almost 10 times taller than it is wide. By lengthening the columnar structure in this final version and carefully tapering the sculpture near the base, Brancusi made this simple sculpture fly.

As with all design decisions, choosing the right scale and proportion greatly increases expressive power. Giovanni Bologna's *Apennine* (9.28) is scaled to overwhelm the viewer with a sense of the mountain spirit's presence. His human frame is monumental, and the surrounding trees and cliff appear to diminish by comparison.

Proportional extremes can be equally expressive. Standing just over 5 feet tall, Alberto Giacometti's *Chariot* (9.29) offers a somber analysis of the human condition. The solitary figure is delicately balanced on gigantic wheels, which then rest on two small pedestals. The entire form is linear, as if distilled down to the barest essentials. Both the chariot and the life it transports are precariously balanced and seem fragile and vulnerable.

Key Questions

- What would happen to your composition if you dramatically changed its scale?

- What would happen if you dramatically changed the proportions in your composition?

- Imagine that your design can be stretched or compressed in any direction. What are the advantages of a very tall, thin composition, compared with a short, cubic composition?

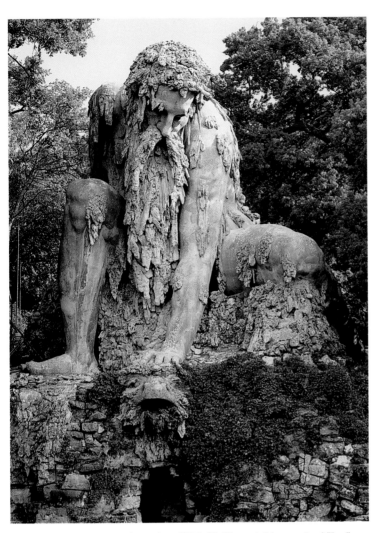

9.28 Giovanni Bologna, *Apennine,* 1580–82. Stone, bricks, mortar. Villa di Pratolino, Florence region, Italy.

9.29 Alberto Giacometti, *Chariot,* 1950. Bronze, 57 × 26 × 26⅛ in. (144.8 × 65.8 × 66.2 cm).

EMPHASIS

Emphasis gives particular prominence to part of a design. A **focal point** is a compositional device used to create emphasis. For example, the bishop's hat in Slodtz's version of St. Bruno (figure 9.19, page 229) is the focal point of the composition. Both emphasis and focal point are used to attract attention and increase visual and conceptual impact.

Emphasis by Isolation

Any **anomaly,** or break from the norm, tends to stand out. Because we seek to connect the verbal and visual information we are given, a mismatched word or an isolated object immediately attracts attention. In *I Never Liked Musical Chairs* (9.30), metalsmith Joana Kao established the norm through

9.30 Joana Kao, *I Never Liked Musical Chairs.* Bracelet, sterling, 24K, 2¾ × 1¾ in. (7 × 4 cm).

seven tiny chairs connected by a silver chain. The figure at the end of the chain breaks the pattern. This break conveys the isolation felt by a child who has been ejected from the game.

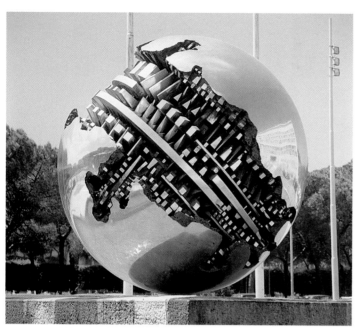

9.31 **Arnaldo Pomodoro,** *Sphere,* **1965.** Bronze, 47 in. (119.4 cm) diameter. Ministero degli Esteri, Rome.

9.32 **Mary Ann Scherr,** *Loops,* **1988.** Sterling silver neckpiece, 8½ × 4¾ × 5 in. (21.6 × 12.1 × 12.7).

Emphasis Through Contrast

Contrast is created when two or more forces operate in opposition.

By reviewing the elements and principles of design discussed thus far, we can quickly create a long list of potential adversaries, including static/dynamic, small/large, smooth/textured, and curvilinear/rectilinear. When the balance is just right, powerful compositions can be created from any such combination. Many artists and designers devote most of their compositional area to one force and a much smaller amount to a contrasting force. The larger force sets the standard, while the smaller force creates the exception.

Contrast can appear in many forms and in varying degrees. Two opposing forces dominate Arnaldo Porudoro's *Sphere* (9.31). The imposing spherical form seems to have been eaten away by an external force, leaving a pattern of rectilinear teeth across its equator. This creates a strong contrast between the massive structure and the invading space, and adds rhythm and texture to the spherical form.

Loops (9.32), by Mary Ann Scherr, presents a contrast between movement and constraint. A curving plane encircles the user's throat, providing protection but restricting

9.33 Pol Bury, *Fountains at Palais Royal,* Paris, 1985.

motion. Below, the suspended rings sway with every movement of the body, creating a dynamic counterpoint to the constraining collar.

Water animates Pol Bury's *Fountains at Palais Royal* (9.33). The design relies on three major elements. The site itself is dominated by the regularly spaced columns that are so characteristic of neoclassical architecture. The polished steel spheres, poised within the bowl of each foundation, reflect these columns and the shimmering water, which provides the third element in the design. In a sense, the spheres serve as mediators between the rigid columns and the silvery water. Like the columns, they are simple volumes, arranged in a group. Like the water, they seem fluid as they reflect the moving water and the passing clouds. In this project, unity and variety have been combined to create an elegant and ever changing sculpture.

Key Questions

- Is there a focal point in your composition? If not, should there be?

- What is the most prominent form in your composition? If so, is it the form you most *want* to emphasize?

- What would happen to your composition if you dramatically increased the amount of contrast?

REPETITION AND RHYTHM

As noted at the beginning of this chapter, *repetition* occurs when we use the same visual element or effect any number of times within a composition. **Rhythm** can be defined as the organization of these multiple elements or effects into a deliberate pattern. Just as a musician creates a deliberate pattern connecting sound and silence, so the artist can create rhythm using positive form and negative space. Using the CD-ROM, you can experiment with regular, alternating, progressive, and complex rhythm.

As with music, the number and distribution of beats create the rhythm. In David Watkins' *Torus 280*

9.34 David Watkins, *Torus 280 (B2)*, 1989. Neckpiece, gilded brass, 11 in. (28 cm).

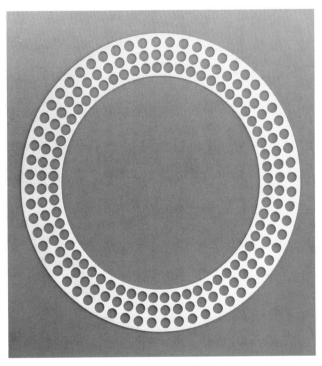

9.35 David Watkins, *Torus 280 (B1)*, 1989. Neckpiece, gilded brass, 11 in. (28 cm).

(B2) (9.34), the consistent order of the circular shapes creates a slow, regular pattern. When the number of circles multiplies in *Torus 280 (B1)* (9.35), the tempo, or pace, increases. As the neckpiece expands outward, the space between the circular openings also expands, creating greater variety in form. Rhythm plays an even greater role in figure

9.36 Tanija & Graham Carr, *Untitled*, 2001. Wet-formed leather, acrylic paint, 13¾ × 29¼ × 29¼ in. (35 × 74 × 74 cm).

9.36. The woven herringbone pattern in the bottom suggests first a clockwise then a counterclockwise visual movement. A similar pattern at the top accentuates the spatial variations in the piece. Tapered rectilinear shapes create a border, around both the interior and the exterior edges. Like a complex musical piece, three types of rhythm have been skillfully woven together.

The multiple views offered by physical objects accentuate the importance of rhythm. The movement of four women around an exuberant musician creates a joyous dance in Jean-Baptiste Carpeaux's *The Dance* (9.37). Our eyes follow the turning heads, clasped hands, and swirling arms as they move in, out, and around in space. A similar rhythm ani-

mates Steve Woodward's *Model of Proposal for Concourse Commission* (9.38). The plywood vortex seems to rise out of the floor to collect in a spinning disk at the top, then descend again, in an endless pattern. When combined with the spinning effect, this up-and-down movement gives the design great vitality.

Repetition is often used to increase compositional unity. It can also be used to quantify an elusive idea. For example, the 30 statues in Magdalena Abakanowicz's *Standing Figures* (9.39) are unified by their similarity in size, shape, and solemnity. Variations in each cast bronze surface provide a degree of individuality. Often interpreted as victims of war, the hollow, headless figures seem frozen in time, offering a silent testimony to a tragic past. The 6,000

9.37 Jean-Baptiste Carpeaux, *The Dance (After Restoration),* **1868–69.** Marble, 7 ft 6½ in. (2.3 m).

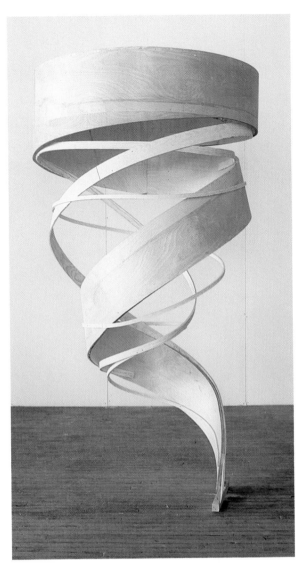

9.38 Steve Woodward, *Model of Proposal for Concourse Commission,* **1987.** Wood, 13¾ × 8 × 7½ in. (34.9 × 20.3 × 19 cm).

9.39 Magdalena Abakanowicz, *Standing Figures (30),* **1994–99.** Bronze, overall 54 ft 3 in. × 19 ft 8 in. (16.55 × 6 m).

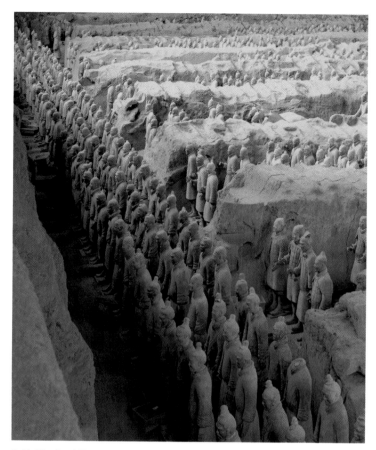

9.40 Tomb of Emperor Shih Huang Ti, 221–206 B.C. Painted ceramic figures, life size.

clay soldiers filling the tomb of Emperor Shih Huang Ti (9.40) demonstrate a different use of repetition. As he faced his death, the emperor may have sought companionship or protection from his army. Sherrie Levine's *La Fortune* (9.41) demonstrates a third use of repetition. Our sense of reality is challenged when we encounter these four pool tables. The identical arrangement of the balls seems impossible: the balls would be randomly distributed in four actual games. Here, a very ordinary scene becomes mysterious, even nightmarish, due to relentless repetition.

Key Questions

- Try repeating any element in your design. What does this repetition contribute, conceptually and compositionally?

- What happens when simple repetition is changed to specific rhythm?

- Does the rhythm remain constant in your design, or is there a change in pace? What is the advantage of each approach?

9.41 Sherrie Levine, *La Fortune* (After Man Ray) **1–6, 1990.** Felt, mahogany, resin, 33 × 110 × 60 in. (84 × 280 × 153 cm).

SUMMARY

- Through composition, we can combine multiple parts to create a unified whole.

- Grouping, containment, proximity, repetition, continuity, and closure are six common strategies for increasing unity. Difference in any aspect of a design increases variety.

- A grid is created through a series of intersecting lines. A matrix is a three-dimensional grid.

- Symmetry, radial symmetry, and asymmetry are three common forms of balance. A dominant, or primary, form is often balanced by one or more subordinate, or secondary, forms.

- Scale and proportion are two types of size relationships. Proportion refers to size relationships within an image, while scale involves a size comparison with our physical size.

- Emphasis gives prominence to a specific part of a design. A focal point is a compositional device used to create emphasis.

- Contrast is created when two or more forces operate in opposition. Many artists and designers devote most of their compositional area to one force and a much smaller amount to a contrasting force. The larger force sets the standard, while the smaller force creates the exception.

- Repetition occurs when we use the same visual element or effect any number of times within a composition. Rhythm is the organization of these multiple elements or effects into a deliberate pattern. Just as a musician creates a deliberate pattern connecting sound and silence, so the artist can create rhythm using positive form and negative space.

Keywords

anomaly	contrast	human scale	rhythm
asymmetrical balance	dominant	matrix	scale
balance	emphasis	monumental	subordinate
closure	focal point	proportion	symmetrical balance
composition	grouping	proximity	unity
containment	grid	radial symmetry	variety
continuity	hand-held	repetition	

Profile:
David MacDonald, Ceramicist

A Passion for Pottery

Internationally renowned ceramicist David MacDonald is best known for his work with utilitarian vessels. His work has been included in over 60 exhibitions, including the Torpedo Factory Art Center in Alexandria, Virginia; The Studio Museum in Harlem; and the Afro-American Historical and Cultural Museum in Philadelphia. He is also renowned as community leader, with work in an adult literacy program, a summer ceramics intensive program for high school students, and work with inmates at the Green Haven Maximum Security Correctional Facility in New York State to his credit.

MS: How did you start making art?

DM: Initially, it was a way to create some private space. As the third in a family of nine children, I always shared a bedroom with at least three of my brothers. I would help my parents unpack the groceries, then unfold the paper bags so that I could use the inside as drawing paper. Through hours of drawing, I was able to create my own little world.

MS: In our conversations and in viewing your work, I am struck by your passion for ceramics in general and functional vessels in particular. What is special about clay?

DM: I was introduced to ceramics during my second year in college. I was immediately fascinated by clay: it is responsive to the slightest pressure and can record the finest impression. After my first mug came out of the kiln and I made my first cup of tea, I was hooked. The idea of turning a lump of dirt into a useful object amazed me. Since I grew up with very little material wealth, I loved the idea of transforming nothing into something.

Now, I am drawn to functional ceramics because I like playing with the interaction between the object and the user. Having to produce a functional object makes the creative act much more interesting and challenging for me. When a teapot has just the right weight, balance, and proportions, it makes the act of pouring tea a celebration of the physical world.

MS: What is the source of your ideas?

DM: Anything can become a conscious or unconscious inspiration. I can get lost in the produce section of the supermarket: the shapes and colors of the vegetables give me all sorts of ideas.

On a more scholarly level, I was influenced by Japanese and Chinese ceramics during college, and for the past 20 years, I have been strongly influenced by African art and culture.

MS: Yes, I notice that a dramatic change in your work occurred around 1978. Before that time, your work was sculptural, representational, and highly charged politically; afterward, it became more utilitarian and abstract. What happened?

DM: At the opening for a solo show in Syracuse, I was asked a question by an elderly white woman that dramatically changed my attitude about my work. She innocently asked if there was anything positive about being black in America or was it just one frustration and humiliation after another. The question haunted me for months afterward. I realized that my creative work had been based on anger and a feeling of victimization. As I matured as an individual, I realized that my experiences weren't limited to anger — there is much more to my life than that! I then decided to tap the rich and varied cultural and artistic tradition to which I am heir. Now I am most interested in expressing the magnificence and nobility of the human spirit and in celebrating my African heritage.

MS: What distinguishes a great pot from a mundane pot?

DM: There is no simple answer to this question. We can talk endlessly about form, surface, line, and so forth and still not gain any real insight into what makes one pot great and another mundane, yet we immediately feel it when the mixture of physical elements is just right. Out of the 30 similar bowls a potter produces, 2 or 3 always seem to stand apart, as something special.

The search for this elemental quality makes my art magical and compels me to make the next piece. Ironically, if I ever identify exactly what it is that makes an exceptional piece, the excitement will be sucked out of the creative process. The search is as compelling as the solution.

MS: Tell me about the vessel pictured here.

DM: *Carved Stoneware Jar* was inspired by the bulbous form of a melon or gourd. The body is full and round and the lid handle is suggestive of a stem. I like the sense of an internal force or energy stretching the outer shell almost to the point of bursting.

First, I considered the function of the jar. To a large extent, the function determines the form. A certain size range facilitates everyday use. If the size is increased, the object is more suitable for ceremonial use, or as a decorative object. Certain shapes offer more storage capacity and better accessibility to whatever is being stored. Finally, the base must be big enough to provide stability.

The surface was carved when the jar was leather-hard, a couple of days after being thrown on the potter's wheel. A form this large can "carry" a fairly complex pattern, composed of smaller shapes in combination with larger design areas. By leaving some areas uncarved, I was able to create an overlapping effect and increase the illusion of space. The slashing diagonal lines help to unify the design and move the viewer's eye around the form, reinforcing the spherical volume.

MS: What were the most valuable lessons you learned from your teachers?

DM: From Joseph Gilliard at Hampton University, I learned the history and technique of ceramics and gained greater patience and self-control. I developed my self-awareness and passion for communication through my work with Robert Stull at the University of Michigan. From Henry Gernhardt, my Syracuse University colleague for 24 years, I learned that teaching is also an art. In nearly 40 years of teaching, Henry's commitment to his art and his students never faltered.

MS: Is there any advice you would like to give to my students?

DM: An artist has to believe in him- or herself. The dedication, courage, and energy my students bring to the classroom are more important than anything I can offer. If you want to stand above the crowd, your passion for your art must be manifest through a willingness to work harder than anyone else. The students who succeed see their art as a way of life and not simply as a way of earning a living. My job as a teacher is to help my students realize their potential and to bring eloquence to their unique voice.

David MacDonald, *Carved Stoneware Storage Jar*, 1997. 15 in. (38.1 cm).

chapter ten

Materials and Methods

An incredible range of materials and methods can be used to produce three-dimensional objects. Paper, metal, fibers, clay, and plastic are among the most versatile materials used by artists and designers; folding, casting, carving, weaving, and stamping are just a few of the production methods. A separate course specifically devoted to materials would be needed if we were to explore this subject in depth.

The purpose of this chapter is more pragmatic. As a beginner, you need both practical advice and a basic introduction to the aesthetic implications of various materials. We will begin with a discussion of the essential characteristics of materials, then consider ways in which contemporary artists use traditional materials. The last section is devoted to student materials used in many three-dimensional design courses.

CHOICE OF MATERIALS

Each material has specific strengths and limitations. For example, rubber cement is a temporary adhesive for ordinary paper, while white glue is an effective permanent adhesive for heavier paper and cardboard. Carpenter's glue works well for wood, while hot glue is an effective adhesive for assemblage materials. Misuse of any material can ruin a great design. By understanding the physical characteristics of common materials, we can produce better work in less time and at less cost. The following considerations are crucial:

- *Strength.* How much weight can a given material support? What is its breaking point when twisted, folded, or bent?

- *Workability.* How difficult is it to alter the shape of a material? Does it cut and bend easily? Can it be melted and cast or dripped to create a new form?

- *Durability.* What range of forces can this material withstand and for how long? Is it impervious to heat, water, wind, and ultraviolet light?

- *Weight.* A material that is too light for a given purpose can be as problematic as a material that is too heavy. What is the function of the project, and how can material weight serve that function?

- *Cost.* Can the material chosen be obtained easily and at a reasonable cost? If your budget is limited, expensive materials may have to be removed from consideration.

- *Toxicity.* Many plastics produce toxic gases when cut, etched, or burned. Paints and solvents may require the use of masks and gloves and often present significant disposal problems. Is the ventilation of your workplace appropriate for your work process? Are less toxic materials available?

- *Function.* Most important, how appropriate is a given material for a particular purpose? A teapot will be useless if the material used is porous, and a chair that is too difficult to construct will never be mass-produced. Any material chosen must serve the structural and aesthetic needs of the object you plan to produce.

Increasing Material Strength

Composites

A **composite** is created when two or more materials of differing strengths are fused together. Fiberglas (which combines glass filaments with plastic resin) and ferro-concrete (which is made from metal mesh embedded in concrete) are familiar examples. Foamcore (which is made from a sheet of polystyrene sandwiched between sheets of coated paper) and duct tape (constructed from three layers of "skin") are composites that are commonly used in three-dimensional design classes. Composites are often used when light weight, low cost, and increased strength are required.

Structural Strength

After years of experimentation, nature has developed an amazing array of effective structures. Two major types are skeletons (also called endoskeletons) and exoskeletons. A **skeleton** provides the internal structure needed by mammals and fish, while insects and many sea creatures rely on an external **exoskeleton** for support.

Architects are masters of both skeletal and exoskeletal structures. In his Guggenheim Museum Bilbao (10.1), architect Frank Gehry created a complex "skeleton" to support the building's gleaming titanium skin. The Gothic cathedral in figure 10.2 demonstrates the use of an exoskeleton. To increase

10.1 Computer-generated Catia image used for the Solomon R. Guggenheim Museum Bilbao, finished 1997.

10.4 Alexander-Gustave Eiffel, diagram of the construction of the Statue of Liberty.

1 Bay
2 Nave
3 Side aisle
4 Nave arcade
5 Clerestory
6 Cluster pier
  with colonettes
7 Triforium
8 Buttress
9 Flying buttress
10 Wooden roof

10.2 Perspective diagram and cross-section of Chartres Cathedral.

building height while reducing mass, medieval architects developed the **flying buttress** used in hundreds of cathedrals throughout Europe. These external structures provided the primary support for many remarkable buildings.

Artists and designers often use an **armature** to create internal structure. For example, a wire or wooden armature is often used to support the cloth or paper used in lampshades. Designers from around the world have created an amazing range of variations on this simple object (10.3). Engineer Gustav Eiffel developed a much more elaborate armature to support Auguste Bartholdi's *Statue of Liberty* (10.4). Standing over 150 feet tall and weighing 225

10.3A–C **Shoji Design,** Three Japanese floor lamps. Steel, bamboo, paper size variable.

tons, this monumental sculpture has to withstand wind, rain, and brisk sea winds. Without a strong internal structure, the statue could never have been built.

Distributing Force

As shown in figure 10.5, the five major forces are **compression, tension, bend, torque,** and **shear.** The equilateral triangle is the linear shape that best resists deformation by all of these forces, and the tetrahedron, or pyramid, is the strongest three-dimensional form. A triangular support, such as a corner brace on the back of a painting, can distribute force effectively and greatly increase strength. On a larger scale, a network of crossbeams in Thorncrown Chapel (10.6) adds both strength and beauty to a sacred space. R. Buckminster Fuller's geodesic

10.5A–E Major physical forces.

10.6 E. Fay Jones & Associates, Thorncrown Chapel, Eureka Springs, Arkansas, 1981.

10.7 R. Buckminster Fuller, U.S. Pavilion, Expo-67, Montreal, 1967.

10.8 Joseph Cornell, *Untitled (Medici Princess)*, c. 1948. Construction, 17⅝ × 11⅛ × 4⅜ in. (44.8 × 28.3 × 11.1 cm).

dome (10.7) expands this idea even further. Typically constructed using hundreds of tetrahedrons, the dome is relatively easy to build and creates a large volume using a minimal amount of mass. A model of beauty and efficiency, the geodesic dome has been widely used for large, open buildings, such as greenhouses and airplane hangars.

Methods of Construction

Compositional choices are strongly influenced by the method of construction. The two most common methods are addition and subtraction.

In **additive sculpture,** the artwork is created from separate parts that have been connected, usually using glues, joints, stitching, or welds. **Assemblage** is one additive method. Using objects and images that were originally designed for another purpose, Joseph Cornell created a whole series of evocative box structures (10.8). Many of these assemblages were designed to honor specific people, past or present. **Modeling** is an additive process often used by ceramicists. Pinching and pushing the pliable clay, skillful ceramicists can make both functional and sculptural objects of great complexity. To create his *Head Series* (10.9), Jean-Pierre Larocque stamped slabs of clay with various textures from cloth, then modeled and carved a head that is both activated and imposing.

In **subtractive sculpture,** the artist removes materials from a larger mass. Carving, drilling, cutting, and turning on a lathe are all subtractive processes. The Tlingit man shown in figure 10.10 follows a methodical process, beginning by drawing on the cedar pole, making a rough cut, then refining and finishing the totem pole.

Plastic and metal forms are often produced using two additional methods. With **solidification,** a liquid material is poured into a mold or extruded through a pipe, then allowed to harden. For example, when we squeeze cake frosting through a shaped nozzle, we can create a wide range of extruded forms. This same basic principle can be applied to materials that are more permanent and less tasty. With **displacement,** a solid material is physically forced into a new configuration. The stamping process used to mint coins is a familiar example of displacement.

10.9 Jean-Pierre Larocque, *Untitled (Head series),* 2002. Stoneware, 36¾ × 21 in. (93.3 × 53.3 cm).

10.10 Tlingit Totem Carver, 1996. Southeast Alaska.

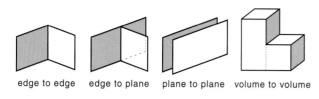

edge to edge   edge to plane   plane to plane   volume to volume

edge to edge   edge to plane   plane to plane   mass to mass

10.11A Connections Through Contact.

10.11B Connections Through Junctions.

ball and socket   hinge   pivot

10.11C Connections Through Joints.

CONNECTIONS

Physical and visual connections are equally important in three-dimensional design. Visual connections compositionally unify multiple surfaces, while physical connections can increase strength, flexibility, functionality, and stability. Connections can be created

- Through contact (10.11A)
- Through junctions (10.11B)
- Through joints (10.11C)

Physical connections are especially important to woodworkers. Carpenters and furniture designers learn dozens of specific joints, hinges, and splices. Mary Miss's *Staged Gates* (10.12A) was largely constructed using three types of joints (10.12B). Nails, screws, bolts, or glue is required when lap or butt joints are used. Interlocking joints can often create a simple connection without such additional reinforcement.

Employed to create functional objects, industrial designers pay particular attention to all types of connections. Because of the various joints used,

10.12A Mary Miss, *Staged Gates*, 1979. Wood, 12 × 50 × 120 ft (3.6 × 15.2 × 36.6 m).

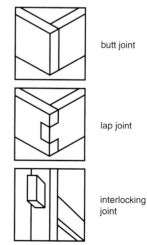

butt joint

lap joint

interlocking joint

10.12B Three Types of Joints.

the simple camera tripod can be expanded or collapsed, and the top can be rotated and reoriented. A model of a human figure (10.13) presents an even wider array of possibilities. Ball-and-socket joints at the shoulders and hips create rotating forms, while the hinge joints in the fingers, knees, and elbows permit a folding and unfolding movement. The spine is a marvel of engineering. Comprised of 24 stacked vertebrae, it provides a highly flexible framework for the entire torso.

Visual connections are just as important as physical connections. A split yellow-orange circle dominates the center of John Okulick's *Wind Wizard* (10.14). Through closure, we mentally connect the halves, despite their physical separation. A second broken circle echoes the interior circle and creates a dynamic boundary for the composition as a whole. The two gold spheres at the upper left and lower right seem poised for movement. Every form is connected to at least one other form, enhancing overall continuity.

10.13 Human figure models include a variety of joints.

10.14 John Okulick, *Wind Wizard*, 1987.
Painted wood, gold leaf, oil stick, 22 × 25 × 6 in. (55.9 × 63.5 × 15.2 cm).

TRANSITIONS

Many types of transitions can be created in three-dimensional design. The various angles and joints in Eduardo Chillida's *Asbesti Gogora III* (10.15) create an abrupt transition from surface to surface, while a fluid transition helps unify the various sections of Liv Blåvarp's *Bird* (10.16). Fluid transitions are often created through gradual change from one form or surface to another. Such **gradation** creates sequential change within a consistent pattern. Figure 10.17 shows a few of the many types of gradation.

TRADITIONAL MATERIALS, CONTEMPORARY USES

Stone

Limestone, basalt, marble, and other dense, fine-grained stones have been used since prehistory to create durable and imposing objects. Hand-held stone amulets have been worn to ward off evil, while monumental sculptures, such as Mount Rushmore and the pyramids at Giza, have been used to commemorate political and religious figures and beliefs. Using chisels, mallets, and rasps, stone carvers can create remarkably delicate forms using an amazing array of textures.

Contemporary artist Anish Kapoor is especially intrigued by the relationship between space and substance. Rather than viewing these forces as simple opposites, he often creates sculptures and installations exploring the essential connection between the two. *Void Field* (10.18) is one example. Kapoor notes:

> It's a work about mass, about weight, about volume, and then at the same time seems to be weightless, volumeless, ephemeral; it's really turning stone into sky. The darkness inside the stones is the darkness of black night, the darkness of sky.[1]

10.15 Eduardo Chillida, *Asbesti Gogora III*, 1962–64. Oak, 81½ × 136⅜ × 73⅛ in. (207.3 × 346.4 × 184.2 cm).

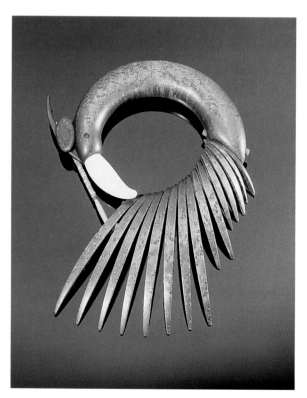

10.16 Liv Blåvarp, *Bird*, 1991. Neckpiece, birdseye maple, satinwood, whaletooth, 12½ × 10¼ in. (32 × 26 cm).

By drilling small, cylindrical openings into 16 massive block of sandstone, Kapoor was able to exaggerate the physicality of a durable stone and emphasize the significance of the interior space.

Wood

Traditional cultures worldwide use wood to create functional structures, such as buildings, furniture, and utensils, as well as sculptural objects, such as masks, ancestor poles, and walking sticks. Readily available in most areas, wood is inherently beautiful, easily painted, relatively light-weight, and surprisingly versatile. It can be carved, steam-formed, and assembled using various hinges and joints.

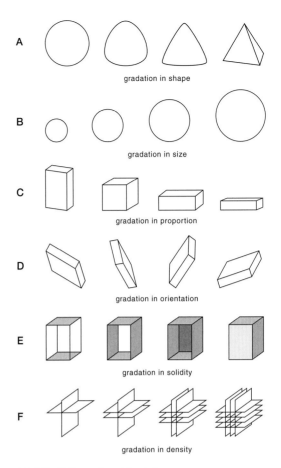

A   gradation in shape

B   gradation in size

C   gradation in proportion

D   gradation in orientation

E   gradation in solidity

F   gradation in density

10.17A–F Examples of Gradation.

10.18 Anish Kapoor, *Void Field,* **1989.** Sixteen sandstone elements.

10.19 Mariko Kusumoto, *Tansu no Oku.* Copper, nickel, silver, brass, bronze, resin, 15½ × 14 × 14 in. (39.4 × 35.6 × 35.6 cm) open.

Metals

Bronze casting, refined during the Renaissance, has traditionally been used for large-scale sculptures of all kinds. Gold, silver, copper, pewter, and brass are more commonly used for jewelry and utensils. Most metals can be cast, forged, soldered, etched, and stamped.

Mariko Kusumoto used copper, nickel silver, sterling silver, resin, bronze, and brass to create *Tansu no Oko* (10.19). A lotus blossom, seashells, butterflies, and an open hand extend out from an etched sheet of turn-of-the-century advertisements. A plastic resin adds color and sparkle to the butterflies. The structure is based on a children's pop-up book, while the images recall the Victorian fascination with mechanical and natural objects.

Clay

Clay is perhaps the most basic and versatile of all materials. Essentially made from refined earth, it can be hand-formed using coil, slab, and carving techniques; poured into molds; and "thrown," using a potter's wheel. When fired, it becomes extremely durable and can be decorated with beautiful colored glazes. All of these qualities are exploited fully by contemporary ceramicists and potters.

Glass

Glass, which is made primarily from silica, has been used for containers of all kinds since the time of the pharaohs. It can be transparent or opaque and, with the addition of copper, cadmium, cobalt, and other materials, can take on a complete range of colors. In its molten state, it can be poured, blown, pressed into molds, drawn into threads, stamped, and extruded.

The transparency of glass is emphasized in Eric Hilton's *Innerland* (10.20). Constructed from 25 cubes of clear glass, the sculpture appears to shift with each change in the viewer's position. Hilton combined the transparency and brilliance of glass with its density and mass to create an artwork that is both formidable and evocative.

Fibers

The term *fibers* covers a wide range of linear materials, including strips of willow, bamboo, and reeds, as well as the more familiar cotton, linen, silk, and wool. As with the other traditional materials, fibers have been used for basketry, quilts, clothing, and other commonplace objects, as well as prayer rugs and ritual clothing, from shrouds to wedding dresses. Most fibers can be painted or dyed and can be constructed in many ways, including weaving, braiding, knotting (as with macramé), knitting, and felting.

Two qualities most distinguish contemporary fibers. First, the traditional separation between

10.20 Eric Hilton, *Innerland,* **1980.** Engraved by Ladislav Havlik, Lubomir Richter, Peter Schelling, and Roger Selander, cut by Mark Witter. Cast, cut, engraved, sandblasted, and polished, 3⅞ × 19⅜ × 19⅜ in. (9.9 × 49.3 × 49.3 cm).

sculpture and fiber arts has largely disappeared. As demonstrated by Red Forest (see figure 8.27, page 193), fibers are often used for large-scale designs. Second, the definition of *fibers* has become increasingly broad. For example, Cathy Strokowsky wove together glass, wire, artificial sinew, and horsehair to create *Glass Pod with Hair,* shown in figure 10.21.

10.21 Cathy Strokowsky, *Glass Pod with Hair,* **2001.** Blown glass, sand-blasted, woven artificial sinew, wire, horse hair, 4¾ × 12½ × 4¾ in. (12 × 31.75 × 12 cm).

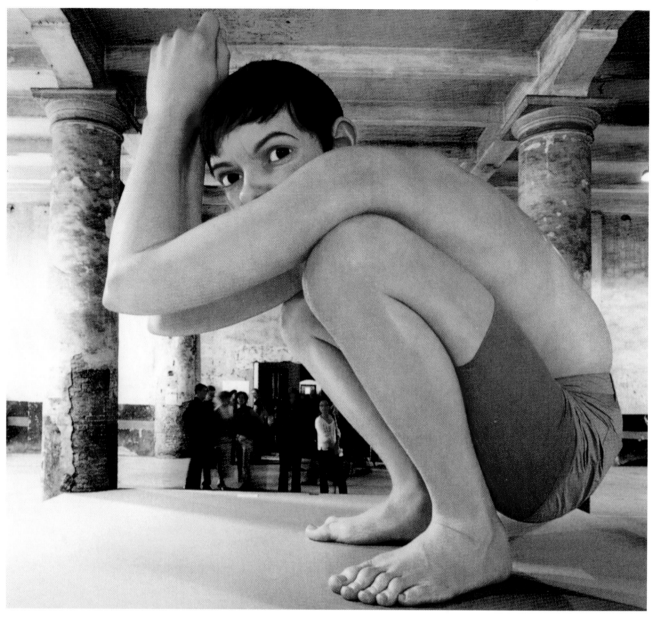

10.22 Ron Mueck, *The Boy*, 1999. Site-specific work installed in the Mind Zone at the Millenium Dome, London, United Kingdom. 16 ft (190 in, 490 cm).

Plastics

Since the 1920s, plastics have provided a plethora of possibilities for both artists and designers. Transparent, translucent, or opaque, plastics can be formed into sheets and then cut and assembled. Many types of plastic can be extruded, cast, vacuum-formed, and stamped. Light in weight, varied in color, and relatively cheap to produce, plastics have fueled a revolution in the design and distribution of household products.

Using a variety of plastics, Ron Mueck has made many large-scale sculptures of human figures. One of the most compelling is *The Boy* (10.22), installed in London's Millennium Dome. Nearly 20 feet high, the adolescent boy seems vulnerable and defensive, despite (or perhaps because of) his enormous size. As with all of Mueck's work, the details are astounding: every hair is defined, and the eyes seem to glisten with moisture as well as apprehension.

STUDENT MATERIALS

To minimize cost and expedite exploration, three-dimensional design projects are often constructed from common materials, such as bristol board, corrugated cardboard, plywood, wire, plaster gauze, and plaster. The following section describes the most basic types of boards and adhesives.

Boards

Bristol board is like thick, stiff paper. It is available in various thicknesses from 1-ply (similar to drawing paper in weight) to 5-ply (which is similar in weight to illustration board). A *cold-pressed* (or vellum) surface is slightly textured, while a *hot-pressed* (or plate) surface is very smooth. The vellum surface is best for graphite, charcoal, pastels, and colored pencils. The smooth surface is good for felt markers and pen and ink. Either can be used for model building, book arts, and planar structures.

Chipboard is a dense, gray, uncoated board made from recycled paper. Most drawing pads have a chipboard backing. Single-thickness chipboard can be cut with an exacto knife or a heavy-duty paper cutter; use a utility knife for all heavier board.

Foamcore is light, strong, and rather unforgiving. It must be cut with a very sharp exacto knife or a scroll saw, and dents in the surface or cutting errors are difficult to repair.

Corrugated cardboard is strong, light-weight, cheap, and amazingly versatile. It is often used for large-scale projects. Through careful planning, you can use the grain (corrugation direction) to create curving planes or even expose it to add texture.

Glues

White glue is nontoxic and water-soluble when wet. It can be used with most porous materials, including all of the boards described in the previous section. It is not suitable for paper-to-paper adhesion, as most papers adhered with white glue will buckle when dry.

Glue stick is water-soluble, acid-free, and nontoxic. Designed as an adhesive for thin paper, glue stick is generally ineffective for gluing any kind of board.

Rubber cement is a traditional paper adhesive that can be "erased" when misapplied, using a special pick-up tool. However, because rubber cement is highly toxic, flammable, and impermanent, it has limited use in three-dimensional design classes.

Hot glue is a wax-based, translucent material that is heated in a gun and applied as a hot, viscous fluid. It is most effective in adhering nonporous materials, and it provides a quick way to create an assemblage. It can also be used to tack cardboard structures together while the white glue dries.

Dry mounting tissue is distributed in sheets of thin, clear plastic. Adhesion occurs when this material is heated, either in a drymount press or using an iron. This is an excellent adhesive for most papers and light-weight cloth, and it is widely used in photography and bookarts.

Tapes

Transparent tape ("Scotch tape") is an all-purpose, light-weight, temporary adhesive for paper. It is not an effective adhesive for boards.

Masking tape is tough, flexible crepe-paper tape. It is designed to mask off unpainted areas, as with painting a car. It is a good temporary adhesive for boards, especially during the model-building stage.

Drafting tape and *artist's tape* are similar to masking tape but with less glue. They can be removed without damaging the surface to which they are applied.

Double-sided encapsulating tape has acrylic adhesive on both surfaces. A layer of thin paper protects one side until the tape is actually applied. An archival version of this material is sold by bookbinding stores, and it can be used for well-crafted final projects.

MATERIALS AND MEANINGS

The materials used in most three-dimensional design classes are inexpensive, can be easily manipulated and are conceptually neutral. As you begin to expand your ideas through more advanced assignments, you can more fully explore the meaning of materials.

Every material has unique psychological associations as well as physical properties. Mirrors are fragile, reflective surfaces commonly used for observation of the self and others. A pile of autumn leaves suggests decay and exudes an earthy aroma. Powdered turmeric spice is yellow and pungent and suggests both cooking and travel.

Whether we are making sculpture or designing products, materials have meaning. For example, the thorny branches at the base of Michele Oka Doner's *Terrible Table* (10.23) are sure to change the emotional atmosphere of any room this table occupies. The wood and wire Deborah Butterfield used to create *Large Horse #4* (10.24) forces us to reconsider our understanding of both horses and nature. A love of materials and an understanding of their characteristics are essential aspects of all three-dimensional work.

10.23 Michele Oka Doner, *Terrible Table.* Bronze and glass, 15¾ × 26 × 22 in. (40 × 66 × 56 cm).

Key Questions

- Why did you choose a particular material for your project? Considering its strength, workability, cost, and so forth, is it really the best material for your purpose?

- What would your project look like if it were done in a different material?

- How would a change in material affect the meaning of your project?

- What nontraditional materials could you use? How can they enhance meaning?

10.24 Deborah Butterfield, *Large Horse #4*, 1979. Steel, wire, sticks, 77 × 124 × 33 in. (195 × 315 × 84 cm).

SUMMARY

- Choice of material substantially affects both the structure and the meaning of a three-dimensional object.

- Strength, workability, durability, weight, cost, toxicity, and function are major considerations when an artist or a designer chooses a material.

- Materials can be strengthened by using composites, by distributing force, and by using skeletons or exoskeletons.

- Common construction methods include addition, subtraction, solidification, and displacement.

- Connections and transitions can increase visual impact as well as structural strength.

- Traditional materials, such as stone, wood, metal, clay, glass, fibers, and plastics, are used by contemporary artists to express a wide range of ideas.

- Student materials, including various types of boards and adhesives, work best when used for the purpose intended.

Keywords

additive sculpture	compression	gradation	solidification
armature	displacement	modeling	subtractive sculpture
assemblage	exoskeleton	shear	tension
bend	flying buttress	skeleton	torque
composite			

Profile:
Todd Slaughter, Sculptor
Materials and Metaphors

Todd Slaughter was born in Memphis, Tennessee, in 1942. After majoring in chemistry and then in mathematics, he transferred into the art program at University of Texas where he earned a BSA (Bachelor of Science in Art) degree. He subsequently earned a Masters degree in Industrial Design at Pratt, in New York City, and is now a professor in the sculpture program at The Ohio State University. He has had solo shows at the Wexner Center for the Arts, PS 1, and the Chicago Cultural Center, and his major commissions include "The Body of Lake Michigan," in Chicago, Illinois, and La Mano y La Balo (figure 8.13, page 187) near Algeciras, Spain.

MS: Abstract forms dominated your early work. For the past fifteen years, you have shifted more toward representational and narrative work. What is the advantage of each approach?

TS: There is a simple beauty in formal relationships. Like music, lines, planes, volumes and spaces can be organized into wonderful and expressive visual patterns.

However, as I have gotten older, I have become more attuned to human relationships and more interested in the power of metaphor. Metaphors can create a bridge between an object and an idea. Using metaphor, I can add layers of meaning to physical structures.

Representational imagery helps the viewer understand the metaphor in a specific way. For example, the 150 aluminum milkweed castings I used for *Hospice* may suggest a single season of growth, the richness of mundane objects around us, and both the fragility and tenacity of life. A roomful of non-referential forms would not carry the same specificity and layering of meaning.

MS: I'm fascinated by your use of everyday objects, such as hats and domestic objects such as sofas, chairs, and houses.

TS: I want to create the strongest, most personal connection possible between the audience and the artwork. Transforming known objects has become more effective for me than introducing forms that are outside of common experience. I am interested in exploring complex relationships within this world rather than in creating an escape into an alternative world.

MS: Your use of materials is especially distinctive. Many of your works have been constructed using graphite, sulfur, salt, paprika, and turmeric. Why use these unusual materials?

TS: They carry meanings and references that I want my artwork to reflect. I am especially interested in transience. Nothing is permanent; even the most massive chunk of steel changes over time. When I cast a thousand pounds of salt to create a full-sized sofa and then place it in a steam room, or set two opposing graphite fists in motion grinding each other to a powder (figure 8.13, page 187), the rate of change becomes accelerated and highly visible. Work is produced and the hands are consumed.

Materials have their own unique physical and conceptual properties based on how they are commonly used. Ancient spices such as turmeric and paprika bring a particular sense of human experience to an artwork in a way that a red chalk could not. With its ability to both preserve and to corrode, salt has long been used as a metaphor for the human body, and can have the delicate appearance of marble.

MS: You have recently used video, taxidermied birds, plastic and rubber-like materials. Why are you using these materials now?

TS: I am attempting to use these synthetic materials to comment on synthetic realities of our time. In my mind, artificial aspects of our life are proliferating and expanding. We are becoming excessively self-protective, seeking perfectly imagined and constructed fantasy homes, malls, theme parks, religious cults, and Internet relationships. I believe these constructions are without vitality, and are simulated reality.

The Upstate Dream Home: Domestic Fortress is a critical symbol of a fantasy home. This work is an isolated, home defensive complex of buildings and walkways protected by three synthetically constructed guard-swans, set atop a cake stand. The cake stand, paved with a landscape of siicone berries and elevated by a circular plinth, protectively isolates a domestic world.

MS: *Protected Comforts* seems to embody many of your major concerns in one complex installation. Please talk us through this piece.

TS: The house's foundation is constructed of brick-like cast graphite pairs of hands. The interior of the foundation walls is felt padded. There is just enough room for a single chair within this interior space. A three-minute looped video, projected onto the translucent roof and seen from within, depicts an increasing number of people "on" the roof; the blue light gradually decreases and the strong bass sound track intensifies. This scenario culminates in a blackening out of the projection and the interior of the house.

This artwork is a dramatization of our often itself-isolating and self-destructive attempts to create comfort and security within an uncomfortable and insecure world. We say that "a man's home is his castle," which suggests that a man is in control and that the home is powerful and protected. But we need only to read a newspaper to see that domestic tensions and external forces insure a level of insecurity.

MS: I'm intrigued by your placement of the viewer inside of the artwork.

TS: Direct experience is very powerful. By placing the viewer in a chair inside the bottom room, I created a primary experience rather than a secondary, symbolic experience. The viewer is held in place, feeling both isolation and an enclosing external threat.

Todd Slaughter, *Protected Comforts*, 2002. Lexan plastic, graphite, DVD projection with soundtrack, 131 in × 69 in × 56 in.

Physical and Cerebral

What is the difference between the pile of wood in figure 11.1 and the sculpture in figure 11.2? The size, orientation, and location of the pile of wood are based on its purpose. It provides the raw material needed for building a house. Positioned at the edge of a construction site, the boards are arranged in a roughly parallel position so that workers can easily grasp and remove individual planks. The pile of wood is purely functional. Its organization has no aesthetic intention.

At first glance, figure 11.2 may seem very much like a pile of wood. The rough planks are clustered together, in close proximity to the house and in a parallel position. On closer examination, we see the perpendicular boards that elevate the structure. Balanced on stilts, the mass of wood seems suspended and in transition. It continues around the house and into the windows. Is the house expelling or inhaling the boards? The entire structure seems poised, ready to shift at any moment.

How and why was this sculpture made? Sculptor Tadashi Kawamata begins by collecting scrap wood from demolished buildings. He then constructs temporary installations, which he describes as "cancers," on conventional buildings. With no predetermined end point, the structures grow like weeds, often enveloping the building. At the end of the exhibition, Kawamata continues onward, dismantling the construction to create another sculpture else-

11.1 Pile of Wood from a Construction Site.

11.2 Tadashi Kawamata, *Tetra House N-3, W26 Project*, 1983. Sapporo, Japan.

where. Using scrap material to build temporary structures, his work demonstrates the fluidity and circulation of urban structures. His design is based on aesthetic rather than functional criteria.

All three-dimensional work gains power from its physical presence. Sculpture, however, is much more than brute force. It is through the transformation of tangible material into ideas and emotions that a sculpture gains significance. The planks in figure 11.1 begin and end as physical material. A pile of wood is just a pile of wood. By contrast, sculpture, such as *Tetra House N-3, W26 Project,* uses physical material to explore and express ideas.

CONSTRUCTED THOUGHT

From Life to Art

Contemporary sculpture is constructed from a wide range of materials, including ice, fire, blood, spools of thread, and crushed automobiles. In her *Ceremonial Arch* (11.3), Mierle Ukeles combined the metal and wood used in traditional sculpture with gloves, lights, metal springs, and asphalt to create an artwork that is both visually exuberant and structurally sound. Sculpture is now shown in parks, subway stations, and public plazas, as well as in galleries and museums. Because contemporary sculpture is so reliant on familiar materials and public settings, the relationship between art and life has become especially close.

This can be an advantage or a disadvantage. Connection to life gives art its vitality. Authenticity is essential. For example, when a play expresses actual feelings in a compelling way, it connects to our personal experience. Too direct a connection is deadly, however. A pile of wood is just a pile of wood. For art to have meaning, commonplace experiences must be distilled, reexamined, or transformed. It has often been said that a play is "life

11.3 Mierle Ukeles, *Ceremonial Arch Honoring Service Workers in the New Service Economy,* **1988.** Steel arch with materials donated from New York City agencies, including gloves, lights, grass, straps, springs, and asphalt; overall structure 11 ft × 8 ft × 8 ft 8 in. (3.35 × 2.43 × 2.44 m), plus glove branches ranging from 2 to 4 ft long (61 × 122 cm).

with the boring parts left out." A play that simply replicates everyday experience can never transport an audience beyond the commonplace. Likewise, sculpture requires a heightened experience, *beyond* everyday life. Through a combination of insight and hard work, the sculptor transforms even the most resistant material into compelling communication. When all elements in a sculpture support the central concept, the viewer is simultaneously connected by the reality of the material and transported by the power of the idea.

Degrees of Representation

Representational artworks often depict persons or objects in such exquisite detail that they seem to come to life. Michelangelo's *Pietà* (11.4) is a good example. In this massive sculpture, Mary grieves as she cradles the dead Jesus. Every crease in the fabric is defined and every nuance of gesture is deliberate. Mary's right hand extends Jesus' flesh as she gently lifts his right shoulder. She tilts her head slightly, and her left hand echoes the position of his feet. Sculptures such as the *Pietà* seem to embody life. They engage our thoughts and emotions through their compelling realism and narrative implications.

Nonobjective artworks can be appreciated for their pure physical form. For example, the simple metal rings Sandra Enterline constructed for her *Caged Sphere Bracelet Series* (11.5) work beautifully as ends in themselves. We can appreciate their economy and grace without knowing a story or pursuing any additional ideas they may suggest.

Most sculptural objects fall somewhere between these two extremes. These **abstract artworks** have been distilled down from a recognizable source. Myra Mimlitsch-Gray's *Timepiece* (11.6) simultaneously suggests the mechanism and movement of a clock, a pendulum, and a musician's metronome. By reducing these familiar timepieces to their essential form, she was able to create an economical design that conveys a universal sense of time.

11.4 Michelangelo, *Pietà*, 1498–1500. Marble, 5 ft 8 in. (1.74 m) h.

Each approach has its advantages. Nonobjective forms are often used in situations that require universality or simplicity. Barnett Newman's *Broken Obelisk* (11.7) is a monochromatic structure constructed from a simple pyramid and an inverted

11.5 Sandra Enterline, *Caged Sphere Bracelet Series,* 1992. Sterling silver, 18-karat gold, hollow-formed, fabricated. Left to right, 5 × 5 × 1⅛ in. (12.7 × 12.7 × 3 cm), 4 × 4 × ¾ in. (10.2 × 10.2 × 1.9 cm), 4 × 4 × ¾ in. (10.2 × 10.2 × 1.9 cm).

11.6 Myra Mimlitsch-Gray, *Timepiece,* 1988. Kinetic brooch, 14-karat gold, lens, diamonds, abrasive disk. Fabricated, 2¼ × 1½ × ¼ in. (6 × 4 × .5 cm).

11.7 Barnett Newman,
Broken Obelisk, **1963–67.**
Cor-Ten steel, 26 × 10½ ×
10½ ft. (66 × 26.7 × 26.7
meters).

obelisk. The point of contact between the two sections becomes charged with energy, as the top half seems to balance on the point of the pyramid. Caught in this moment of equilibrium, the sculpture is as carefully balanced as a ballerina on point.

On the other hand, the representational approach can stimulate the imagination by providing a fresh interpretation of a familiar object. In *Of Bodies Born Up by Water* (11.8), Walter Martin and Paloma Muñoz used a similar structure to create a very different effect. The poised obelisk is now a grandfather clock. When it topples, time, memory, and family history may be erased.

**11.8 Walter Martin and
Paloma Muñoz,** *Of Bodies
Born Up by Water,* **1987.**
Plaster, oil paint, sheet metal,
and wood, 111½ × 20 ×
16½ in. (283 × 51 × 42 cm).

CONSTRUCTED THOUGHT

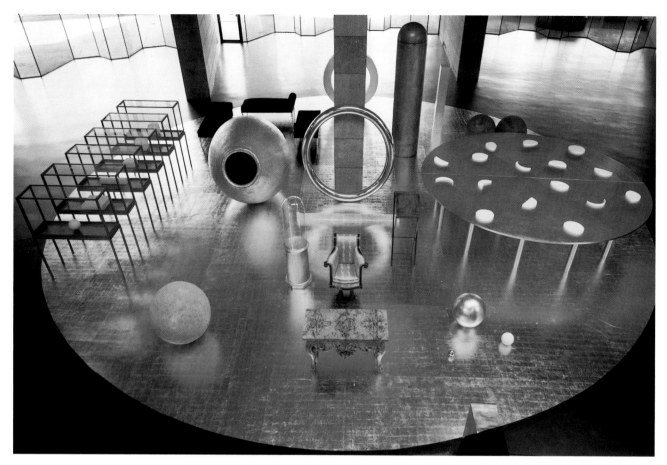

11.9 James Lee Byars, *The Perfect Thought,* 1990 (installation shot). Various objects covered with gold leaf, composed in one of two circles of gold leaf, large circle 40 ft (12.2 m) diameter, small circle 27 ft (8.2 m) diameter.

Boundaries

Because the art/life connection is so important, sculptors must be especially attentive to the physical and psychological boundaries in each piece. As the dividing line between objects, images, or experiences, the boundary is charged with energy. It can serve three major purposes.

Boundaries Can Connect

A simple shape can create a boundary. To define *The Perfect Thought* (11.9), James Lee Byars painted two gold-leaf circles on the floor. The larger circle enclosed 23 separate works from earlier exhibitions, while the smaller circle remained empty. This simple strategy unified a collection of individual artworks while leaving a second space open, to be filled by the viewer's imagination.

A physical boundary is used to create a psychological connection in *My Mother 3,* by Cho Duck-

Hyun (11.10). The strip of fabric that extends out from the drawing and rolls onto the floor enters our space. Combined with the gentle gesture of the woman, the unfurled fabric invites our entry into her world. Here, the tangible world of sculpture and the illusory world of drawing work in perfect harmony.

Boundaries Can Separate

Constructed from nine 12-foot-wide bushes within the median of a busy highway, Maya Ying Lin's *Topo* (11.11) uses a boundary to separate as well as to connect. Enclosed within the mile-long median, the bushes provide a series of visual steppingstones, inviting us to move down the line diagonally. Shifting circles at either end of the sculpture appear to rotate the last two bushes, directing our attention back down the line. Through this illusion of per-

11.10 Cho Duck-Hyun, *My Mother 3* (Memory of the Twentieth Century), **1996.** Graphite and charcoal on canvas, Halogen light, 48 × 57 in. (122 × 145 cm).

11.11 Maya Ying Lin, *Topo*, 1991.

petual motion, the simple design becomes highly activated.

Psychological separation adds power to George Segal's *The Subway* (11.12). Developed as a three-dimensional painting, Segal's construction replicates a familiar setting, using actual subway seats, handrails, and a window, which flashes with the lights of "passing" trains. The ghostly white plaster figure seems familiar but remains distant, the shell of a living, breathing person. Here, a psychological boundary transforms the commonplace into an expression of alienation.

11.12 George Segal, *The Subway,* **1968.** Plaster, metal, glass, rattan, electrical parts with lightbubs, and map. 7 ft 4 in. × 9 ft 5 in. × 4 ft × in. (2.25 × 2.88 × 1.3 m).

11.13 Susan Trangmar, *Blue Skies*, 1990. Installation view.

11.14 Hiroshi Teshigahara, One-Man Show Bamboo Installation at Metropolitan Plaza in Ikebukuro, Tokyo, June 10–15, 1993.

Boundaries Can Enclose

Increasingly, sculptors are using every square inch of gallery space and surface to create complex installations. In *Blue Skies* (11.13), Susan Trangmar used the gallery walls as four large projection surfaces. Surrounded by the projections and by his or her own cast shadow, the viewer becomes a participant in the installation.

The sculpture itself can also envelop the viewer. The boundaries in Hiroshi Teshigahara's *Monumental Ikebana* (11.14) create a passage through a bamboo maze. The patterns of light and shadow combined with the graceful arch entice and enchant the visitor. The physical sensation of enclosure brings magic to the delicate structure.

Bases and Places

Traditional sculpture is generally mounted on a **plinth,** which provides a horizontal base, or on a **pedestal,** which provides a vertical base. Either can serve three purposes:

- To physically separate the sculpture from the surrounding space
- To provide strength and structural stability
- To elevate an object psychologically, distinguishing it from its surroundings and increasing its impact

11.15 Barbara Chase-Riboud, *Malcolm X #3*, 1970. Polished bronze and silk.

11.16 Edgar Hilaire Germain Degas, *Horse Galloping on Right Foot*, c. 1881. Bronze cast of wax model, 11⅛ in. (30 cm).

11.17 Benvenuto Cellini, *Perseus and Medusa*, 1545–54. Bronze, 18 ft h.

Seemingly insignificant, the plinth or pedestal can actually become an essential component of three-dimensional design, both physically and aesthetically. In figure 11.15, the marble base adds elevation as well as a marked contrast in material. As a result, Barbara Chase-Riboud's *Malcolm X #3* now has a solid platform from which to speak. The plinth in *Horse Galloping on Right Foot* (11.16), by Edgar Degas, provides a visual context for the galloping horse, as well as physical stability. The sculpture would collapse, physically and aesthetically, if the base were removed. The pedestal for Benvenuto Cellini's *Perseus and Medusa* (11.17) elevates the heroic statue and creates an architectural connection to the surrounding buildings.

For Constantin Brancusi, the base was an essential element rather than a passive support. He used a specific pedestal form to enhance the power and grace of each of his variations on birds (figures 9.25, 9.26, 9.27, page 232), Seeking dynamism rather than stability, Umberto Boccioni split the base in half

11.18 Umberto Boccioni, *Unique Forms of Continuity in Space*, **1913.** Bronze (cast in 1931), 43⅞ × 34⅞ × 15¾ in. (111.2 × 88.5 × 40 cm).

when he composed *Unique Forms of Continuity in Space* (11.18). The abstracted figure strides forward in space, too energetic to be constrained by conventional boundaries.

In contemporary sculpture, the base often extends to include an entire architectural site. Resting directly on the surface of the plaza, the granite boulders in Elyn Zimmerman's *Marabar* (11.19) are intended to suggest continents, while the channel of water suggests the ocean. Combining large scale with a "baseless" design, the artist has dissolved the traditional boundary between the stones and the surroundings. The entire plaza is thus transformed into a sculptural site.

Key Questions

- How is your artwork similar to everyday life? How is it different?

- What can a boundary or base add to your design?

- How will the content change if your project is placed in a specific setting?

11.19 Elyn Zimmerman, *Marabar,* **1984.** Boulders (natural cleft and polished granite) and water. Plaza: 140 × 60 ft (42.7 × 18.3 m). Pool: 60 ft × 6 ft × 18 in. (18.3 m × 1.8 m × 45.7 cm). Boulders: 2 to 10½ ft. (61 cm to 3.2 m).

11.20 Dennis Oppenheim, *Device to Root Out Evil,* 1997. Galvanized structural steel, anodized perforated aluminum, transparent red Venetian glass, concrete foundations, 20 × 15 × 8 ft (6.1 × 4.57 × 2.44 m).

11.21 Antony Gormley, *Learning to Think,* 1991. Lead, fiberglass and air, five figures, each 68 × 41¾ × 122 in. (173 × 106 × 310 cm).

PHYSICAL FORCES

Weight and Gravity

Of the forces of nature, gravity is the most immediately noticeable when we begin to construct a three-dimensional structure. Lines, spaces, and volumes must be organized according to the laws of physics while simultaneously meeting our aesthetic objectives. Balance is a structural necessity as well as a compositional force. After watching several prototypes collapse, it is easy to conclude that gravity is our enemy, to be conquered at all costs. But is it?

When we begin to analyze the uses of gravity in sculpture, we soon find that it is an asset rather than a liability. Just as a ballet dancer relies on gravity to provide a solid launching pad for each leap and a predictable support for each landing, so the sculptor uses gravity to express ideas and generate emotions.

Downward gravity animates *Device to Root Out Evil* (11.20). The inverted church structure seems to have been propelled aloft, finally driving into the ground upon landing. As noted by sculptor Dennis Oppenheim, this inversion of a familiar structure creates a reversal of content. The steeple is now pointing to hell rather than to heaven. Even without any cultural associations, however, we would still respond to the improbable balance and intense color in this large piece.

A combination of weight and weightlessness gives Antony Gormley's *Learning to Think* (11.21) its impact. Constructed from a mold made from the artist's own body, the hollow lead figures are basically identical. Hovering 10 feet off the ground, they seem weightless. At the same time, because they are suspended from the ceiling, each figure seems as heavy as a convict at the end of a hangman's noose. This paradox gives the sculpture great physical force and communicates an elusive concept. Clearly, the knowledge embodied in this sculpture is not easy to attain!

11.22 John Chamberlain, *The Hedge*, 1997. Painted milled steel, chromium-plated steel, and stainless steel, overall installed 44½ in. × 44½ in. × 46 ft 4 in. (113 cm × 113 cm × 14.12 m); 16 units, each 44½ × 44½ × 12 in. (113 × 113 × 30.5 cm).

Compression and Expansion

Most materials tend to compress as weight increases. As shown in figure 9.21 (on page 230), physical compression can be used to evoke a visceral response. We feel the pressure as the top log pushes down on the log below. Compression plays an especially important role in the works of John Chamberlain, who began making sculptures from crushed automobiles in the 1960s. In *The Hedge* (11.22), crushed pieces of metal have been transformed into an improbable garden. The contradiction between the materials and the meaning suggests a new definition of *nature*.

Expansion is an equally compelling force. Constructed from the charred fragments of a church that had been struck by lightning, Cornelia Parker's *Mass* (11.23) seems to present the event in suspended animation. Supported by fine steel wire and cotton thread, the hovering sculpture appears weightless, caught at the moment of explosion.

11.23 Cornelia Parker, *Mass (Colder Darker Matter)*, 1997. Charcoal retrieved from a church struck by lightning, suspended from steel wire and cotton thread, 10 × 10 × 10 ft (3.5 × 3.5 × 3.5 m).

Tension and Torsion

Tension can be used to stretch or bend an object, while torsion creates a twisting movement. Either can add physical and cerebral strength to a sculpture. Stretched taut, the steel cables in Kenneth Snelson's *Free Ride Home* provide the force needed to elevate the aluminum tubes that dominate the sculpture. Tension is equally important for the designer. It is the tension in the bent metal rods that creates the structure in the *Peregrine Tent* from The North Face (11.24). In Maren Hassinger's *12 Trees No 2* (11.25), cables and wires have been twisted together, then clamped at the top. Based on our experience in the physical world, we can feel the force in the twisted strands and imagine the explosive result if this power were released.

11.24 *Peregrine Tent* by The North Face, San Leandro, CA

11.25 Maren Hassinger, *12 Trees No 2*, 1979. Galvanized wire rope, 10 × 150 × 5 ft (3.1 × 45.7 × 1.5 m).

11.26 Rachel Whiteread, *House*, 1993. Commissioned by Artangel Trust and Beck's (corner of Grove Rd. and Roman Rd., London, destroyed 1994).

Presence and Absence

Presence is another important aspect of physicality. When we confront a massive sculpture, like the Olmec portrait on page 197, it exudes a strength that is far beyond anything a small photograph can convey. Equally, the space surrounding a sculpture or the absence of an anticipated object can have great impact.

Many sculptors have used this quality of presence and absence to explore the passage of time and the nature of memory. British sculptor Rachel Whiteread explores presence and absence in many of her works. Using hundreds of gallons of cement to create a solid cast from an empty house, she accentuates absence by making the space within the house very solidly present (11.26). In his *Writing on the Wall* series, Shimon Attie used slide projections to remind us of shops and families destroyed during the Holocaust. Figure 11.27 shows one of the many slides from the 1930s that he projected onto various buildings in Berlin. The actual bookstore depicted disappeared long ago.

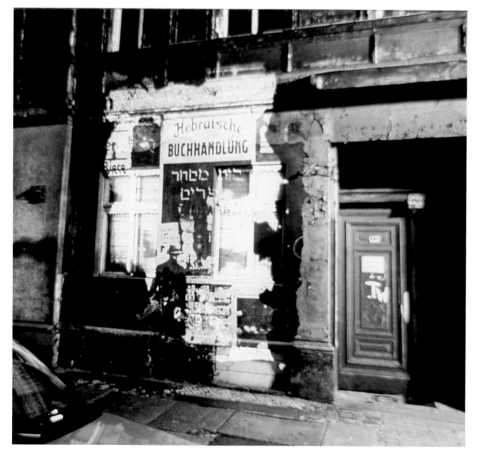

11.27 Shimon Attie, *Almstadtstrasse 43 (formerly Grenandierstrasse 7): Slide Projection of Former Hebrew Bookstore, Berlin,* 1930, from the series *The Writing on the Wall,* 1992. Ektacolor print of site-specific slide-projection installation, 20 × 24 in. (50.8 × 60.9 cm).

11.28 Todd Slaughter, *Grinding Knuckles,* 1993. One RPM Graphite and motors, 12 × 20 × 12 in.

Process and Product

In the past 50 years, sculptors have expanded their choice of materials to include many physical and chemical processes:

- *Friction.* The graphite hands in Todd Slaughter's *Grinding Knuckles* (11.28) slowly rotate, grinding the sculpture away every time this artwork is displayed.

- *Condensation.* Sealed inside the Hans Haacke *Weather Cube* (11.29), water evaporates or condenses based on the ambient temperature inside the gallery.

- *Oxidation.* Ronald Dahl transformed the familiar ladder when he placed his sculpture in the

11.29 Hans Haacke, *Weather Cube,* 1963–65. Acrylic plastic, water, climate in area of display, 12 in. cube (30.5 cm).

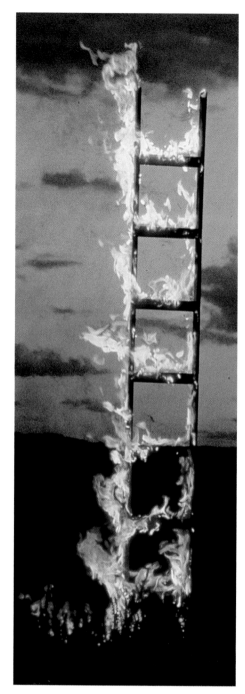

Nevada desert and set it aflame to create *Seven Windows to a Sky on Fire* (11.30).

- *Filtration.* Located next to a wastewater treatment plant, Lorna Jordan's *Waterworks Gardens: The Grotto* (11.31) purifies up to 2,000 gallons of oil-laced storm water per minute. The 8-acre site includes stone mosaics, natural filtration systems, and colorful bands of sedges, yellow irises, and red-twig dogwoods.

11.30 Ronald Dahl, *Seven Windows to a Sky on Fire,* **1982.** Wood/flame, 9 × 12 × 3 in. (22.7 × 30.5 × 7.6 cm).

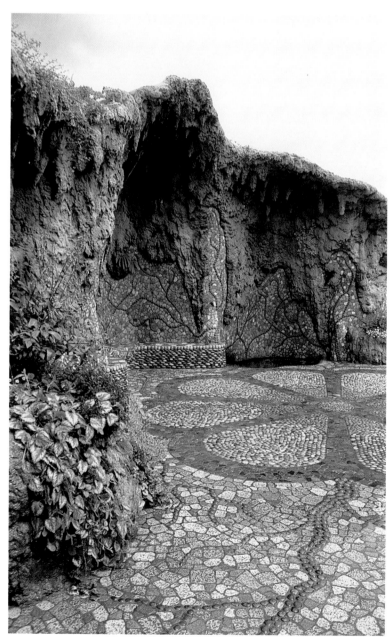

11.31 Lorna Jordan, *Waterworks Gardens: The Grotto,* **1996.** Third of five public garden rooms in the King County East Division Reclamation Plant, Renton, WA.

11.32 Covered Effigy Jar with Removable Head. From Teotihuacan, Mexico. Ceramic, 10¾ in. (27.3 cm).

11.33 Raymond Duchamp-Villon, *The Great Horse*, 1957 version of a 1914 work. Bronze, 39¼ × 24 × 36 in. (99.7 × 60.9 × 91.4 cm).

CEREBRAL QUALITIES OF SCULPTURAL OBJECTS

Building on a Tradition

Traditional sculpture has been characterized by four qualities. First, mass, or solid substance, rather than open space, is the primary concern. Traditional sculptures, such as Michelangelo's *Pietà* (see 11.4, page 262), are relatively solid. In this masterpiece, a sense of profound resignation is created through the use of gravity. The mother has fully accepted her grief. The position of the limbs and the folds in the fabric create a dynamic surface on a stable pyramidal mass. Second, the human figure is the primary subject. Sculptors have long sought to capture in wood, metal, or stone the vitality of a living person. Third, as a means to this end, traditional sculpture is overwhelmingly representational. Indeed, attention to detail and the ability to animate marble have long been the hallmarks of Western sculpture, from the Renaissance to Romanticism. Even a less detailed pre-Columbian effigy jar (11.32) gains eloquence from the use of representation.

Finally, traditional sculptures often tell stories. Public monuments have often been commissioned by kings or by communities of ordinary people to tell national stories. For example, the Statue of Liberty, designed to embody the democratic ideal shared by France and the United States. It was financed through a public lottery, theatrical events, and even prizefights. The poem describing "huddled masses yearning to breathe free," combined with the heroic figure, distills the history of immigration to America into a few words.

Reinventing Sculpture

In Europe, the four qualities of traditional sculpture reached their climax during the nineteenth century. Seeking fresh ideas and new approaches, artists in Russia, Italy, and France then began a process that would transform sculpture forever.

Four major changes followed. First, space became a major concern. As shown in Antoine Pevsner's *Torso* (see 8.28, page 194), sculpture began to be constructed from the inside out, rather than being carved from the outside in. Second, abstraction and transformation became more important than description and representation. For example, Raymond Duchamp-Villon's *The Great Horse* (11.33), constructed from a mix of organic and mechanical parts, bears little resemblance to an actual horse. Third, while the human figure continued to dominate early-twentieth-century sculpture, by midcentury almost any subject matter could be used.

11.34 Marcel Duchamp, *Bicycle Wheel,* **1951.** (Third version, after lost original of 1913.) Assemblage, metal wheel, 25½ in. (63.8 cm) diameter, mounted on painted wood stool 23¾ in. (60.2 cm); overall 50½ × 25½ × 16⅝ in. (128.3 × 63.8 × 42 cm).

Indeed, many significant artworks from this period, including Mark de Suvero's *Ik Ook Eindhoven* (see figure 8.17, page 189), are nonobjective, without external subject matter. Weight, balance, and the dynamics of space are the only content such works require. Most importantly, sculptors began to break down the traditional separation between art and life. Commonplace objects, such as Marcel Duchamp's *Bicycle Wheel* (11.34), were placed in galleries and defined as art.

CONTEMPORARY QUESTIONS, CONTEMPORARY ANSWERS

The evolution of sculpture has accelerated in the past 30 years. Earthworks, which transform natural sites into sculptural settings, have become a powerful force in both art and ecology. An installation, which may combine time, space, and sound, can present both artist and audience with new opportunities for communication and expression. Performance art (which is discussed at greater length in Chapter Fourteen), combines art, technology, and theater. The traditional has become the transformative. Four of the manifestations of change are described in the following sections.

Sculpture as Place

Traditionally permanent, sculpture has always been placed in a wide variety of significant settings. Stonehenge (11.35), constructed from massive limestone blocks weighing up to 50 tons, may have been used as a gigantic sundial by its Neolithic builders. The avenue approaching the stone circle is carefully aligned to the summer solstice, while stones within the circle are aligned with the northernmost and southernmost paths of the rising moon.

Likewise, contemporary sculptors add meaning to their work by exploring the physical, psychological, and temporal characteristics of each site. Glen Onwin's *Nigredo* (11.36) is one of four works in a series titled *As Above, So Below.* Placed in an abandoned chapel, this concrete pool, filled with water,

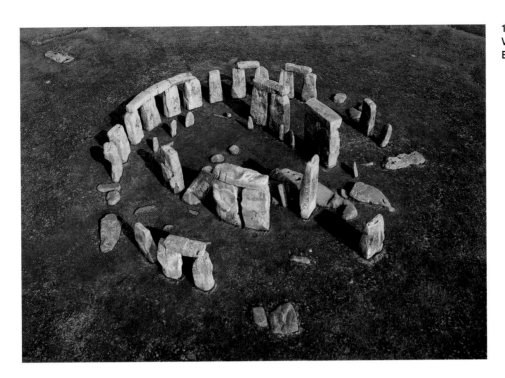

11.36 Glen Onwin, *Nigredo,* 1992. Installation view of exhibition *As Above, So Below,* at the Square Chapel, Halifax, May 9–June 15, 1992. Exposed timbers of the roof reflected in an artificial concrete pool filled with black brine and wax.

11.37 Karen Giusti, *White House/Greenhouse,* New York City, 1996. Recycled steel beams, vinyl, Plexiglas, and rose bushes, 40 × 15 × 14 ft (12 × 4.5 × 4.3 m).

black brine, and wax, seems especially ominous in the once-sacred site. The personal and the political were combined in Karen Giusti's *White House/Greenhouse* (11.37). Placed in Battery Park in New York City, the transparent one-quarter scale model of the White House had both Wall Street and the Statue of Liberty in the background. Made of recycled steel beams, clear vinyl, and large paintings on Plexiglas, the structure presented a scathing commentary on American politics while providing a greenhouse for 200 rose bushes.

Sculpture as Journey

As sculptures have expanded in size, the manner in which the viewer enters, exits, and explores the site has become increasingly important. When the audience participates, a sculpture can be transformed from an object into an experience.

Christopher Janney's *Sonic Plaza* (11.38) at Eastern Carolina University is an especially enticing example. Composed of four distinct sculptures, the site offers a variety of sensory experiences. Various melodic sounds greet participants at the *Sonic Gates.* The 64 water jets on the *Percussion Water Wall* spew forth complex patterns of water to a percussive accompaniment. Four smaller sculptures emerge from the large doors of the *Media Glockenspiel* each day. Finally, a cloud of water vapor created by *Ground Cloud* hovers over the plaza, responding to pedestrian movement and wind direction.

11.38 Christopher Janney, *Sonic Plaza,* Eastern Carolina University, 1998. Sound, light, water, and interactive elements, total length 400 ft (122 m). Top: *Sonic Gates;* middle row left to right: *Media Glockenspiel* and *Percussion Water Wall;* bottom, *Ground Cloud.*

Sculpture as Time

A fascination with time pervades contemporary sculpture. Many sculptures demonstrate the changes that occur as time passes. The amount, frequency, and means of change vary widely. Placed atop the corporate offices of a lighting company, Fumaki Nakamura's *Light Communication* (11.39) presents a simple metamorphosis in a spectacular way. The 88 neon poles gradually illuminate the interior of the structure in three 30-second cycles. The beauty of the light, combined with the hypnotic sequence of change, animates and illuminates the night sky.

Sculpture is also used to demonstrate the impermanence that is an essential characteristic of time. To create *curcuma sul travertino* (11.40), Shelagh Wakely covered the entrance hall to a British school with a thin layer of yellow turmeric spice. As visitors passed through the room, they gradually erased the dust. Thus, during the week-long exhibition, visitors were marked by their passage through the room, and, with spice on their shoes, subsequently marked each new room they entered.

Time itself is the subject of Jim Campbell's *Digital Watch* (11.41). An ominous ticking noise accompanies the installation. On the massive screen, viewers see themselves twice — in real time to the left of the clock and in a 2-second delay on the clock face itself. The repetition and delay create a disturbing psychological effect. The persistent sound of the watch freezes time with each tick while pushing time forward in a relentless pattern.

11.39 Fumaki Nakamura, *Light Communication*, Oyama Lighting. Installed at Ginza 4-chome (main intersection). Eighty-eight poles on a box frame with 400 flashing lamps and projection lights underneath, front 26 ft 3 in. w. × 19 ft 8 in. d. × 29 ft 4 in. h. (8 × 6 × 12 m). Neon tube total length 546 ft 2 in. (1,500 m).

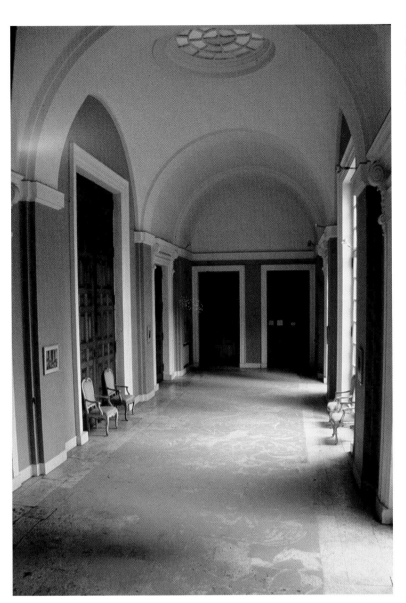

11.40 Shelagh Wakely, *curcuma sul travertino,* **1991.** Turmeric powder on travertine marble floor (smell of turmeric filled the space), swept up after three weeks, 46 ft × 11 ft 6 in. (14 × 3.5 m).

11.41 Jim Campbell, *Digital Watch,* **1991.** Watch, camera, video cameras, electronics. Dimensions variable.

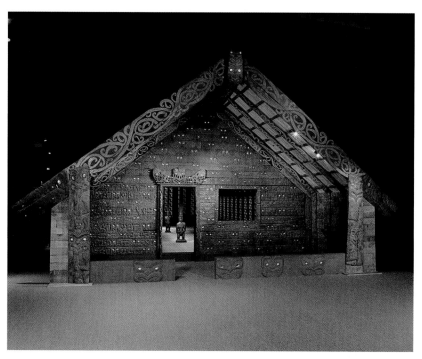

11.42 *Maori Meeting House,* called "Rautepupuke," New Zealand, 1881. 56 ft × 13 ft 10 in. (17 × 4 m).

Sculpture as Self

It has often been said that all artwork is autobiographical. This is especially true of sculpture. As the physical manifestation of thought, sculpture has an immediacy similar to that of a living person.

Both traditional and contemporary sculptors have explored this theme in many marvelous ways. The indigenous people of New Zealand, the Maori, have often combined sculpture with architecture to create a genealogical self-portrait. The face of a prominent ancestor is placed on the front gable of the sacred meeting house (11.42). The ridge at the top of the roof is the ancestor's backbone, the rafters form his ribs, and the four

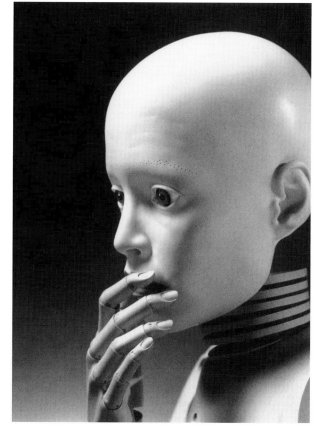

11.43 Katherine Wetzel (photograph), Elizabeth King (sculpture), *Pupil* from *Attention's Loop,* 1987–90. Installation at the Bunting Institute, Radcliffe College, 1997. Porcelain, glass eyes, carved wood, brass. One-half life size.

corner posts represent his arms and legs. Faces of other ancestors are carved on the exterior of the building and on interior posts. Finally, carvings of the Earth Mother and Sky Father are placed over the porch. Through a combination of representation and symbolism, every aspect of the building is designed to honor the past and inspire the present people.

Attention's Loop (11.43), by Elizabeth King, offers another type of self-portrait. In this installation, six highly detailed mannequins are presented in a variety of poses. Carefully articulated arms and hands in three additional display cases line the back wall of the gallery, while an 11-minute video loop shows the mannequins moving. The combination of supreme craftsmanship, robotic machinery, and fluid animation communicates a complex range of ideas. The mannequins are both fascinating and disturbing. It appears that human consciousness has been trapped in a sculptural body.

Eva Hesse's *Laocoön* (11.44) is a more abstract self-portrait. As noted in Chapter Seven, the ancient Greek sculpture *Laocoön and His Two Sons* (see figure 8.21, page 191), depicts a scene from the Trojan War. Laocoön warns against accepting the large wooden horse the Greeks offer as a gift. The Greek goddess Athena sends two serpents to attack and kill Laocoön, thus gaining entry into Troy and victory for the Greeks hidden in the horse. Like the snakes that bind Laocoön and his sons, the cords in Hesse's sculpture are messengers of death. They choke the ladder structure and foreshadow Hesse's own death at age 34 from a brain tumor. As she noted, "My life and art have not been separated."[1]

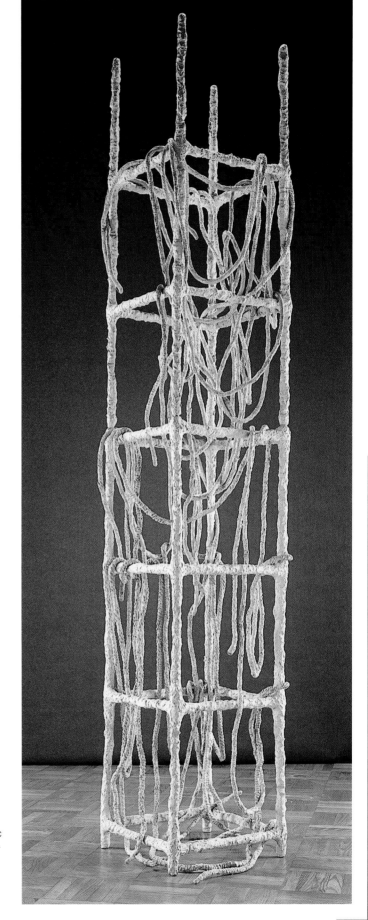

11.44 Eva Hesse, *Laocoön,* 1966. Acrylic paint, cloth-covered cord, wire, and papier-mâché over plastic plumber's pipe, bottom 130 × 23½ × 23 in. (330.2 × 59.7 × 58.4 cm), top 130 × 21½ × 21½ in. (330.2 × 54.6 × 54.6 cm).

EXPRESSING IDEAS IN PHYSICAL FORM

The combination of tangible material and aesthetic complexity gives sculpture a unique power. Like an alchemist, the sculptor transforms ordinary materials into conceptual gold. Tadashi Kawamata's pile of wood becomes a metaphor for urban change. In Mierle Ukeles' *Ceremonial Arch*, the gloves and light-bulbs used by sanitation workers are transformed into a sculpture. A burning ladder becomes a metaphor for a spiritual passage in Ronald Dahl's *Seven Windows to a Sky on Fire*. Through a miracle of invention, the best sculptures simultaneously embrace and transcend their physical nature.

Key Questions

- How might physical forces, such as gravity, tension, and compression, expand the meaning of your artwork?

- How would a change in material affect your artwork, both physically and conceptually?

- What does your artwork reveal about yourself and the world around you?

SUMMARY

- A pile of wood at a construction site is stacked for convenience and accessibility. A pile of wood in a sculpture is designed to communicate ideas and emotions.

- Art gains power from its connection to life. Through art, commonplace experiences are distilled, reexamined, and transformed.

- Physical and psychological boundaries can connect or separate art and life.

- A base can distinguish a sculpture from its surroundings, provide structural stability, and expand aesthetic content.

- Physical forces, such as gravity, compression, expansion, tension, and torsion, can be used to express ideas while providing structural strength.

- The materials a sculptor selects can both heighten and deepen the meaning of the artwork.

- Traditional Western sculpture is massive, representational, figurative, and narrative.

- Contemporary sculpture is often more spatial, abstract, and nonfigurative than traditional sculpture.

- Many contemporary sculptors use specific sites, audience participation, temporal change, and explorations of the self to create powerful artworks.

Keywords

abstract artwork
installation
nonobjective artwork

pedestal
performance art

plinth
representational artwork

Profile:
Rick Paul, Sculptor
Physical, Virtual, and Cerebral

Rick Paul is a professor in the Department of Visual and Performing Arts at Purdue University and chairperson of the Art and Design division. Paul has been involved with foundations design courses throughout the entire 30 years of his teaching career, and for 10 years, he was foundations design coordinator at Purdue.

Paul received his BFA in sculpture from the University of Florida and his MFA in sculpture from Pennsylvania State University. During the 1980s, he made room-sized architectural installations, including exhibitions at The Contemporary Arts Center, Cincinnati; The Cultural Center, Chicago; The Fort Wayne Museum of Art; and The Institute of Contemporary Art, Philadelphia. In 1992, Paul was awarded a Master's fellowship by the National Endowment for the Arts.

Paul's earliest computer work dates from 1974. It was the advent of the personal computer and CAD software that prompted him to use computers to make sculpture. His current work is almost entirely virtual but still maintains many of the characteristics of earlier, site-related sculptures. The relationship between structure and form, the use of environmental context, and the significance of symbolic substitution continue to be issues addressed by his art.

MS: How and why did you start making art?

RP: I started making art as a sophomore in college. At that time I was majoring in another creative area, chemistry, and taking art courses as electives. The first two art courses I enrolled in were photography and three-dimensional design. I enjoyed these classes so much that I continued to take at least one art course each subsequent semester. It took me five years of undergraduate school to decide my major. Once I realized that art could be as creative and challenging as the sciences, I changed my major from chemistry to art and finished my BFA in two semesters.

MS: You have been making sculpture for some 35 years. What qualities attract you to three-dimensional art and design?

RP: As a child I found building my own toys much more interesting than playing with packaged toys. The raw materials for my projects came from the neighborhood trash cans. I had a large walk-in closet full of all sorts of mechanical and electrical parts cataloged and stored in columns of shoeboxes. I was totally fascinated with the variety of materials and forms used by industry and the many ways to combine the parts.

I also made large dioramas and miniature architectural structures. These were often based on the book I was reading at the time. My father forbade me to use his workshop and tools but that did not stop me from using them when he was not around. Looking back, I am convinced that these childhood experiences helped me to develop my intuitive sense of space and dexterity. It also led me to understand the specific physical properties of each material (strength, hardness, malleability, color, texture, grain), which every sculptor uses to advantage.

I have always enjoyed posing questions and solving complex problems. I enjoy the challenges of construction — how can I design an object which possesses structural integrity and withstands the forces of gravity? And, every sculptural question has an ideal as well as a pragmatic answer. When and where do you compromise the ideal solution to get the job done?

MS: Tell me about your creative process. How do you generate, develop, and implement an idea?

RP: My creative process starts with an initial spark usually a response to an intriguing idea, site, material, or process. Ideas usually come from looking at an ordinary everyday experience from an unusual viewpoint. For example, my 10 years of working with Gatorfoam started with a scrap I carried with me in my truck for over a year. Occasionally I would examine it while stopped at a red light. I was convinced that it had very special properties that I could take advantage of to make very special sculptures. I was right. Gatorfoam, which is like foamcore with a hard surface, permitted me to construct very large, light structures very easily. *Kepler's Dream* at The Contemporary Arts Center in Cincinnati (1981) was the first piece I built with this material.

My virtual objects usually start as sketches. Some of my best ideas occur when I am traveling. During travel, I am physically and psychologically free of my usual daily routine and obligations. I have time for new ideas and more freedom to explore. I have one simple rule for using my sketchbook: there are no rules! Drawings are combined with text and computer pseudocode. My sketchbook is a record of where my head has been and where ideas might lead me in the future. Brainstorming on paper is a great way of generating new ideas.

MS: What do you do when you hit a wall?

RP: I guess I am a contrarian. Often I deliberately turn left where other people would go forward. I make a point of searching for the less obvious. In the process I am willing to obliterate or discard an approach I've worked on for hours.

MS: What is the importance of scale?

RP: I consider two kinds of scale when building a sculpture. The first is the scale of the work itself. How big is it relative to the viewer or space it occupies? If I use architectural elements, they are two-thirds scale. This scale makes for a more intimate environment and can provide for more information within a limited space. Rarely is the viewer aware that such elements as stairs are subhuman

Rick Paul, *DC Object*, 1998. Virtual sculpture, wood and canvas (virtual materials), 36 × 13 × 13 ft (virtual size).

in scale. In this way they accept the various architectural elements as larger than they really are.

The second kind of scale is "material scale." Material scale is actually a scale range that is defined by the physical characteristics of the material. For example, corrugated cardboard works fine for small-scale constructions, but it is an unlikely material for a tiny matchbox sculpture or for construction of an object 20 feet tall. You learn what the scale range of a material is by working with it. Typically students are unaware of the potential of a material. This is why I encourage them to study and experiment with unfamiliar materials before using them.

MS: In our discussions of teaching, you talked a lot about the advantages of limitations, which can help students focus their energy and explore an idea more deeply. What are the limitations in your own work? How do you push past the boundaries?

RP: I accept the limits of a problem as a challenge rather than a hindrance. The most significant limits to creativity are self-imposed, rather than external. Knowing yourself and how to work around self-imposed limits is an important asset to creativity that takes a long time to develop.

MS: How do you compare your tangible art with your virtual objects?

RP: For me there is no boundary separating the material world from the virtual world. My work moves back and forth between the two, drawing from both. I am currently working on a series of virtual objects built for specific real environments. Compare *Object at Rest* and *DC Object*, for example. Both were conceived with a specific site in mind. They are roughly equal in size. They are made of the same materials (wood and fabric). Both were conceived as floating objects to be exhibited in an out-of-context environment. There are advantages and disadvantages to both ways of working.

MS: Do you have any advice for my students?

RP: Realize that there is no substitute for experience. Art and design require mastery of many skills, investigation of many emotions, and exploration of many ideas. There are no shortcuts. Persistence is much more important than talent. No matter how much talent you have, nothing will happen without a sincere and sustained commitment to your work.

Rick Paul, *Querschnitt*, 1989 installation. Gator foam™, wood and fabric, 36 × 24 × 20 ft.

Top: Rick Paul, *Object at Rest,* 1994 installation. Wood and fabric, 24 × 24 × 12 ft. Bottom: Rick Paul, *Expanding History,* 2000. Virtual sculpture, wood and fabric (virtual materials), 36 × 26 × 14 ft (virtual size).

Part Three
Multimedia Resources

Take advantage of the multimedia resources for Part Three in order to test and expand your understanding of three-dimensional design elements.

Resources	Contents
www.mhhe.com/launching2	Learning objectives for each chapter
Student Center Chapter 8 Chapter 9 Chapter 10 Chapter 11	Study outlines for each chapter Quizzes with instant feedback Flashcards for studying art vocabulary Internet exercises for developing critical viewing skills Book suggestions for your personal library and research projects
Core Concepts in Art CD-ROM 	Exercises to explore how 3D elements are used to create works of art Videos illustrating sculpture, glass, and jewelry-making techniques

Studio projects for Part Three are described and illustrated for teachers on the Web and on a CD-ROM.

Resources	Projects
www.mhhe.com/launching2 **Instructor Center** IM Part Three **Instructor's Resource CD-ROM** Part Three	*Spheres of Influence #1 and #2:* Planar construction problems *Head Case:* Planar construction and tunnel books *Calderesque Self Portrait:* A linear problem using wire *Linear Athlete:* Gesture, balance, and implied motion *Becoming Borg:* The skin and the skeleton of human and machine *Discovering Mass:* Modeling a sculptural object and carving a form *Wooden Wizardry:* Transforming a wooden plank into a wizard's staff *Superhero Mask/Headgear Design:* From the personal to the improbable *Audio Assemblage:* Creating a sculptural musical instrument *Myths and Masks:* Exploring concept and construction *Book Transformed:* Content based construction *Abstracted Object, Fragmented:* Work with scale, craft, and concept

Creativity

Bohm, David. *On Creativity.* New York: Routledge, 2000.

Briggs, John. *Fire in the Crucible: Understanding the Process of Creative Genius.* Grand Rapids: Phanes Press, 2000.

Csikszentmihalyi, Mihaly. *Creativity: Flow and the Psychology of Discovery and Invention.* New York: Harper Collins, 1996.

Dewey, John. *Art as Experience.* New York: Capricorn Books, 1958.

Gardner, Howard. *Art, Mind and Brain: A Cognitive Approach to Creativity.* New York: Basic Books, 1982.

Gardner, Howard. *Creating Minds: An Anatomy of Creativity Seen Through the Lives of Freud, Einstein, Picasso, Stravinsky, Eliot, Graham, and Gandhi.* New York: Basic Books, 1993.

Gardner, Howard. *Frames of Mind: The Theory of Multiple Intelligences.* New York: Basic Books, 1985.

Lamott, Anne. *Bird by Bird: Some Instructions on Writing and Life.* New York: Anchor Books, 1998.

Le Boeuf, Michael. *Imagineering.* New York: McGraw-Hill, 1980.

Prince, George. "Creativity and Learning as Skills, Not Talents," *The Philips Exeter Bulletin,* 1980.

Shekerjian, Denise. *Uncommon Genius: How Great Ideas Are Born.* New York: Penguin Books, 1991.

Wallace, Doris B., and Howard E. Gruber, eds. *Creative People at Work.* New York: Oxford University Press, 1989.

Concept Development

Adams, James L. *Conceptual Blockbusting.* Reading, MA: Addison-Wesley, 1986.

de Bono, Edward. *Lateral Thinking.* London: Ward Educational Limited, 1970.

Grear, Malcolm. *Inside/Outside: From the Basics to the Practice of Design.* New York: Van Nostrand Reinhold, 1993.

Johnson, Mary Frisbee. *Visual Workouts: A Collection of Art-Making Problems.* Englewood Cliffs, NJ: Prentice Hall, 1983.

Lakoff, George, and Mark Johnson. *Metaphors We Live By.* Chicago: University of Chicago Press, 1981.

Shahn, Ben. *The Shape of Content.* Cambridge, MA: Harvard University Press, 1957.

Von Oech, Roger. *A Kick in the Seat of the Pants.* New York: Harper and Row, 1963.

Von Oech, Roger. *A Whack on the Side of the Head.* New York: Harper and Row, 1986.

Wilde, Judith and Richard. *Visual Literacy: A Conceptual Approach to Graphic Problem Solving.* New York: Watson-Guptil, 2000.

Critical Thinking

Barnet, Sylvan. *A Short Guide to Writing About Art,* 6th ed. New York: Addison, Wesley, Longman, 2000.

Barrett, Terry. *Criticizing Photographs: An Introduction to Understanding Images,* 3rd ed. New York: McGraw-Hill, 2000.

Barrett, Terry. *Interpreting Art.* New York: McGraw-Hill, 2003.

Sayre, Henry M. *Writing About Art,* 3rd ed. Upper Saddle River, NJ: Prentice Hall, 1999.

Smagula, Howard, ed. *Re-visions: New Perspectives of Art Criticism.* Englewood Cliffs, NJ: Prentice Hall, 1991.

Tucker, Amy. *Visual Literacy: Writing About Art.* New York: McGraw-Hill, 2002.

Three-Dimensional Design

Andrews, Oliver. *Living Materials: A Sculptor's Handbook,* Berkeley: University of California Press, 1988.

Bachelard, Gaston. *The Poetics of Space,* trans. Maria Jolas. Boston: Beacon Press, 1969.

Beardsley, John. *Earthworks and Beyond: Contemporary Art in the Landscape.* New York: Abbeville Press, 1998.

Ching, Frank. *Architecture: Form, Space, and Order,* 2nd ed. New York: Van Nostrand Reinhold, 1996.

de Oliveria, Nicolas, Nicola Oxley, and Michael Petry. *Installation Art.* Washington, DC: Smithsonian Institution Press, 1994.

Dormer, Peter, and Ralph Turner. *The New Jewelry: Trends and Traditions.* London: Thames and Hudson, 1985.

Frantz, Suzanne. *Contemporary Glass: A World Survey from the Corning Museum of Glass.* New York: Harry N. Abrams, 1989.

Koplos, Janet. *Contemporary Japanese Sculpture.* New York: Abbeville Press, 1991.

Lane, Peter. *Ceramic Form: Design and Decoration,* rev. ed. New York: Rizzoli, 1998.

Lewin, Susan Grant. *One of a Kind: American Art Jewelry Today.* New York: Harry N. Abrams, 1994.

Lidstone, John. *Building with Wire.* New York: Van Nostrand Reinhold, 1972.

Luecking, Stephen. *Principles of Three Dimensional Design.* Upper Saddle River, NJ: Pearson Education, 2002.

Lynn, Martha Dreyer. *Clay Today: Contemporary Ceramicists and Their Work.* Los Angeles: Los Angeles County Museum of Art, and San Francisco: Chronicle Books, 1990.

Manzini, Ezio. *The Material of Invention: Materials and Design.* Cambridge, MA: MIT Press, 1989.

Miller, Bonnie J. *Out of the Fire: Contemporary Glass Artists and Their Work.* San Francisco: Chronicle Books, 1991.

Nunley, John W., and Cara McCarty. *Masks: Faces of Culture.* New York: Harry N. Abrams in association with the Saint Louis Art Museum, 1999.

Penny, Nicholas. *The Materials of Sculpture.* New Haven: Yale University Press, 1993.

Selz, Peter Howard. *Barbara Chase-Riboud, Sculptor.* New York: Harry N. Abrams, 1999.

Wallschlaeger, Charles, and Cynthia Busic-Snyder. *Basic Visual Concepts and Principles for Artists, Architects and Designers.* New York: McGraw-Hill, 1992.

Williams, Arthur. *Sculpture: Technique, Form, Content.* Worcester, MA: Davis, 1993.

Wong, Wucius. *Principles of Form and Design.* New York: Van Nostrand Reinhold, 1993.

Wyatt, Gary. *Spirit Faces: Contemporary Native American Masks from the Northwest.* San Francisco: Chronicle Books, 1994.

key readings

Works Cited, Chapter Two

1. Johannes Itten, *The Art of Color* (New York: Van Nostrand Reinhold, 1974), p. 16.
2. Alexander Theroux, *The Primary Colors: Three Essays* (New York: Henry Holt and Company, 1994), p. 6.

Works Cited, Chapter Three

1. Jean L. McKechnie, *Webster's New Universal Unabridged Dictionary* (New York: Simon and Schuster, 1983), p. 373.

Works Cited, Chapter Twelve

1. David Bordwell and Kristin Thompson, *Film Art: An Introduction*, 5th ed. (New York: McGraw-Hill, 1997), pp. 277–78.
2. Scott McCloud, *Understanding Comics* (New York: HarperPerennial, 1994), pp. 70–74.
3. Keith A. Smith, *Structure of the Visual Book* (Fairport, NY: The Sigma Foundation, 1991), pp. 102–4.

Works Cited, Chapter Thirteen

1. Keith A. Smith, *Structure of the Visual Book* (Fairport, NY: The Sigma Foundation, 1991), p. 106.
2. Robert McKee, *Story: Substance, Structure, Style and the Principles of Screen Writing* (New York: HarperCollins, 1997), pp. 37–41.

Works Cited, Chapter Fourteen

1. Jean L. McKechnie, *Webster's New Universal Unabridged Dictionary* (New York: Simon and Schuster, 1983), p. 1011.
2. Maynard Mack, *World Masterpieces* (New York: W.W. Norton and Company, 1965), p. 478.
3. Rachel Carson, *Under the Sea Wind* (New York: Viking Penguin, 1996), p. 23.

notes

Glossary
by Mary Stewart and Peter Forbes

A

abstract form 1. a form derived from visual reality that has been distilled or transformed, reducing its resemblance to the original source. 2. a multiple image structure, such as a film, in which the parts are related to each other through repetition and visual characteristics, such as shape, color, scale or direction of movement.

abstract shape a shape that is derived from a visual source, but is so transformed that it bears little visual resemblance to that source.

abstraction the reduction of an image or object to an essential aspect of its form or concept.

accent a specific shape, volume, color, musical note, etc. that has been emphasized. Using an accent, a designer can bring attention to part of a composition and increase rhythmic variation within a pattern.

accent color a color that stands out from its surroundings. Often used to attract attention to a specific part of a design.

achromatic color a color (such as black and white) that has no hue.

act a major division in a film or theatrical event. Acts are generally constructed from a group of sequences that increase in intensity.

action-to-action transition in comic books, the juxtaposition of two or more panels showing a sequence of actions.

actual lines lines which are physically present in a design.

actual motion motion that physically occurs in a design.

actual time the duration of an actual temporal event. For example, it takes less than a minute for the bowling ball to roll down the ramps in Jean Tinguley's *Chaos 1*.

additive color color created by combining projected beams of chromatic light. The additive color primaries are red, green and blue and the secondaries are cyan, magenta, and yellow.

additive sculpture a physical object constructed from separate parts that have been connected using glues, joints, stitching, welds and so on.

aesthetics the study of human responses to art and beauty.

afterimage in color theory, a ghostly image that continues to linger after the actual image has been removed.

ambient light the quality of light within an entire space or setting. For example, when we enter an open courtyard on a sunny summer afternoon, we are surrounded by warm ambient sunlight. Everything we see is colorful and bright.

amplified perspective the exaggerated use of linear perspective to achieve a dramatic and engaging presentation of the subject. Amplified perspective is often created using an unusual viewing position, such as a bird's eye view, accelerated convergence, or some form of distortion.

analogy a similarity or connection between things which are apparently separate and dissimilar. For example, when a teacher describes wet plaster as having the "consistency of cream," she is using an analogy.

analogous color a color scheme based on hues that are adjacent on a color wheel, such as red, red-orange and orange.

anesthetic a chemical or action used to induce insensitivity or unconsciousness.

anomaly an obvious break from norm in a design.

approximate symmetry a form of balance that occurs when roughly similar imagery appears on either side of a central axis.

aspect-to-aspect transition in comic books, the juxtaposition of two or more panels showing different views of a single setting or event. This transition is often used in Japanese comic books.

armature an internal structure created to strengthen and support a three-dimensional object.

assemblage an additive method in which the artist or designer constructs the artwork using objects and images which were originally created for another purpose. Essentially, assemblage can be defined as three-dimensional collage.

asymmetrical balance equilibrium among visual elements that do not mirror each other on either side of an axis.

atmospheric perspective a visual phenomenon in which the atmospheric density progressively increases, hazing over the perceived world as one looks into its depth. Overall definition lessens, details fade, contrasts become muted and, in a landscape, a blue mist descends.

attached shadow a shadow that directly defines a form.

B

backlight a light source positioned behind a person or object that can either create a silhouette or separate the person or object from the background.

balance the equal distribution of weight or force among visual units.

base a horizontal support for a physical object, such as a stone block supporting a bronze sculpture.

beat 1. a unit of musical rhythm which creates the pulse of a sound, 2. in acting, the most basic element in a story. A beat is an exchange of behavior, based on action and reaction.

bend one of the five major forces affecting structural strength.

Bezold effect a change in a single color that substantially alters our perception of the entire composition.

boundary the dividing line or edge between objects, images, or experiences.

brainstorming any of a number of problem solving techniques which are designed to expand ideas and encourage creativity. List making, mapping, associative thinking, and metaphorical thinking are common strategies used.

C

glossary

calligraphic line derived from the Greek words for beautiful and writing, a flowing, and expressive line that is as personal as handwriting. Calligraphic lines generally vary in thickness and velocity.

camera angle the angle at which an object or event is viewed. An aerial view can provide the sweeping panorama needed to convey the enormity of a battle, while a low camera angle can provide an expansive view of the sky.

carving the removal of materials from a larger mass, gradually revealing an image or object. Carving is a subtractive process.

cast shadow a dark shape that results from placement of an opaque object in the path of a light source.

causality the interrelation of cause and effect, based on the premise that nothing occurs without cause. Narrative film is based on causality: because the starting pistol was shot, the footrace began.

cause/effect critique a critique in which the viewer seeks to determine the cause for each visual or emotional effect in a design. For example, the dynamism in a design may be caused by the diagonal lines and asymmetrical balance used. Also known as formal analysis.

categorical form in film, a multiple image structure that is based on categories, or subsets of a topic. For example, a film on predators might begin with a discussion of wolves, then move on to lions, and conclude with a discussion of hawks.

centricity as identified by Rudolph Arnheim, a compressive compositional force.

characteristic texture the inherent or familiar texture of a material. The gleaming reflective surface of a steel teapot, the transparent and reflective qualities of glass, and the gritty texture of clay are all characteristic textures.

chiaroscuro (from Italian meaning **"light-dark"**). The gradual transition of values to create the illusion of light and shadow on a three-dimensional form.

chroma the purity, intensity, or saturation of a color.

chromatic gray a gray made from a mixture of various hues, rather than a simple blend of black and white.

chronology the order in which events occur.

cliché an overused expression or a predictable visual treatment of an idea.

close-up in film, a type of framing in which the scale of the object shown is relatively large, as in a close-up of an actor's face.

closure the mind's inclination to connect fragmentary information to produce a completed form. Closure is an essential aspect of Gestalt psychology.

collage an image constructed from visual or verbal fragments initially designed for another purpose.

color harmony use of compatible colors to help unify a composition.

color interaction the way colors within a composition influence one another.

color key a color that dominates an image and heightens its psychological and compositional impact.

color overtone a secondary hue "bias" in a primary color. For example, alizarin crimson is a red with violet overtones, while scarlet is a red with orange overtones.

color theory the art and science of color interaction and effects.

compare/contrast critique a critique in which similarities and differences between two designs are analyzed. Often used in art history classes to demonstrate differences in approach between artists.

comparison recognition of similarity in two or more compositions. Often used in art history to demonstrate connections between images done by different artists or in different periods.

complementary color hues that oppose one another on a color wheel. When paired in a composition, complementary colors create contrast; when mixed, complementary colors produce a wide range of browns.

composite a new material created when two or more materials of differing strengths are fused together. Examples include fiberglas and formcore.

composition the combination of multiple parts into a unified or harmonious whole.

compression the forcing or crushing of material into a smaller, denser condition and its visual dynamics and implied psychological effects.

condensation to be reduced to a denser form, as with the transition from a vapor to a liquid.

cone of vision in perspective drawing, a hypothetical cone of perception originating at the eye of the artist and expanding outward to include whatever he or she wishes to record in an illusionistic image, such as a perspective drawing. The cone's maximum scoping angle is 45-60 degrees anything outside of the cone of vision is subject to distortion.

contact the meeting point between visual or structural elements in a design.

containment a unifying force created by the outer edge of a composition or by a boundary within a composition.

content the emotional and/or intellectual meaning or message of an artwork.

continuity degree of connection or flow among compositional parts.

contradictory texture the unfamiliar use of a texture or the addition of an unusual texture to the surface of an object.

contrast the degree of difference between compositional parts or between one image and another. Contrast is created when two or more forces operate in opposition.

contrasting colors colors that are substantially different in hue, value, intensity or temperature.

contour line a line that describes the edges of a form and suggests three-dimensional volume.

convergent thinking a problem-solving strategy in which a pre-determined goal is pursued in a linear progression using a highly focused problem-solving process. Six steps are commonly used: 1. define the problem, 2. do research, 3. determine your objective, 4. devise a strategy, 5. execute the strategy, 6. evaluate the results.

critique any means by which the strengths and weaknesses of designs are analyzed.

cropping the manner in which a section of an image or a fragment of observed reality has been framed. For example, photographers select a fragment of reality every time they look through the view finder of the camera. Part of the scene is included, while the remainder is cut away. Photographs are often cropped further in the darkroom, leaving only the most significant information.

cross contour multiple lines running over the surface of an object horizontally and/or vertically which describe its surface configuration topographically, as in mapping. This process is much like wire-framing in three-dimensional computer modeling. Cross contours can also be used in drawing to suggest three-dimensional form through tonal variation.

cross–hatching a technique used in drawing and print-making to shade an object using two or more networks of parallel lines. Darker values are created as the number of networks increases.

crosscut in film, an abrupt alternation between two or more lines of action.

curvilinear shape a shape whose contour is dominated by curves and flowing lines.

cut in film, the immediate change from one shot or frame to another.

definition 1. the degree to which a shape is distinguished from both the ground area and from other shapes within the design. 2. the degree of resolution or focus of an entire image. Sharply defined shapes tend to advance while blurred shapes tend to recede.

denouement the outcome, solution or point of clarification in a story.

density the extent to which compositional parts are spread out or crowded together. Visual connections generally occur easily in high-density compositions, while visual connections may be less obvious in low-density compositions.

depth of field the range of focus in a photographic image, from foreground to background. In a photograph with great depth of field, an object that is fifteen feet from the camera is in focus, as well as an object that is ten feet from the camera.

descriptive shape a shape that is derived from specific subject matter and strongly based on perceptual reality.

diegesis the world created in a film or video.

descriptive critique a critique in which the viewer carefully describes what he or she sees when observing a design.

directed light localized and focused light, such as a spot-light on a singer.

direction actual or implied movement of an element within a design.

displacement a forming method in which a solid material is physically forced into a new configuration. The stamping process used to mint coins is an example of displacement.

dissolve a transition between two shots during which the first image gradually disappears while the second image gradually appears.

dissonance the absence of harmony in a composition. Often created using disharmonious colors, shapes, textures or sounds.

distribution the manner in which colors, shapes or other visual elements are arranged within the format.

divergent thinking an open-ended problem-solving strategy. Starting with a broad theme, the artist or designer expands ideas in all directions.

dominance the principle of composition in which certain elements assume greater importance than others. Also see **emphasis.**

duration 1. the length of time required for the completion of an event; as in the running time of a film, video, or performance. 2. the running time of events depicted in the story (plot duration), 3. the overall span of time the story encompasses (story duration).

dynamic energetic, vigorous, forceful; creating or suggesting change or motion.

dynamic form a form that implies change.

earthwork Commonly, an artwork that has been created through the transformation of a natural site into an aesthetic statement.

eccentricity as identified by Rudolph Arnheim, an expansive compositional force.

economy distillation of a design down to the essentials in order to increase impact.

editing in film, selecting and sequencing the details of an event to create a cohesive whole.

elements of design basic building blocks from which designs are made. For example the essential elements of two-dimensional design are line, shape, texture, color and value.

environmental work (or environment) an artwork that must be entered physically. Installations, (which are usually presented indoors) and earth-works (which are usually presented outdoors) are two major types of environmental works.

emotional advertising use of emotion to sell a service, product, or idea. This strategy is often used when a product is neither unique nor demonstrably better than a competing product.

elevation in orthographic projection, the front, back and side views of an object or architectural structure.

emphasis special attention given to some aspect of a composition to increase its prominence.

exaggerated advertising pushing an idea to an extreme to make a point.

exoskeleton an external support structure.

expansion the extending outward of materials to fill more space.

eye level or eye line in linear perspective, the eye level is determined by the physical position of the artist. Sitting on the floor creates a low eye level while standing at an easel creates a higher eye level. Also know as the horizon line. All vanishing points in one and two point perspective are positioned on the eye level.

F

fade a gradual transition use in film and video. 1. In a fade-in, a dark screen gradually brightens as a shot appears. 2. In a fade-out, the shot gradually darkens as the screen goes black.

fidelity the degree of connection between a sound and its source. For example, when we hear the sound of a helicopter and see a helicopter on the screen, the sound matches with image, creating tight fidelity.

figure the primary or positive shape in a design; a shape which is noticeably separated from the background. The figure is the dominant shape in a figure-ground relationship.

figure/ground reversal an arrangement in which positive and negative shapes alternatively command attention.

fill light a diffused light used to lower the contrast between light and dark areas in cinematic and theatrical lighting.

filtration the process of separating a solid from a liquid by passing it through a porous substance such as cloth, charcoal or sand.

flashback in film, an alternation in chronology in which events that occur later in a story are shown first.

floodlight a softly defined light with a broad beam.

flying buttress a type of exoskeleton commonly used by medieval architects in creating cathedrals.

focal point primary point of interest in a composition. A focal point is often used to emphasize an area of particular importance or to provide a strong sense of compositional direction.

format the outer edge or boundary of a design.

form 1. the physical manifestation of an idea, as opposed to the content, which refers to the idea itself. 2. the organization or arrangement of visual elements to create a unified design 3. a three-dimensional composition or unit within a three-dimensional composition. For example, a sphere, cube and pyramid are all three-dimensional forms.

formalism an approach to art and design that emphasizes the beauty of line, shape, texture, etc. as ends in themselves rather than as means to express content. Strictly formalist works have no explicit subject matter.

fractured space discontinuous space that is created when multiple viewpoints are combined within a single image.

frame a single static image in film or video.

freestanding work an artwork that is self-supporting and is designed to be viewed from all sides.

function the purpose of a design or the objective which motivates the designer. For an industrial designer, the primary purpose of a design is often utilitarian. For example, he or she may be required to design a more fuel-efficient automobile. For a sculptor, the primary purpose of a design is aesthetic: he or she seeks to create an artwork that engages the viewer emotionally and intellectually.

fusion the combination of shapes or volumes along a common edge.

G

geometric form a three-dimensional form derived from or suggestive of geometry. Examples include cubes, spheres tetrahedrons, etc.

geometric shape a shape derived from or suggestive of geometry. Geometric shapes are characterized by crisp, precise edges and mathematically consistent curves.

Gestalt psychology a theory of visual perception that emphasizes the importance of holistic composition. According to this theory, grouping, containment, repetition, proximity, continuity, and closure are essential aspects of visual unity.

gesture drawing a vigorous drawing that captures the action, structure and overall orientation of an object, rather than describing specific details. Often used as a basis for figure drawing.

gloss 1. in writing, words of explanation or translation inserted into a text. 2. a secondary text within a manuscript that provides comments on the main text.

gradation any gradual transition from one color to another or from one shape or volume to another. In drawing, shading created through the gradation of grays can be used to suggest three-dimensional form.

graphic relationship the juxtaposition of two or more separate images that are compositionally similar. For example, if a basketball is shown in the first panel, an aerial view of the round free-throw zone is shown in the second, and the hoop of the basket itself is shown in the third, a graphic relationship based on circles has been created.

gravity the force that tends to pull all bodies toward the center of the Earth.

grid a visual or physical structure created from intersecting parallel lines.

grisaille a gray underpainting, often used by Renaissance artists, to increase the illusion of space.

group in sequential structure, a collection of images that are related by subject matter, composition, or source. For example the trombone, trumpet and tuba are all members of the group know as the brass section in an orchestra.

grouping visual organization based on similarity in location, orientation, shape, color and so on.

gutter in bookbinding, the center line of a book, where the two pages are joined.

H

Happening an assemblage of improvised, spontaneous events performed by the artist and audience alike, based on a general theme. There is no rehearsal and any location, from a parking lot to a factory interior can be used. The Happening is most commonly associated with Alan Kaprow and is a precursor to Performance Art.

hard sell advertising an advertising approach in which a major point is presented in a clear, direct manner. The narrative is usually linear, and the message is usually explicit.

harmony a pleasing or soothing relationship among colors, shapes, or other design elements.

hatching A technique used in drawing and printmaking to create a range of gray tones using multiple parallel lines.

high definition sharply focused visual information that is easily readable. High definition creates strong contrast between shapes and tends to increase clarity and immediacy of communication.

horizon line in linear perspective, the line on which all vanishing points are positioned. More accurately described as the eye line or eye level.

hue the name of a color (such as red or yellow) that distinguishes it from others and assigns it a position in the visual spectrum.

human scale a design that is roughly our size.

humorous advertising use of humor to sell a service, product, or idea. By entertaining the viewer, the designer can make the message more memorable.

Iconography the study of symbolic visual systems.

illusionary space the representation of an object or scene on a two-dimensional surface so as to give it the appearance of three-dimensionality.

imbalance the absence of balance.

implied line 1. a line that is suggested by the positions of shapes or objects within a design. 2. a line that is suggested by movement or by a gesture rather than being physically drawn or constructed.

implied motion the suggested change in location of a figure or object.

implied time the suggested location or duration of an event.

installation an artwork or a design that presents an ensemble of images and objects within a three-dimensional environment.

intensity 1. the purity, saturation, or chroma of a color. For example, fire engine red is a high intensity color, while brick red is a low intensity color. 2. in time design, the power, concentration and energy with which an action is performed or the quality of observation of an event.

interdisciplinary art the combination of two or more different disciplines to create a hybrid artform.

interdisciplinary thinking use of skills and knowledge from more than one discipline.

in the round a three dimensional object that is self-supporting and is designed to be viewed from all sides, as in free-standing sculpture.

invented texture a form of visual texture that has been created without reference to perceptual reality.

joint a physical connection between elements or parts in a three-dimensional object. Some joints are fixed, such as ones that are bolted together, while others can be moved, as with a hinge or a ball and socket joint.

junction 1. the place at which objects or events meet. 2. a physical intersection between elements or parts in a three-dimensional object.

key light a primary source of illumination.

kinetic form a form that actually moves.

kinesthetics the science of movement.

lap dissolve in film, a dissolve in which two shots are temporarily superimposed.

layed space compositional space that has been deliberately separated into foreground, middle ground and background.

line 1. a point in motion, 2. a series of adjacent points, 3. a connection between points, 4. an implied connection between points. Line is one of the basic elements of design.

line weight variation in line thickness.

linear perspective a mathematical system for projecting the apparent dimensions of a three-dimensional object onto a flat surface. Developed by artists during the Renaissance, linear perspective is one strategy for creating the illusion of space.

long shot in film, a type of framing in which the scale of the subject shown is relatively small, as with an image of a human figure within a landscape.

loudness the amplitude of a sound wave; the volume of a sound.

low definition blurred or ambiguous visual information. Low definition shapes can increase the complexity of the design and encourage multiple interpretations.

maquette a well developed three-dimensional sketch, comparable to a two-dimensional thumbnail sketch.

matrix a three-dimensional grid.

mass a solid three-dimensional form.

medium shot a type of framing in which the scale of the subject shown is of moderate size, as in view of an actor from the waist up.

meter the basic pattern of sound and silence in music or positive and negative in design.

metaphor a figure of speech in which one thing is directly linked to another dissimilar thing. Through this connection, the original word is given the qualities of the linked word. For example, when we say "she's a diamond in the rough" we attribute to a woman the qualities of an unpolished gem.

metaphorical thinking the use of metaphors or analogies to create visual or verbal bridges.

model in three-dimensional design, a model is a technical experiment or a small-scale version of a larger design.

modeling the process of manipulating a pliable material (such as clay) to create a three-dimensional object.

moment-to-moment transition in comic books, a transition in which a character or situation is simply being observed over time. This transition is often used in Japanese comic books but rarely in American comic books.

monochromatic color scheme a color scheme based on variations in a single hue. For example, a light, pastel blue, a medium navy blue and a dark blue-black may be used in a room interior.

monumental objects objects that are much larger than humans.

movement in design, the use of deliberate visual pathways to help direct the viewer's attention to areas of particular interest.

myth a traditional story collectively composed by many members of a society. The creation of the world, sources of evil, the power of knowledge and even the nature of reality may be explained through these grand expressions of the imagination.

N

negative shape (or **space**) 1. a clearly defined area around a positive shape or form 2. a shape created through the absence of an object rather than through the presence of an object.

non-objective shape shapes created without reference to specific visual subject matter.

non-sequitur transition the juxtaposition of multiple frames or shots that have no obvious conceptual relationship.

O

objective criticism the assessment of strengths and weakness in a design solely based on the visual information presented.

one-point perspective a form of linear perspective in which the lines receding into space converge at a single vanishing point of the eye level or horizon line.

opponent theory an explanation for the electric glow that occurs when two complementary colors are placed side by side.

orientation the horizontal, vertical, or diagonal position of a composition or design element.

organic shape a shape that visually suggests nature or natural forces. also know as biomorphic shape.

organizational lines lines used to create the loose linear "skeleton" on which a compositional can be built. Also know as structural lines.

orthographic projection a drawing system widely used by artists and designers to delineate the top, bottom and four side views of a three-dimensional object. Unlike perspective drawing, which is designed to create the illusion of space, an orthographic projection is constructed using parallel lines that accurately delineate six surfaces of an object.

overlap placement of one shape in front of another to create the illusion of space.

oxidation a common form of chemical change used in creating a patina (or colored surface) on a metal sculpture.

P

panel a single frame in a comic book.

pattern a design created through systematic repetition. Many patterns are based on a module, or repeated visual unit.

pedestal a vertical support for a sculptural object.

performance art a live presentation, often including the artist, usually combining elements from a variety of art forms, such a film, video, theater and dance.

permanence the degree of durability, or resistance to decay, in a given material or design.

physical texture actual variation in a surface.

picture plane in linear perspective, the flat surface on which a three-dimensional image is mentally projected.

pitch in music, the relative highness or lowness of a sound. Pitch is determined by wave frequency, as compression and expansion occurs within the sound wave.

plane a three-dimensional form that has length and width but minimal thickness.

plan view the top view of a three-dimensional object or architectural structure, drawn orthographically or freehand.

plinth horizontal support for a sculptural object.

plot duration the running time of the events depicted in a story.

polyhedra (or **polyhedrons**) multi-faceted volumes.

positive form an area of physical substance in a three-dimensional design.

positive shape the principle or foreground shape in a design and the dominant shape or figure in a figure-ground relationship.

primary colors colors from which virtually all other colors can be mixed. The additive (or light) color primaries are red, green and blue. The subtractive (or pigment) color primaries are yellow, magenta red and cyan blue.

primary contour the defining edges of a physical object, such as the extremities of a carved sculpture.

principles of design the means by which visual elements are organized into a unified and expressive arrangement. Unity and variety, balance, scale and proportion, rhythm, illusion of space and illusion of movement are commonly cited as the principles of two-dimensional design.

proportion the relative size of visual elements within an image.

prototype a well-developed model, as with the fully-functional prototype cars developed by automobile companies.

proximity the distance between visual or structural elements or between an object and the audience.

pure forms circles, spheres, triangles, cubes and other forms created without reference to specific subject matter.

R

radial symmetry a form of balance that is created when shapes or volumes are mirrored both vertically and horizontally, with the center of the composition acting as a focal point.

rational advertising a type of advertising in which logic and comparisons of quality are used to sell a service, product, or idea. A rational approach is most effective when the message is compelling in itself or the product is truly unique.

realistic advertising use of a familiar setting or situation to involve the viewer and relate a product, service or idea to use in everyday life.

rectilinear shape a shape composed from straight lines and angular corners.

refracted light light that has been bent as it passes through a prism.

relief sculpture in which forms project out from a flat surface. The degree of projection ranges from low to high relief.

repetition the use of the same visual element or effect a number of times in the same composition.

representation commonly, the life-like depiction of persons or objects.

representational shape a shape derived from specific subject matter and strongly based on visual observation.

rhetorical form a type of sequential organization in which the parts are used to create and support an argument. Often used in documentary films.

rhythm 1. presentation of multiple units in a deliberate pattern. 2. in filmmaking, the perceived rate and regularity of sounds, shots, and movement within the shots. Rhythm is determined by the beat (pulse), accent (stress) and tempo (pace).

rhythmic relationship the juxtaposition of multiple visual elements or images to create a deliberate pulse or beat.

S

saturation the purity, chroma, or intensity of a color.

scale a size relationship between two separate objects, such as the relationship between the size of the Statue of Liberty and a human visitor to the monument.

scene in film, continuous action in continuous time and continuous space.

scene-to-scene transition in comic books, the juxtaposition of two or more frames showing different scenes or settings.

scope conceptually, the extent of our perception or the range of ideas our minds can grasp. temporally, scope refers to the range of action within a given moment.

screenplay the written blueprint for the film; commonly constructed from multiple acts.

secondary colors hues mixed from adjacent primaries. In paint, the secondary colors are violet, green and orange.

secondary contour the inner edges of a physical object, such as the internal design and detailing of a carved sculpture.

section in orthographic projection, a slice of an object or architectural structure that reveals its internal structure and detail.

sequence 1. in filmmaking, a collection of related shots and scenes that comprise a major section of action or narration, 2. in narrative structure, any collection of images that have been organized by *cause and effect*. In a simple sequence, action number two is caused by action number one. In a complex sequence, there may be a considerable delay between the cause and the effect.

series in sequential structure, a collection of images that are linked simply, as with cars in a train.

setting the physical and temporal location of a story, the props and costumes used in a story, and the use of sound.

serious advertising advertising which treats a topic in a somber or solemn manner. Often used for public service announcements, such as drunk driving commercials.

shape a flat, enclosed area created when a line connects to enclose an area, an area is surrounded by other shapes, or an area is filled with color or texture.

shade a hue that has been mixed with black.

shading in drawing, a continuous series of grays that are used to suggest three-dimensionality and create the illusion of light.

shear a force that creates a lateral break in a material.

shot in film, a continuous group of frames.

side light a light positioned to the side of a person or object. Can be used to dramatically increase the sense of dimensionality.

sight line 1. a viewing line that is established by the arrangement of objects within one's field of vision, 2. a straight line of unimpeded vision.

simile a figure of speech in which one thing is linked to another dissimilar thing using the word "like" or "as." Through this connection, the original word is given the qualities of the linked word. For example, when we say "he's as strong as an ox," we attribute to a man the strength of an animal.

simultaneous contrast the optical alteration of a color by a surrounding color.

site-specific artwork an artwork is specifically designed for and installed in a particular place.

skeleton (or endoskeleton) a structure that provides internal support.

soft sell advertising an advertising approach that uses emotion, rather than reason, to sell a service, product, or idea. The narrative is often non-linear and ideas or actions may be implied.

solidification a forming method in which a liquid material is poured into a mold or extruded through a pipe, then allowed to harden.

space the area within or around an area of substance The artist/designer defines and activates space when constructing a three dimensional object.

spatial context the space in which a sound is generated. A sound that is played outdoors behaves differently than a sound that is played in a small room.

spatial relationship the juxtaposition of two or more images that are spatially different, such as a close-up, medium shot, and a long shot.

split complementary a complementary color plus the two colors on either side of its complement on the color wheel.

spotlight a light that creates a small, clearly defined beam.

story duration the overall length of a story.

static a composition that is at rest or an object that appears stationary.

static form a form that appears to be stable and unmoving.

stereotype a fixed generalization based on a preconception.

subordinate of secondary importance. See **emphasis.**

subtractive color hue created when light is selectively reflected off a colored surface.

subject the person, object, event or idea on which an artwork is based.

subject-to-subject transition in comic books, the juxtaposition of two or more frames showing different subject matter.

subjective criticism the assessment of strengths and weaknesses in a design based on non-objective criteria, such as the narrative implications of an idea, the cultural ramifications of an action or the personal meaning of an image.

subtractive sculpture a forming method in which materials are removed from a larger mass, Carving, drilling, cutting and turning on a lathe are all subtractive processes.

symbolic color a color that has been assigned a particular meaning by the members of a society. For example, in the United States, the white color of a wedding gown symbolizes purity, while in Borneo, white symbolizes death.

symmetrical balance a form of balance that is created when shapes are mirrored on either side of a central axis, as in a composition that is vertically divided down the center.

tangibility the substantiality of an object or the degree to which an object or a force can be felt.

take in film or video, one version of an event.

temperature the physical and psychological heat suggested by a color's hue.

tempo the pace at which time-based art and music occurs. A fast tempo is generally used in action films while a slow tempo is usually used in a dramatic film.

temporal relationship how the shots in a film relate in time.

tension the extension of an object through stretching or bending.

tertiary color a hue that is mixed from a primary color and an adjacent secondary color.

testimonial advertising use of a trust worthy character or celebrity to provide endorsement for a product, service or idea.

texture the visual or tactile quality of a form. Texture can be created visually using multiple marks, physically, through surface variation, or through the inherent property of a specific material, such as sand as opposed to smooth porcelain.

timbre the unique sound quality of each instrument. For example, a note of the same volume and pitch is quite different when it is generated by a flute rather than a violin.

three-point perspective a form of linear perspective in which the lines receding into space converge at a two vanishing points of the eye level (one to the left of the object being drawn and one to the right of the object being drawn) plus a third vanishing point above or below the eye level. Used when the picture plane must be tilted to encompass an object placed above or below the eye level.

three-quarter work a physical object that is designed to be viewed from the front and sides only.

tint a hue that has been mixed with white.

tone a hue that has been mixed with black and white.

torque the distortion of an object through a twisting movement. Also know as **torsion.**

transition the process of changing from one state or form to another. For example, the surface of a metal sculpture as it shifts from a smooth to a rough surface or the manner in which a computer drawing morphs from one form to another.

triadic harmony a color scheme based on three colors which are equidistant on a color wheel.

tromp l'oeil a flat illusion that is so convincing the viewer believes the image is real. From a French term meaning "to fool the eye."

two-point perspective a form of linear perspective in which the lines receding into space converge at a two vanishing points of the eye level (or horizon line), one to the left of the object being drawn and one to the right of the object being drawn.

typestyle the distinctive quality of the letterforms within a given font. For example, Helvetica has a very different look than Palatino type.

unity compositional similarity, oneness, togetherness, or cohesion.

value the relative lightness or darkness of a surface.

value distribution the proportion and arrangement of lights and darks in a composition. Also know as **value pattern.**

value scale a range of grays that are presented in a consistent sequence, creating a gradual transition from white to black.

variety the differences which give a design visual and conceptual interest; notably, use of contrast, emphasis, differences in size, and so forth.

vanishing point in linear perspective, the point or points on the eye line at which parallel lines appear to converge.

viewing time the time an audience devotes to watching or exploring an artwork.

visual book an experimental structure which conveys ideas, actions and emotions using multiple images in an integrated and interdependent format. Also known as an artist's book.

visual movement use of continuity to create deliberate visual pathways. Often used to direct the viewer's attention to areas of particular importance in the composition.

visual texture texture created using multiple marks or through a descriptive simulation of physical texture.

visual weight 1. the inclination of shapes to float or sink compositionally 2. the relative importance of a visual element within a design.

vitalistic sculpture a sculpture which appears to embody life in an inanimate material, such as Fiberglas, stone or wood.

volume 1. an empty three-dimensional form. 2. in two-dimensional design, a three-dimensional form that has been represented using the illusion of space. 3. in time design, the loudness of a sound.

volume summary a drawing which communicates visual information reductively, using basic volumes, such as sphere, cubes and cylinders to indicate the major components of a figure or object.

W

weight the visual or physical heaviness of an object.

wipe in film, a transition in which first shot seems to be pushed off the screen by the second. Wipes were used extensively in *Star Wars*.

introduction

i.1, Collection: Edition 1: Museo Nacional Centro de Arte Reina Sofia, Madrid. Edition 2: Los Angeles County Museum of Art, Modern and Contemporary Art Council Fund. Photo: Gary McKinnis.

i.2, Collection Toni Greenbaum, NY. Photo: Keith E. LoBue.

i.3, Designers: Bill Cannan, Tony Ortiz, H. Kurt Heinz. Design Firm: Bill Cannan & Co. Client/Mfr. NASA Public Affairs

i.5, Installation,Venice Bienniale, Chiesa de San Stae, Venice, Italy. Courtesy of Paula Cooper Gallery, NY.

i.6, Photograph © The Museum of Modern Art, Film Stills Archive. By permission of the Estate of Alfred Hitchcock.

i.7, Designers: James E. Grove, John Cook, Jim Holtorf, Fernando Pardo, Mike Boltich. Design Firm: Designworks/ USA. Client/Mfr: Corona Clipper Co.

i.9, Denver Art Museum Collection: Funds from Helen Dill bequest, 1935.14. © Denver Art Museum 2005.

i.10, © 2005 The Estate of Sam Francis/Artists Rights Society (ARS), NY.

i.11, Collection, University of Illinois at Urbana, Champaign. Photo courtesy of the artist © Alice Aycock, 1994.

i.12, TM & © 2005 Marvel Characters, Inc. Used with permission.

i.13, Courtesy of the author.

part two

Page 114: © 1996 Georgiana Nehl. Photo by David Browne.

Page 115: Courtesy of Jason Chin.

chapter four

4.2, © 2005 Cordon Art B. V. Baarn, Holland.

Page 125: © 1996 Georgiana Nehl. Photo by David Browne.

Profile, pages 126-127: © Nancy Callahan and Diane Gallo.

chapter five

5.1, Cooper-Hewitt National Design Museum, Gift of Gary Laredo, 1956.10.1 Smithsonian Institution/Art Resource, NY.

5.2, The Museum of Modern Art, New York. Gift of Edgar Kaufman, Jr. Photo © 2005 Art Resource, NY.

5.5, The Museum of Modern Art, New York. Gift of Herman Miller Furniture Company. Photo © Museum of Modern Art/Art Resource, NY.

5.6, Photo courtesy of Knoll, Inc.

5.8, Courtesy of Ray Rogers.

5.9, The Corning Museum of Glass, Gift of Vera Liskova.

5.10, Courtesy of Chronicle Books.

5.11, The Museum of Modern Art, New York. Mrs. Simon Guggenheim Fund. Photograph © 2005 The Museum of Modern Art/ © 2005 Estate of Yves Tanguy/Artists Rights Society (ARS), NY.

5.12, © 2005 Artists Rights Society (ARS), NY, SIAE, Rome. Allan Mitchell Photography.

5.15 A-B, Courtesy of the author.

5.16 A-C, Honolulu Academy of Arts, Gift of James Michener, 1991 (21.971). Photo © Honolulu Academy of Arts.

5.17, Photo: Leslie Leupp.

5.18, Private Collection; Collection Stedelijk Museum, Amsterdam. Photo: George Erml.

Profile, pages 144-145: © Heidi Lasher-Oakes.

chapter six

6.1 A-B, © The Art Institute of Chicago, Charles H. and Mary F. S. Worcester Collection. All Rights Reserved.

6.2, Stanza della Segnatura, Vatican Palace, Vatican State. Scala/Art Resource, NY.

Self Assignment, pages 154-155: Courtesy of Jason Chin.

6.10, The Nelson-Atkins Museum of Art and The Kansas City Sculpture Park including Shuttlecocks, by Claes Oldenburg and Coosje van Bruggen, 1994; Purchase: acquired through the generosity of the Sosland Family. Photograph: E.G. Schempf, F94-1/2-4.

6.15, Moderna Museet, Stockholm. © Robert Rauschenberg/Licensed by VAGA, NY.

6.16, © Robert Rauschenberg/Licensed by VAGA, NY. Photo: Harry Shunk.

6.17, © Robert Rauschenberg/Licensed by VAGA, NY.

Profile, page 162: Courtesy of the artist.

Page 163: From a cover of *Miriam's Cup* by Fran Manushkin, illustrated by Bob Dacey. Published by Scholastic Press, a division of Scholastic Inc. Illustration © 1998 by Bob Dacey. Used by permission.

chapter seven

7.1, Collection of the National Palace Museum, Taipei, Taiwan.

7.2, Courtesy of the artist.

7.3, © Milton Glaser.

7.4, The Menil Collection, Houston.

7.5, © Kenny Kiernan, Mendola Ltd.

7.6, Courtesy of Jacqui & Sherry Matthews Advocacy Marketing.

7.7, Michael A. Mello, *Dead Wrong: A Death Row Lawyer Speaks Out Against Capital Punishment.* © 1997. Cover design and illustration by Mark MacCaulay. Reprinted by permission of The University of Wisconsin Press.

7.8, Courtesy of Georgiana Nehl.

7.10, Courtesy of the artists.

7.11, Ruhr/Paragon, Minneapolis.

7.12, Courtesy of the artist.

7.13, Courtesy of Richard Saul Wurman, wurmanrs@aol.com and Pentagram.

7.14, © Robert Rauschenberg/Licensed by VAGA, NY.

7.15, Margaret Bourke-White/TimePix/Getty Images.

7.16, Alfred Eisenstadt/TimePix/Getty Images.

7.17, Michael Bierut & Tracey Cameron/Pentagram. Photo: Don F. Wong.

7.18, Courtesy of Sean O'Meallie. Photo: Ric Helstrom.

7.19, © 1999 Iomega Corporation.

7.20, Museo Nacional Centro de Arte Reina Sofia, Madrid/Bridgeman Art Library, NY. © 2005 Estate of Pablo Picasso/Artists Rights Society (ARS), NY.

Profile, page 176: Courtesy of the artist.

Profile, page 177: *The Bicycle Rider,* author Guy Davenport, 1985, Red Ozier Press. Letterpress printing, 5 x 5 x 9.5 inches. Courtesy of the artist.

part three

Page 178: Collection of the Hirshhorn Museum, Washington, DC. Photo © 1997 Katherine Wetzel, of Sculpture "Pupil" by Elizabeth King.

Page 179 T: Solomon R. Guggenheim Museum, New York, purchased with funds contributed by the Louis and Bessie Adler Foundation, Inc., Seymour M. Klein, President, 1985 (85.3276).

Page 179 B: Private Collection. Photo: M. Mimlitsch-Gray.

chapter eight

8.1, Musée d'Orsay, Paris. Réunion des Musées Nationaux/Giraudon/Art Resource, NY.

8.2, Photo: Andy Heidt. *The Republic,* Columbus, OH.

8.3, © David Muench/CORBIS.

8.4, © Bob Evans, Force Fin, www.forcefin.com.

8.8, Courtesy of Metro Pictures, NY.

8.9, Musée Rodin/Art Resource, NY.

8.10, © Muntadas 1987, Courtesy of Kent Gallery. © 2005 Artists Rights Society (ARS), NY/VEGAP, Madrid.

8.11, Installation, Venice Bienniale, Chiesa di San Stae, Venice, Italy. Courtesy Paula Cooper Gallery, NY.

8.12, Estate of Robert Smithson, Courtesy of the John Weber Gallery, NY. © Licensed by VAGA, NY. Photo: Gianfranco Gorgoni.

8.13, Commissioned by the port city of Algeciras, Spain. Courtesy of the artist.

8.14, Photo: Steve Vidler. Superstock.

8.15, Storm King Art Center, Mountainville, NY, Gift of the Ralph E. Ogden Foundation. Photo: Jerry L. Thompson.

8.16, Courtesy of Rudi Stern.

8.17, Hirshhorn Museum and Sculpture Garden, Smithsonian Institution. Courtesy of the artist and Spacetime C.C.

8.18, Peter Pierobon, Designer, Ladderback Chair. Firm & Manufacturer: Snyderman Gallery. Client: Cinetrix. Photo: Tom Brummett. From Product Design 3, 1988 by PBC International, by Joe Dolce.

8.19, Art Institute of Chicago, Gift of Mr. and Mrs. Howard Goldsmith (1961,46).

8.20, © Chris Burden.

8.21, Musei Vatican, Rome. BildArchiv Preussischer Kulturbesitz, Berlin/Art Resource, NY.

8.22, Nikolai Fine Art, New York.

8.23, Courtesy David Zwirner Gallery. © 2005 Estate of Gordon Matta-Clark/Artists Rights Society (ARS), NY.

8.24, Loggia del Lanzi, Florence. Scala/Art Resource, NY.

8.25, © Nancy Holt/Licensed by VAGA, NY.

8.26, The Image Bank/Getty Images.

8.27, Bank One Art Collection.

8.28, The Museum of Modern Art, New York. Katherine S. Dreier Bequest. © 2005 Artists Rights Society (ARS), NY/ADAGP, Paris. Photo © 2005 Museum of Modern Art/Art Resource, NY.

8.29, Time Life Pictures/Getty Images.

8.30, Calder Plaza, Vandenberg, Center, Grand Rapids, MI. Maynard Williams/Superstock.

8.32, Charles Wallschlaeger, Professor Emeritus, The Ohio State University, Department of Industrial, Interior and Visual Communication Design.

8.33, Ginevra Carafe. Manufactured by Alessi, Crusinallo, Italy, Design Ettore Sottsass, 1997.

8.36, Tate Gallery, London, UK. The work illustrated has been reproduced by permission of the Henry Moore Foundation.

8.37, Superstock.

8.38, Collection, University of Illinois at Urbana, Champaign. Photo courtesy of the artist © Alice Aycock, 1994.

8.39, Solomon R. Guggenheim Museum, New York, by exchange, 1967 (67.1862). © Estate of David Smith/Licensed by VAGA, NY.

8.40, Museo Arqueologico del Banco Central, Quito, Ecuador. © 2005 Dirk Bakker.

8.41, Los Angeles County Museum of Art, Gift of Howard and Gwen Laurie Smits. Photograph © 2005 Museum Associates/LACMA.

8.42, © FMGB Guggenheim Bilbao Museo. All Rights Reserved. © 2005 Artists Rights Society (ARS), NY.

8.43, Courtesy Dia Center for the Arts and Walter De Maria.

8.44, Courtesy Anish Kapoor and Lisson Gallery, London.

8.45, Albright-Knox Art Gallery, Buffalo, New York, Gift of Seymour H. Knox, Jr., 1966.

8.46, The Margulies Collection at the Warehouse. Photo: Peter Aaron.

8.47, Museum of Indian Arts and Culture/Laboratory of Anthropology, Museum of New Mexico, Santa Fe.

8.48-8.49, Los Angeles County Museum of Art, Gift of Howard and Gwen Laurie Smits. Photograph © 2005 Museum Associates/LACMA.

8.50, Courtesy of Alexander and Bonin, NY.

8.51, Dept. of Archaeology and Anthropology, University of Ibadan/The Bridgeman Art Library, NY. Photo: Heini Schneebeli.

8.52, Courtesy of Gallery Nii, Ginza, Tokyo.

8.53, Chesterwood Museum Archives. Chesterwood, a National Trust Historic Site, Stockbridge, MA.

8.54, Courtesy of Stan Rickel.

8.55, Busch Lobby, MIT Permanent Collection, Gift of the Albert and Vera List Family Collection.

8.56, September 1998-June 1999 Installation at Dia Center for the Arts, NY.

8.57, Designers: Bill Cannan, Tony Ortiz, H. Kurt Heinz. Design Firm: Bill Cannan & Co. Client/Mfr. NASA Public Affairs.

8.58, As installed at the Whitney Museum of American Art, New York, 1980. Courtesy of Barbara Gladstone, NY.

8.59, © 2005 Artists Rights Society (ARS), NY/ADAGP, Paris.

8.60, Edition 1: Collection of Marion Stroud Swingle. Edition 2: Collection of the Artist. Photo: Roman Mensing.

8.62, Courtesy of Fisher-Price.

8.63, Courtesy of Toshiyuki Kita/IDK Design Laboratory, LTD, Japan.

8.64, © Keith Edmier. Courtesy of Sadie Coles HQ, London.

8.65, Courtesy of Michael Graves & Associates. Photo: William Taylor.

8.66, © Andy Goldsworthy.

8.67, Photo by Robert Stave, 1989. © Adele Linarducci, 1989.

8.68, Whitney Museum of Art, NY. Purchase, with funds from the Louis and Bessie Adler Foundation, Inc., Seymour M. Klein, President, the Gilman Foundation, Inc., the Howard and Jean Lipman Foundation, Inc., and the National Endowment for the Arts (79.4). Photo: Duane Preble. © The George and Helen Segal Foundation/Licensed by VAGA, NY.

8.69, Museo del Templo Mayor, Mexico City. Instituto Nacional de Antropologia e Historia (INAH).

8.70, © University of Cincinnati Fine Arts Collection.

8.71, Courtesy of Erwin Hauer.

Profile, pages 217-219: Courtesy of the artist.

chapter nine

9.1, Courtesy of Humanscale, NY.

9.2, Solomon R. Guggenheim Museum, New York, purchased with funds contributed by the Louis and Bessie Adler Foundation, Inc., Seymour M. Klein, President, 1985 (85.3276).

9.3, Courtesy Marian Goodman Gallery, NY.

9.4, Courtesy of Matthew Marks Gallery, NY.

9.5, Giraudon/Art Resource, NY. © 2005 Estate of Louise Nevelson/Artists Rights Society (ARS), NY.

9.6, © Aaron Macsai.

9.7, Courtesy of Alexander and Bonin, NY.

9.8, Photo: Timothy Hursley. Holocaust Memorial Museum, Washington, DC.

9.9, Collection, University of Illinois at Urbana, Champaign. Photo courtesy of the artist © Alice Aycock, 1994.

9.10, UCLA Fowler Museum of Cultural History. Photo: Don Cole.

9.11, Detroit Institute of Arts, Detroit, MI. © 2005 Sol Le Witt/Artists Rights Society (ARS), NY.

9.12, Mixed media installation at the Albright-Knox Art Gallery, September 1982. Albright-Knox Art Gallery, Buffalo, NY.

9.13, Courtesy of Mary Boone Gallery, NY.

9.14, Superstock.

9.15, Installation: Capp Street Project, S.F. Courtesy of Alexander and Bonin, NY.

9.16a, Courtesy the Library, American Museum of Natural History, NY, Trans. 2104(2)

9.18, Courtesy of Theodore Gall.

9.19, Ludovica Canali De Rossi, Milano, Italy.

9.20, Santa Maria degli Angeli, Rome, Italy/Mauro Magliani/Superstock.

9.21, Kukje Gallery, Chrong Ku, Seoul, Korea.

9.22, Courtesy of Patricia A. Renick.

9.24, Designers: James E. Grove, John Cook, Jim Holtorf, Fernando Pardo, Mike Boltich. Design Firm: Designworks/USA. Client/Mfr: Corona Clipper Co.

9.25, Solomon R. Guggenheim Foundation, New York, Peggy Guggenheim, Venice (76.2553.50). © 2005 Artists Rights Society (ARS), NY/ADAGP, Paris. Photo: David Heald, © Solomon R. Guggenheim Museum Foundation, NY.

9.26, Art Institute of Chicago. Partial gift of the Arts Club of Chicago; restricted gift of various donors, through prior bequest of Arthur Rubloff; through prior restricted gift of William Hartmann; through prior gifts of Mr. and Mrs. Carter H. Harrison, Mr. and Mrs. Arnold H. Maremont through the Kate Maremont Foundation, Woodruff J. Parker, Art Institute of Chicago. Photo © 2005 Art Institute of Chicago. All Rights Reserved. © 2005 Artists Rights Society (ARS), NY/ADAGP, Paris.

9.27, The Museum of Modern Art, New York, given anonymously. © 2005 Artists Rights Society (ARS), NY/ADAGP, Paris. Photograph © Museum of Modern Art/Art Resource, NY.

9.28, Fratelli Alinari/Superstock.

9.29, The Museum of Modern Art, New York/ Art Resource, NY. © 2005 Artists Rights Society (ARS), NY.

9.30, Photo: Doug Yaple.

9.31, Ludovica Canali De Rossi, Milano, Italy.

9.32, Courtesy of the National Ornamental Metal Museum, Memphis, TN. Collection of the artist.

9.33, © 2005 Artists Rights Society (ARS), NY/ADAGP, Paris. Photo © CNAP Command Publique, Ministére de la Culture, Paris.

9.34, Museum fur Kunst und Gewerbe, Hamburg.

9.35, Private Collection.

9.36, Courtesy of Tanija & Graham Carr. Photo: Victor France.

9.37, Musée d'Orsay, Paris. Réunion des Musées Nationaux/Art Resource, NY.

9.38, Collection Walker Art Center, Minneapolis. Acquired with Lannan Foundation support in conjunction with the exhibition Sculpture Inside Outside, 1991.

9.39, The Nelson-Atkins Museum of Art, Kansas City, Missouri. Gift of the Hall Family Foundation, F99-33/1 A-DD. Photo: E. G. Schempf.

9.40, Photo: Don Hamilton.

9.41, San Francisco Museum of Modern Art. Courtesy of Paula Cooper Gallery, NY.

Profile, pages 240-241: Photos courtesy of the artist.

chapter ten

10.1, Guggenheim Bilbao © 1997, The Solomon R. Guggenheim Foundation, Bilbao. © FMGB Guggenheim Bilbao Museo, 2001. All rights reserved.

10.3, Courtesy of Shoji Design.

10.6, Photo: Whit Slemmons, Courtesy of Thorncrown Chapel.

10.7, © Lee Snider/CORBIS.

10.8, Courtesy Agnes Gund Collection. © The Joseph and Robert Cornell Memorial Foundation/Licensed by VAGA, NY.

10.9, Courtesy of Garth Clark Gallery, NY. Photo: Pierre Longtin.

10.10, Photo: Don Pitcher. Alaska Stock.

10.12, Wright State University, Dayton, OH.

10.13, Photo supplied by Blick Art Materials.

10.14, Collection Majorie & Arnold Platzker.

10.15, Art Institute of Chicago, Grant J. Pick Purchase Fund (1967.386). © 2005 Artists Rights Society (ARS), NY/ VEGAP, Madrid.

10.16, Kunstindustrimuseet I Oslo (Museum of Decorative Arts & Design) Norway.

10.18, Courtesy Anish Kapoor and Lisson Gallery, London.

10.19, Private Collection.

10.20, Corning Museum of Glass, Corning, NY (86.4.180).

10.21, Courtesy Galerie Elena Lee, Montreal.

10.22, Courtesy of James Cohan Gallery.

10.23, Collection of the Art Institute of Chicago. Courtesy of the artist.

10.24, Courtesy of Deborah Butterfield.

Profile, pages 258-259: Courtesy of Todd Slaughter.

chapter eleven

11.1, George Glod/Superstock.

11.2, Photo: Shigeo Anzai, Tokyo.

11.3, Courtesy of Ronald Feldman Fine Arts.

11.4, Saint Peter's Basilica, Vatican, Rome. Alinari/Art Resource, NY.

11.5, Private Collection; Collection Martha Stewart; Collection Oakland Museum of Art.

11.6, Private Collection. Photo: M. Mimlitsch-Gray.

11.7, Collection: Rothko Chapel, Houston, dedicated to Reverend Martin Luther King, Jr. © 2005 Barnett Newman Foundation/Artists Rights Society, NY.

11.8, Courtesy of P.P.O.W., NY.

11.9, University of California, Berkeley Art Museum. Photographed for the UC Berkeley Art Museum by Ben Blackwell.

11.10, Kukje Gallery, Chrong Ku, Seoul, Korea.

11.11, Photo: Henry Arnold, © Maya Lin.

11.12, Private collection. © The George and Helen Segal Foundation/Licensed by VAGA, NY.

11.13, Courtesy of Susan Trangmar.

11.14, Courtesy of the Sogetsu Foundation.

11.15, On loan to The Philadelphia Museum of Art, Philadelphia, PA.

11.16, The Metropolitan Museum of Art, Bequest of Mrs. H.O. Havemeyer, 1929. The H.W. Havemeyer Collection.

11.18, The Museum of Modern Art, New York. Acquired through the Lillie P. Bliss Bequest. Photograph © The Museum of Modern Art/Art Resource, NY.

11.19, National Geographic Society Headquarters, Washington, DC.

11.20, Collection of The Denver Art Museum, Denver, CO. Gift of Ginny Williams. Photo: Edward Smith. Courtesy Joseph Helman Gallery, NY (BH 1912).

11.21, Courtesy Jay Jopling Gallery/White Cube, London. © Antony Gormley.

11.22, Courtesy of Pace Wildenstein. Photo: Ellen Page Wilson. © 2005 John Chamberlain/Artists Rights Society (ARS), NY.

11.23, Installation at SITE Santa Fe, 1999.

11.24, Courtesy of The North Face, San Leandro, CA.

11.25, Collection: Caltrans, City of Los Angeles, San Diego Freeway Northbound, Mulholland Drive Exit, Los Angeles.

11.26, (Corner of Grove Rd. and Roman Rd., London, destroyed 1994). Commissioned by Artangel Trust and Beck's.

11.27, Courtesy of Jack Shainman Gallery, NY. © 2005 Artists Rights Society (ARS), NY/VG Bild-Kunst, Bonn.

11.28, Courtesy of Todd Slaughter.

11.29, © 2005 Artists Rights Society (ARS), NY/VG Bild-Kunst. Bonn.

11.30, © Ronald Dahl.

11.31, Third of five public garden rooms in the King County East Division Reclamation Plant, Renton, WA.

11.32, Courtesy of the Library, American Museum of Natural History, NY, Trans. 1448(4).

11.33, Art Institute of Chicago, Gift of Margaret Fisher in memory of her parents, Mr. and Mrs. Walter L. Fisher (1957.165), view 1.

11.34, The Museum of Modern Art, New York. The Sidney and Harriet Janis Collection. Art Resource, NY. © 2005 Artists Rights Society (ARS), NY/ADAGP, Paris/Estate of Marcel Duchamp.

11.35, © Skyscan Balloon Photography.

11.36, Courtesy of the Henry Moore Foundation and the artist.

11.37, Nikolai Fine Art, New York.

11.38, © PhenomenArts,Inc. Christopher Janney, Artistic Director.

11.39, Courtesy of Rudi Stern.

11.40, The British School at Rome. Photo: Shelagh Wakely.

11.41, San Francisco Museum of Modern Art. Doris and Donald G. Fisher Fund. Courtesy Hosfelt Gallery.

11.42, © The Field Museum of Natural History, Chicago. Photo: White & Dorman, Front view, neg #A112518.C.

11.43, © Allen Memorial Art Museum, Oberlin College, OH. Fund for Contemporary Art and gift of the artist and the Fischbach Gallery, 1970.

11.44, Collection of the Hirshhorn Museum, Washington, DC. Photo © 1997 Katherine Wetzel, of Sculpture "Pupil" by Elizabeth King.

Profile, pages 286-289: Courtesy of the artist.

Index

index

index